Emplaced Myth

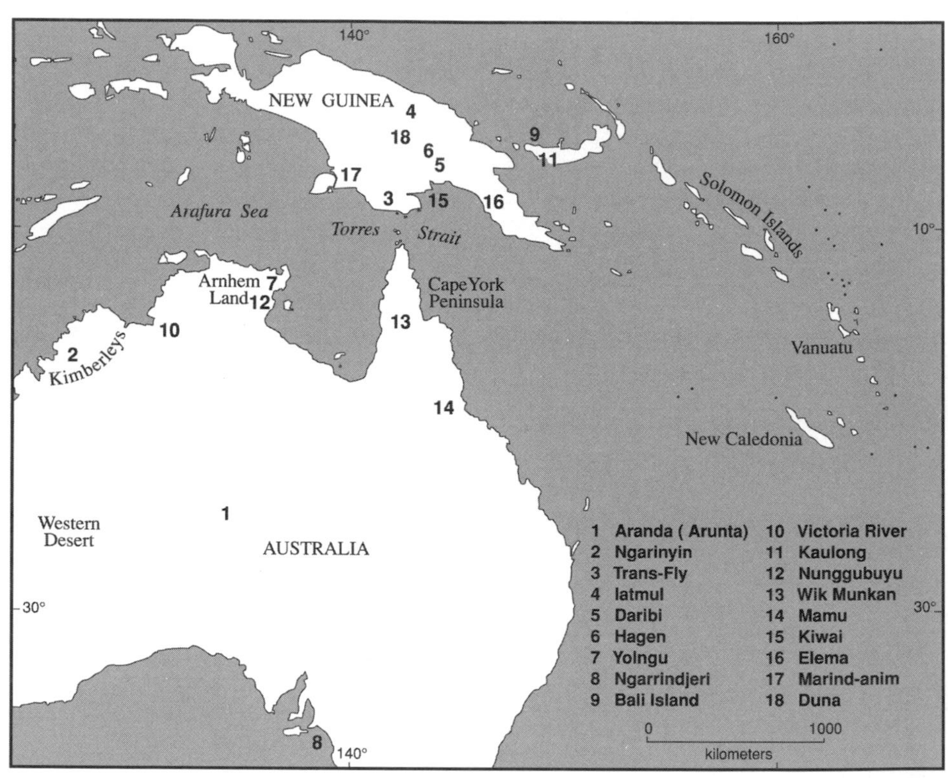

Map 1. Location of Areas and Groups. (Map courtesy of Department of Cartography, Research School of Pacific and Asian Studies, Australian National University)

Emplaced Myth

Space, Narrative, and Knowledge in Aboriginal Australia and Papua New Guinea

Edited by Alan Rumsey and James Weiner

University of Hawai'i Press
Honolulu

Printed in the United States of America

06 05 04 03 02 01 5 4 3 2 1

Library of Congress Cataloging-in-Publication Data

Emplaced myth : space, narrative, and knowledge in Aboriginal Australia and Papua New Guinea / edited by Alan Rumsey and James Weiner.
p. cm.
Includes bibliographical references and index.
ISBN 0–8248–1663–3 (cloth : alk. paper) —
ISBN 0–8248–2389–3 (pbk. : alk. paper)
1. Australian aborigines—Land tenure—Congresses. 2. Papuans—Land tenure—Congresses. 3. Philosophy, Papuan—Congresses. 4. Philosophy, Australian aboriginal—Congresses. 5. Sacred space—Melanesia—Congresses. 6. Sacred space—Australia—Congresses. I. Rumsey, Alan. II. Weiner, James F.

GN666.E52 2001
305.89'915—dc21 00–057691

University of Hawai'i Press books are printed on acid-free paper and meet the guidelines for permanence and durability of the Council on Library Resources.

Book design by Kenneth Miyamoto
Printed by The Maple-Vail Book Manufacturing Group

CONTENTS

ACKNOWLEDGMENTS

The original conference at which most of the papers in this volume were presented, "From Myth to Minerals: Place, Narrative, Land, and Transformation in Australia and New Guinea," was funded by the Wenner-Gren Foundation for Anthropological Research and the Australian National University. We would like to express our deep appreciation to both institutions, and to Laurie Obbink of Wenner-Gren and Professor James Fox and Dr. Chris Ballard of the Australian National University.

The following people also presented papers at the original conference: Aletta Biersack, Mark Donohue, Françoise Dussart, Jane Fajans, Bill Foley, Robert Foster, Jack Golson, Jane Goodale, Chris Gosden, David Hyndman, Hank Nelson, Elizabeth Povinelli, Ingrid Slotte, Brian Stacey, and Leontine Visser.

In addition, the following people acted as chairpersons for the various sessions of the three-day conference: James Fox, Chris Gregory, Margaret Jolly, Shelley Mallett, Andrew Pawley, Nicolas Peterson, Diane Smith, and Nick Thomas.

Peter Toner recorded the presentations and the discussion following each paper. Ann Buller, Diane Kovacs, and Ria Van de Zandt of the Research School of Pacific and Asian Studies provided logistical and administrative support during and after the conference. Margaret Forster provided editorial assistance in preparing the manuscript.

We would also like to thank Pamela Kelley at the University of Hawai'i Press for her support, the anonymous reviewers of the manuscript for their helpful comments, and Australian National University for their contribution toward publication costs.

Introduction

Alan Rumsey

In 1997 the Chevron oil company (through its Papua New Guinea subsidiary Chevron Niugini Limited) engaged in negotiations with the Queensland state government in Australia to construct a pipeline that would bring natural gas from the Kutubu oil fields and other neighboring gas fields to a terminus in Gladstone, Queensland by way of Townsville. In October 1998 an agreement to develop the pipeline was signed by the Australian AGL Gas Company, its partner Petronas of Malaysia, and the PNG Gas Supply Consortium, headed by Chevron Services Australia. What is in progress here is something different from the suboceanic communication cables that have long linked the island of New Guinea to Australia. Here there will be an actual flow of substance. And considering that the Foi people who live in the oil project area in New Guinea see petroleum as originating from women's menstrual blood (Weiner 1995c), which itself has inscriptive, place-making powers, we are witnessing the Western technological equivalent of one of the epic journeys of mythic inscription that in both New Guinea and Australia play central cosmogonic roles in so many communities. The prospect of the creation of this umbilical cord of connection between two landmasses, which until recently in geological terms were one, serves as a way of introducing a range of problems raised by a comparison between Australian and Papua New Guinea lifeworlds.

Most immediately, there is the likely impact of the pipeline upon indigenous peoples whose lands lie in its course on both sides of the

Torres Strait. Of this we may already have an intimation in the work of such anthropologists as John Burton, Tom Ernst, and Bruce Knauft, who have observed what has happened along the new Kutubu-to-Poroma section of the Highlands Highway that was built by Chevron:

> The mountain highway that Chevron constructed in the north [to allow access to the Kutubu oil fields] has become a conduit for New Guinea highlanders wanting to infiltrate the Kutubu area. Liquor, theft, poaching, squatting, and rape have been introduced to thinly populated areas unaccustomed to such problems. (Knauft 1996:98)

Politically, the situation is anything but clear-cut. In the struggle among the Papua New Guinea state, local landowners, and the Kutubu Joint Venture for control of the oil pipeline to the Gulf Coast, the Southern Highlands and Gulf Province landowners sided with Chevron against the Papua New Guinea government, showing that each relationship in these complicated multiparty engagements is contestable.[1] On the Australian side, a similar triangular tension is evident in negotiations among Aboriginal land councils and the landowners they represent, the Queensland government, and the Chevron company. Nevertheless, negotiations are all but complete with Aboriginal landowners along the pipeline's proposed course in northern Queensland, and one cannot help but wonder if their lives will be any less transformed by the outcome. In any case, the example, like other recent developments such as the Bougainville crisis in Papua New Guinea and the recognition of Native Title in Australia, serves to highlight the way in which the landedness of indigenous peoples has become a central issue for the integrity of the state and its relation to international capital on either side of the strait.

This volume arose from a conference at which those issues were a central focus. Titled "From Myth to Minerals: Place, Narrative, Land, and Transformation in Australia and Papua New Guinea," the conference was held in Canberra at the Australian National University in July 1997.[2] It brought together an international group of scholars, including all the contributors to this volume, to discuss indigenous cosmologies of Australia and Papua New Guinea in relation to each other, and the impact of multinational resource extraction on both. The essays concerned most explicitly with the impact of mining are being published in a companion volume to this one, *Mining and Indigenous Lifeworlds in Australia and Papua New Guinea* (Rumsey and Weiner in press).

The present volume focuses more generally upon the indigenous lifeworlds that are being affected and upon the ways in which they are grounded in the very earth that is being dug up. Of course, the pipeline is only the latest in a series of events through which those lifeworlds have been brought in conjuncture with the colonizing West, and thereby, at least indirectly, with each other. But even had they not been, we submit that there are good reasons for a conjoint ethnographic focus on Aboriginal Australia and Papua New Guinea to be of interest. How so?

Not very long ago in the history of anthropology, the most likely answer to that question might have been this: for the interesting examples they offer of contrasting *types* of society or culture—agrarian versus hunter-gatherer, "tribal" versus "band" (Sahlins 1968, Service 1966), "elementary structures" versus "complex structures" (Lévi-Strauss 1969), "prescriptive" versus "performative" structures (Sahlins 1985:x–iv, 26–31), and so on. Each of these sorts of contrasts is grounded in a kind of "whole systems" typology (Schneider 1965) wherein each contrastive case stands for a larger class that includes other, historically unrelated exemplars from elsewhere in the world. So the essential properties that are revealed by an Australia–New Guinea comparison are the same ones that would be revealed by a !Kung-Dinka one, an Australian-Hawaiian one (Sahlins 1985:xii), and so on.

Or, in a closely related rhetoric of reversal, one can argue that (areas of) Australia and New Guinea are really of the same essential type. This argument has been made, for example, by the Dutch comparativist Alex van der Leeden with respect to Lévi-Strauss' distinction between "elementary" structures of kinship/exchange and "complex" ones. Whereas Lévi-Strauss had seen Australian Aboriginal societies as prime exemplars of the former type and Melanesian ones as transitional between the two, van der Leeden argued instead that "elementary structures are as clearly discernible in Melanesia and New Guinea [*sic*] as in Australia" (van der Leeden 1970:84 et passim; cf. van der Leeden 1960), in respect of which they belong with the Asian and other examples discussed by Lévi-Strauss (1969).

Our interest here is not in whole-system comparisons of that kind. We do not use Australian or New Guinea examples to stand for any kind of larger class or to try to shed light on some presumably "underlying" panhuman reality such as "elementary structures."[3] Rather, the analytical strategy we follow here is more like a certain Melanesian one from the New Guinea Highlands that Francesca Merlan and I have studied, namely the Melpa–Ku Waru practice of *pairing,* or what the people there call "making twos" (Merlan and Rumsey 1991:113–116 et passim; Rumsey 1995; cf. Strauss 1962:15–16, Lancy and Strathern 1981). As opposed to schemata that create a fixed order of knowledge by taxonomic classification, Ku Waru people use one of multivalent binary combination as a way of creating alternative perspectives on things, by highlighting what is common to pairs of them. In Ku Waru, *kung* "pig," for example, is alternatively paired with (among other things) *owa* "dog," *sumuyl* "kina shell," and *langi* "vegetable food," highlighting what it has in common with each of the other paired terms, namely "domestic animal," "wealth item," and "food."

Consistent with this schema of pairing, one of the main ways in which novelty is generated is through what we (Merlan and Rumsey 1991:236–238) have called "contingent juxtaposition," the bringing together of previously isolated entities or categories in a way that reveals something theretofore concealed or latent in each. A prime example would be the first arrival of Europeans in the New Guinea Highlands in the 1930s. This was taken by highlanders not just as a revelation of an outside world that they had been unaware of but as something that placed them in a new relationship that revealed things they had not previously known about themselves (Rumsey 1999a).[4] Another example we have studied (Merlan and Rumsey 1991:156–197, 210–214) was the novel pairing of a women's cooperative work group in exchange relationships with both of two sides in a "tribal fight," between whom they had intervened on the battlefield to stop the fight, placing the order of "government law" and "business" in what was perceived to be a new and mutually illuminating relationship with that of "indigenous" *(bo)* male-dominated segmentary business-as-usual.

It is in this spirit of "making twos" that we juxtapose Australia and New Guinea in this volume. That is, rather than starting with given classificatory categories and treating the ethnographic cases as exemplary of them, we start with a certain juxtaposition and see how our understanding of each of the paired terms might be transformed in the event. We do not treat even the paired terms themselves—"Aboriginal Australia" and "New Guinea"—as brute facts about the world but as historically contingent ways of looking at it (cf. Lederman 1998; Foster 1999, regarding "Melanesia"). For us the most immediately relevant historical fact is the existence of distinct "regional traditions" (Fardon 1990) of ethnography associated with opposite sides of the Torres Strait. On the northern side, the relevant region is of course not limited to New Guinea (here used to mean the entire island and the nearby associated smaller islands) but is variously extended to include more remote "Melanesian" locales such as the Solomons and Vanuatu. It is these *ethnographically* defined regions (however fuzzy around some of the edges) that we take as our objects of juxtaposition.

Even allowing us this strategy, the reader may still ask, Why Australia and New Guinea? Our claim is not that this is a uniquely appropriate or privileged pairing—that these two belong together as coordinate taxa in some fixed order of things—any more than do *kung* "pig" and *owa* "dog" in Ku Waru, or hornbill and cassowary in Foi. Alternative pairings are not only possible but have already been made, with considerable success, by other anthropologists concerned with New Guinea: witness the recent volume of papers edited by Michael Lambek and Andrew Strathern (1998), *Bodies and Persons: Comparative Perspectives from Africa and Melanesia,* and the planned volume by Gregor and Tuzin (in preparation) on gender in Amazonia and Melanesia.

For each of the conferences from which those two volumes arose, there was a previous stipulation and narrowing down of the grounds against which similarity and contrast would be considered. Lambek and Strathern selected the body and personhood as fields or categories within which to limit the proliferation of comparison between Africa and Melanesia. The organizers of the Wenner-Gren Amazonia-Melanesia conference chose the topic of gender in order to effect a similar control on comparison.

By contrast, the conference from which the present volume arose did not focus on a single analytical category such as "gender" or "personhood." Rather, it proceeded in part from the questions of mining impact that I raised above, and in part also from the intimation that there were certain rather more specific motifs in the ethnography of each region that seemed to resonate with ones from the other, but that had seldom been considered in conjunction with each other. These themes will be identified below. What I want to note here is that, unlike the other two comparative axes mentioned above, the one we have posited here concerns areas of the world that are immediately adjacent to one another, and part of the interest in comparison lies in questions of historic and possible prehistoric relationships between the two.[5] That is, the relevant relations of contiguity have been established not just in the imagination of the analysts but also at least in part by actual flows of people, power, objects across the wider region.

The importance of such regional connectedness has already been widely recognized by New Guinea specialists, who in recent years have held several comparative conferences focusing on particular regions within Papua New Guinea.[6] Speaking of one such region, Marilyn Strathern has said:

> The societies of the Papua New Guinea Highlands, and elements of their formation, are complex parts and uneven outgrowths of one another. If they are connected, they are only partially so. The continuities I have in mind are less a question of abstract similarities (Parkin 1987) than of proximities in space and time (Fardon 1987).
>
> . . . we could envisage Highland peoples in a constant process of self-substitution, eclipsing or turning one kind of world into another, through (a series of) historical events—comparability is lost in the exercise, but a kind of compatibility remains. Analogy remains possible. The turn is, in fact, one that the anthropologist routinely replicates when he or she writes on one society with a further society in mind. (Strathern 1991:54)

The present volume innovates upon these previous regional exercises by attending to "proximities in time and space" on a much larger scale. I submit that the problems and prospects for comparison at this scale do not differ in kind from the ones that Strathern identifies with respect to the New Guinea Highlands in the quote above. Of course, analogy is *always* possible, and all such connections are "partial," but in the case of Australia and New Guinea, just as within the Highlands on a smaller scale, we are dealing with a region in which it is plausible to think of the relevant connections or transformations as linked up in continuous series.

To see why, it is important to bear in mind that what are now Australia and New Guinea have been a single landmass—known to archaeologists as Sahul—for at least three fourths of the period of human habitation (White 1996; O'Connell and Allen 1998) and that even in the postglacial period when the land bridge across the Torres Strait became inundated, the two have never been separated by more than sixty miles of open sea, across which there has probably always been continuous human traffic. Moreover, the territories that became the independent state of Papua New Guinea in 1975 share important aspects of their colonial history with northern Queensland and Australia's Northern Territory. Both had, of course, been administered as territories of Australia, and there was regular flow of colonists, missionaries, and capital across the Torres Strait and the Arafura Sea.

One of the main reasons for inattentiveness to more long-standing continuities between the lifeways of Australian Aborigines and New Guineans has been the rigid stereotyping of the former as "hunter-gatherers" and the latter as "horticulturists." Not only is this dichotomy irrelevant for most of the prehistoric human past of Sahul; even in historic times it is actually a continuum that extends across the Torres Strait rather than a categorical difference between Australia and New Guinea. That is, there was a gradient in the extent to which agriculture was practiced between the islands to the north and east and those to the south, where, on the islands nearest to Cape York, it was only a marginal source of food as opposed to hunting, foraging, and fishing. And if we stop using the "hunter-gatherer"/"horticulturist" rubrics in a "whole-systems" vein and instead compare areas of Aboriginal Australia and New Guinea with respect to the prevalence of meat versus that of vegetable foods in the indigenous people's diets, it appears that there was a similar continuum extending right across the adjacent landmasses. Jones and Bowler (1980) demonstrated this elegantly, showing that there was more variation both within Australia and within New Guinea in these respects than there was across adjacent regions of northern Australia and southern New Guinea, and that it is more closely correlated with soil types and rainfall than it is with the distribution of horticulture.

Previous Comparative Work on Australian and New Guinea Cosmologies

Though the present volume is the first full-scale comparative work on Australia and New Guinea, we are by no means the first anthropologists to have made comparisons between the two areas. Before elaborating on what we see as the most significant results to emerge from the present project, it will be useful to review some of the work that has been done before.

In general,[7] the part of New Guinea where resemblances to Aboriginal Australia have been most remarked is the south coast, from Elema on the Gulf of Papua to Marind-anim in southwestern Irian Jaya. In 1963 Jan van Baal published a well-known article titled "The Cult of the Bull-Roarer in Australia and Southern New Guinea," in which he compared its ritual uses and associated myths among four south coast peoples: Kiwai, Trans-Fly, Marind-anim, and Elema and two Australian Aboriginal ones: Yolngu and Aranda. The main point of his article is to establish that "in Australia and in the southern part of New Guinea the bull-roarer has to be interpreted as a phallic symbol and, consequently, its cult as a phallic cult" (van Baal 1963: 201). He shows that in all six ethnographic cases "myths are re-enacted by performers who, in a disguised form, bear a phallic symbol identical with the ancestor who is represented" (208). Van Baal sees in this "the suggestion that there are significant similarities [between southern New Guinean cultures and Australian ones]."

"To them," he says in a parting remark, "could be added the apparent similarities found between the totemism of the Marind-anim and the Orokolo on the one hand and that of the Australian tribes on the other, as well as the functional similarities between the Australian system of sections and totem-relationships and the organization of over-all-clans in southern New Guinea" (213).

These points were taken up and elaborated upon by A. C. van der Leeden in his contribution to a Festschrift for van Baal, with specific reference to the Nunggubuyu of southeastern Arnhem Land, with whom he had done fieldwork, and Marind-anim (van der Leeden 1975). While conceding that there are considerable ecological differences between the two, he saw these as relevant mainly in accounting for "the contrast between both regions, in the realization of basically identical structural processes of ritual and kinship organization" (151), namely, in each case the "totemic and fourfold division of the society into moieties, sub-moieties . . . , composed of patrilineal clans, sub-clans and lineages" (151). He says that "in both societies, this four-fold division is ideological rather than formal" in that these social categories are "not strictly differentiated and functionally independent corporate groups," but nonetheless "all categories form a closely integrated whole, and represent different views of a basic set of central ideas underlying the society as a whole" (151). He points out that the major cults in each society are identified with particular moieties and regions, but there is a tight interdependence among them, valorized in myth by the movements across the landscape of the hero figures who brought the ceremonies.

Van der Leeden argues that cult gatherings effect the "consolidation and intensification of the identity of Nunggubuyu society" (156–157), because "the great moiety rituals should be performed by representatives of clans of at least all four sub-moieties" (157). In this he claims, "the tribe presents itself, albeit in a symbolical fashion, as a local and territorial unit" (157). This seems to me a non sequitur, since the sub-moieties (or "semi-moieties," as Australianists nowadays generally call them) are by no means limited to Nunggubuyu territory but are of unbounded extent.

Be that as it may, van der Leeden here draws a parallel with the way Marind-anim territorial groups are "composed of local segments which, in each territorial group, reflect the composition of the tribe as a whole, each phratry being represented among the local clans" (ibid.). Those familiar with the work of Marilyn Strathern (1991), Roy Wagner (1991), and Jadran Mimica (1988) will here recognize the kind of "holographic" or "fractal" relationship of whole-to-whole that has been seen to figure so prominently in Melanesian social life.

In his 1993 book *South Coast New Guinea Cultures,* Bruce Knauft also compares Marind-anim with Aboriginal Australia, with particular attention to the role of the *dema* creator beings. Their pervasiveness in Marind social life, he says, "suggests similarities with the dreamtime ancestors of Australian Aboriginal populations southward across the shallow Arafura Sea" (Knauft 1993:137).

> Yet, there were important differences. The world of the *dema* was not only primordial, but temporal or "in time." Correspondingly, the deep-seated transformation of subjects into totemic objects in Australian ritual, as penetrated by Munn . . . comes to a fuller circle among Marind-anim. *Dema* were subjectified as present beings and Marind objectified themselves as creative embodiments who continued the *dema*'s restless wanderings and vital energy. (Knauft 1993:137–138)

Interestingly, though, other and especially more recent Australian ethnography by scholars such as Rose (1992, 1996, chapter 5 below), Povinelli (1993), and Redmond (chapter 6 below), as well as commentary by Aboriginal people,[8] makes much the same point about Aboriginal dreamings, bringing them much closer to Knauft's characterization of Marind-anim *dema* than he may have supposed.

Knauft also takes up the comparison mentioned above between Aboriginal Australia and the "Trans-Fly" area, drawing upon the restudy done there by Mary Ayres in 1979–1981. He says the similarity in myth and cosmology is strong: "Indeed, links to the Australian dreamtime are stronger here than among any of the other south coast language-culture areas"—even more so than to Marind-anim, for

> whereas Marind *dema* embodied a primordial past, their presence was continuously creative in the present. Marind liked to travel long distances, wreak the vengeance of the *dema* on foreign peoples, proliferate their cults in new incarnations, and transform the social and cultural landscape as *dema* had done. Trans-Fly peoples, in contrast, were conservatively bound to specific ancestral locations. Lacking specific mythological knowledge of neighboring clans, local groups feared to travel on others' land, worried lest they violate its story-places and court sorcery from its human inhabitants. Even if a neighboring language dialect was known, it was inappropriate to speak it, since one lacked ancestral connection with the knowledge it presumed. In contrast to the Marind's ubiquitous cross-cutting ritual linkages, Morehead peoples emphasized the "highly autonomous nature of local section groups." (Knauft 1993:185)

This comparison may not be entirely apposite in what it assumes about Australian Aborigines, since, as van der Leeden emphasizes, they, too, have linked the efficacy of their internal religious life to "cross-cutting ritual linkages." And Australian Aborigines are, as Don Laycock (1979:82) once put it, "the leading contenders for being the most multilingual people in the world." But whatever differences there might be in the extent of their travels, there is an impressive similarity among all three of these kinds of creator figures: the Marind-anim *dema,* the Morehead "story people" *(meintj),* and Aboriginal dreamings.

Traveling Myth: The Sido Tales

It is not only the resemblance in the general form of these cosmologies that has attracted attention from scholars, but also the details of some of the mythology itself. This is true in particular of the so-called Papuan hero tales featuring the character Sido, also known as Sida, Said, Soida, Hido, Soido, Sorouw, or Souw. Roy Wagner has pointed out that "in their continuative aspect, these stories form a striking parallel to the series of myths involving a 'traveling creator' reported from northern Australia." There, too, "the activities of the hero are frequently associated with special landmarks, and the hero is often identified or connected with a snake, as is the case in many of the Papuan stories." Wagner points to some correspondences in the details in the story of Kunukban "Black-Headed Python" from the Victoria River area of the Northern Territory and the Daribi myth of Souw. He concludes that "it is not unlikely that [the Papuan hero tales] draw on a mythic complex of much greater extent that is widely ramified throughout Papua and Australia" (Wagner 1972:20; cf. Wagner 1996).

Of particular interest here are the myths of Aukam and Tiai, told in the western Torres Strait Islands, which Beckett (1975) shows to be related in a continuous series, not only with the Sido tales but also with myths told in the eastern Torres Strait Islands and mainland Australia, as far away as Wik Munkan on western Cape York and Mamu, more than five hundred kilometers down the east coast of Queensland. It is not at all implausible that these myths are all related in a single chain of transmission, since the earliest historical records and oral history attest to regular social contacts among people at every link: mainland and Kiwai Island Papuans with Torres Strait Islanders and western Torres Strait Islanders with Cape York Aborigines. And language relationships in the area show that this must have been the case for a very long time. For the western Torres Strait language shares many elements in common with Australian Aboriginal ones. Indeed, it has generally been taken to *be* an Australian Aboriginal language. This is now being contested by Robert Dixon (forthcoming), who argues that its Australian-seeming features are the result of extensive borrowing from mainland languages.[9] But in either case, extensive social interaction between islanders and Cape York Aborigines is presupposed.

In other words, even now after seven thousand years of separation between the two landmasses, what we see in the Torres Strait is not a sharp boundary between two categorically distinct culture areas but a continuum of related peoples and sociocultural forms. This is not to say that people who are distant from each other along the continuum share a common understanding of how they linked. The Berndts and Roy Wagner, from the Australian and New Guinea sides, respectively, both make the important point that the knowledge of transcultural and transregional Creator Beings was always local and partial, and that only in exceptional circumstances did the entire geographic and narrative dimension of any Being's activities become explicitly apprehended by humans:

> As a rule no local descent group, clan, or dialect unit owns a complete myth. Even though at first it may appear to do so, what it has is usually only a section, dealing with some of the actions of a certain being. (Berndt and Berndt 1952:201)

> An important feature of these myths is that the hero is generally portrayed as journeying across the known world in some significant way, and that this movement is linked to the major action of the plot. . . . Landmarks and curious features along his route are often linked to his passage, and at Karamui he is said to have created many of the prominent landforms. Frequently the hero is supposed to have originated in the territory of a neighboring people. . . . My Daribi informants told me "we know the story up to the Sazabage [a local ridge], if you want to know what happened afterward, ask the people at Iuro." The total effect is one of a series of linked myths, continued from one society to the next, or, in the native view, the continued adventures of a single wandering hero. (Wagner 1972:19–20)

In short, there is a kind of spatialization of knowledge that goes hand in hand with knowledge of places (cf. chapter 1). James Weiner turns again to this twin theme of emplaced knowledge and knowledge of places in his afterword to this volume, showing it to be a prominent feature of sociality in both New Guinea and Aboriginal Australia and arguing that it lies at the heart of what is distinctive to the two in conjunction with each other. This is not to say that it is unique to the two regions, any more than the Ku Waru class of wealth items is limited to pigs and kina shells. But the two regions are salient exemplars of this relationship, and in true Melpa–Ku Waru fashion, the pairing of the two serves to make visible a feature (in this case itself a two-way relationship, between knowledge of places and emplacement of knowledge) that turns out to be of wider import.

Further Lines of Comparison Developed in the Volume

Above, I have been discussing two different sorts of relationships that have been posited in previous essays toward a comparative anthropology of Australia and New Guinea. In the Sido tales, what is at issue is relationships of direct contiguity within a single sociohistorical field. By contrast, the comparisons made by van Baal, van der Leeden, and Knauft may hint at such a relationship, but they do not presuppose it. All three of those comparisons turn up what are taken to be significant resemblances between particular lifeways in specified regions of Australia and New Guinea, and these are taken as a ground of similarity against which differences can also stand out as significant (cf. Stewart and Strathern, chapter 4 in this volume).

In general, the trans-Arafura comparisons made in this volume are of the latter sort rather than the former. That is, the main point of them is not to establish a historical relationship, for all that they may hint at one. Rather, as already suggested by my invocation of the Melpa–Ku Waru practice of pairing, the point is to see what new light can be shed on each term of the comparison by considering it in relation to the other.

To this end, in chapter 1 I trace the relationships among ancestral tracks, myth, and placedness in Australia and areas of Melanesia, focusing particularly on Aranda and Ngarinyin (Australia), Morehead River and Iatmul (New Guinea), and Tanna (Vanuatu). Taking up Deleuze and Guattari's notion of the rhizome as an image of nonhierarchical connectivity, I argue that it is useful for understanding the groundedness of cosmology in landscape that is common to all these cases, but that, in light of them, the opposition that Deleuze and Guattari posit between rhizomatic and supposedly "Western," "arborescent" models is in need of some refinements. Drawing on these cases, and on my experience in working on Aboriginal land claims, I also offer some general conclusions about the relation between indigenous cosmologies, anthropology, and the politics of landedness in Third and Fourth World settings.

In six of the remaining nine chapters, the authors explicitly develop other comparisons, either involving other areas of Australia and Papua New Guinea, other aspects of the cosmologies, or both. In the remainder of this introduction I will briefly summarize those chapters so as to orient the reader to the rest of the book. In this respect my discussion is complementary to James Weiner's in the afterword, since his concern there is not to take up points of comparison made by the other authors but to make his own. His discussion does, however, include good summaries of the three noncomparative chapters, by Wagner, Lattas, and Redmond, to which I refer the reader rather than saying anything further about them here.

In chapter 2 Jürg Wassmann provides an account of the Iatmul system of religious secrecy. He focuses on the ritual knotted cord as an iconic representation both of a spatial sequence of place names adumbrated in important creation myths and of a narrative sequence of names, the knowledge of which provides the basis of political power in Iatmul society. He demonstrates how clans in Iatmul society are focused on the necessity to withhold the knowledge of these names from rival clans who seek to divest them of rights to territory. Drawing on Australian ethnography from Arnhem Land and the central desert, Wassmann shows that there are strong similarities with respect to the role of ancestral movements among named places, and of secret knowledge of them, but that there is among the Iatmul a much greater emphasis on knowledge of the names per se, of which there are many for each place and totemic figure. The sets of alternative names serve as masks to provide a large set of alternative identities for a small number of underlying "essences," and knowledge of these is power.

Wassmann's perspective on Iatmul cosmology, based on his fieldwork with the Western Iatmul (Nyaura) is complemented in chapter 9 by that of Eric Silverman, who has worked among the Eastern Iatmul. Following up on the extended comparison he has drawn elsewhere between Sepik cosmology and Australian Aboriginal (Silverman 1997), Silverman notes the parallels with regard to onomastic topogenesis, ancestral travel, and the resulting landscape of tracks or "strings," but he contrasts the two in the degree of fixity they posit: while the Australian dreamtime is often represented as a "single unchanging, timeless source" (Myers 1986:52), by contrast "Eastern Iatmul rarely envision a fixed cosmos" but instead "view their cosmology in terms of pluralism, disjunction and contradiction." Silverman also provides a wide-ranging view of contemporary dilemmas of cultural property and the dissemination of formerly secret iconographic designs that are themselves keys to control of knowledge in these societies.

Chapter 4, by Pamela Stewart and Andrew Strathern, shows that the "ancestral track" motif is by no means a constant across even small areas of Papua New Guinea. Drawing upon their fieldwork among the Duna people of the Southern Highlands, Stewart and Strathern discuss the extensive system of ritual trackways that crosscut the Huli-Duna-Ipili region (cf. also Biersack 1995:16–19) and note the parallel between these and Australian dreaming tracks. But among the nearby Hageners of the Western Highlands Province, where they have also worked (about a hundred kilometers to the east), no such tracks are evident. The Hageners do have their charter myths, however, and Stewart and Strathern develop a fine-grained comparison between these and those of the Yolngu people of northeastern Arnhem Land. They frame their comparison in terms of a useful ideal-typic distinction between "origin stories," which tell of events that lay down a permanent state of affairs, and "creation stories," which stress human agency and tell of "events that initiate a new state of affairs in historical terms."

In a fitting homage to her teacher Jane Goodale, Deborah Bird Rose, in chapter 5, develops an extended comparison between the cosmology of Aborigines she has worked with in the Victoria River region of the Northern Territory and that of the Kaulong people of West New Britain as described by Goodale (1995). Both posit a realm of "enduring sources," to which living beings must sustain a relationship through their everyday productive activities. Among the Victoria River people the enduring source is the dreaming. Humans are seen as embedded in the habitats that sustain them, through relations of subject-to-subject reciprocity both among themselves and with the nonhuman world. Among the Kaulong the enduring sources of life are seen to lie in the forest, outside the human realm, which is associated with the clearing. Human life is "brought out of the forest and into the garden and clearing, where it is sustained through human action." Rose argues that in comparison to the Aboriginal system "the organization of human responsibility toward the world is thus diminished."

Returning to the theme of secrecy, which is prominent in Wassmann's chapter, James Weiner in chapter 7 takes up the dramatic and critical case of the Hindmarsh Island Aboriginal sacred site application in South Australia. Drawing upon the ethnography of the Australian Aboriginal Yulbaridja and Yolngu and the New Guinea Baktaman and Iatmul, he addresses the issue of restricted knowledge. He suggests that the avowal of nescience, or ignorance of important cultural information, is not a mere lack but is itself an important aspect of cultural and personal localization within regimes that are founded on a difference in access to cosmological knowledge. This chapter addresses not just the disjunction between knowledge and landedness but also how this disjunction itself is often put to creative uses in what appear to be wholly indigenous contexts.

The final chapter, by Lissant Bolton, is based on her fieldwork in Vanuatu and her employment both at the Vanuatu Cultural Centre there and at the Australian Museum in Sydney. Bolton shows how the movement of objects, myths, and designs finds its way into the "sacred places" of the Western world, namely the museums that house the material embodiment of these regimes of narrative and restricted knowledge. She draws attention to the problems of incommensurability between these cultures and standard Western notions of objectification, with implications for how legislation designed to protect the cultural property and viability of these traditions may or may not accomplish what it intends to. Both in the Pacific Islands and at Australian museums, where Aboriginal people now take a leading role in shaping the presentation of their culture, in line with these people's priorities, there has been a lessening of emphasis upon material objects and a correspondingly greater one on the *performance* of culture and on the protection of the *places* that are of continuing cultural significance.

In demonstrating as much, Bolton's chapter brings together two important points that pertain to the volume as a whole. One (elegantly demonstrated by Silverman's chapter also) is that, whatever else they do, people in all the specific locales and regions under discussion here also participate (however unevenly) in global circuits of power, with respect to which the whole world must be taken as the relevant "ethnographic region." The other point is that the lifeways that are discussed in this volume are not mere relics of a premodern past, nor do they exist in an empyrean realm of disembodied images. They are grounded in earthly places no less tangible than the substance that is set to flow from Kutubu to Queensland. Through their detailed comparative examination of the modalities of that emplacement, we hope the essays in this volume will help foster a new appreciation of what is at stake in the ever-intensifying struggles for recognition of the landedness of indigenous peoples in Australia, New Guinea, and beyond.

Notes

For their helpful comments on earlier drafts of this introduction I would like to thank Eric Hirsch, Francesca Merlan, James Weiner, and two anonymous referees. I am especially indebted to James Weiner, who first proposed the main idea of the opening paragraph and was a major stimulus for many of the other ideas developed here. For the discussion of the prehistory of Australia, New Guinea, and Sahul, I am indebted to Chris Gosden, Rhys Jones, and especially Jack Golson, who wrote a lucid paper on the subject for the conference from which this volume arose.

1. See Sagir (in press) for an account of conflict between Foi and Fasu landowners in the Kutubu oil project area over the division of petroleum revenues between them.

2. The conference was funded by a grant from the Wenner-Gren Foundation, and the Resource Management in the Pacific project at the Research School of Pacific and Asian Studies, Australian National University. We thank these benefactors for their support.

3. Compare van der Leeden's concluding proposition that "a comparative study of structural resemblances between Australia and Melanesia can make an important contribution to the knowledge of elementary structures" (van der Leeden 1970:89). From the more nominalist spirit in which analytical frameworks are generally deployed in anthropology nowadays, this way of putting the matter seems otiose. Even Lévi-Strauss, for all his emphasis on universal unconscious mental structures, cautions that "the notions of 'elementary structures' and of 'complex structures' are purely heuristic—they provide a tool for investigation—and . . . cannot be used alone to define a system" (Lévi-Strauss 1965: 18). Rather than ask how our knowledge of elementary structures might be increased by studying resemblances between Australia and Melanesia, most of the contributors to this volume would, I think, be more inclined to ask how our understanding of what goes on in Australia and Melanesia might or might not be aided by any such abstract notion: "elementary structure," "partible person," or whatever.

4. As in many areas of Melanesia, the Ku Waru people took the Europeans to be their own ancestors or distant collateral relatives, and all their marvelous wealth and miraculous technology to be something that they themselves had once had but lost when their white (or, as they say, "red") ancestors absconded with them.

5. The same is potentially true of some of the comparisons made in the Africa-Melanesia volume (Lambek and Strathern 1998), notwithstanding the considerable geographic distance between two areas, for two of the four papers in the volume that concern "African" peoples are about peoples of Madagascar, which is anomalous with respect to the Africa-Melanesia axis, as it bears the strong imprint of prehistoric colonization by Austronesian-speaking people, just as do the eastern reaches of "Melanesia."

6. Within the past two decades there have been conferences focused on the following regions: Mountain Ok (Craig and Hyndman 1990), Sepik (Lutkehaus 1990), southwestern New Guinea Highlands (Biersack 1995; Goldman and Ballard 1998), the Massim area (Leach and Leach 1983; Damon and Wagner 1989), and the Angan region.

7. But see also Mead (1933–1934) and Silverman (1997) for some interesting comparisons involving the Sepik region.

8. See, for example, the remarks by a Western Desert Aboriginal man cited in chapter 1 in this volume, note 4.

9. Aside from the well-established fact of linguistic borrowing across the Torres Strait, one has to ask, given that Australia and New Guinea were one landmass until about ten thousand years ago, whether there are any demonstrable deeper-level genetic relations between presently attested Papuan languages and Australian Aboriginal ones. The answer is, no, not really. An interesting case for such a relationship has been made by a leading Papuanist, Bill Foley (1986), who presented new evidence in support of it at the conference from which this volume arose. But Foley himself still considers his case to be inconclusive. This can, however, by no means be taken as firm evidence that the languages do *not* derive from a common source, since the comparative method used by historical linguists is generally unreliable for reconstructing relations beyond about ten thousand years before the present.

1
Tracks, Traces, and Links to Land in Aboriginal Australia, New Guinea, and Beyond

Alan Rumsey

Does not the east, Oceania in particular, offer something like a rhizomatic model opposed in every respect to the Western model of the tree?

(Deleuze and Guattari 1987)

A commonplace of Australianist ethnography is that people's relationships to country and to each other are seen to have been determined by the founding acts of primordial beings who moved across the land and sea, giving the world its present form by creating named places linked in series. Readily comprehended as instances of Deleuze and Guattari's "rhizomatic model" (Muecke, Benterrak, and Roe 1984), these Australian "dreaming tracks" bear some interesting family resemblances to forms of topographic objectification attested as far away as Amazonia (Hill 1993), North America (Waterman 1920; La Flesche 1925) and eastern Indonesia (Fox 1997a, 1997b). But some of the most striking parallels are found closer to Australia, in New Guinea and island Melanesia. Here I will be describing three such cases, from directly across the Torres Strait in south coast New Guinea, from the middle Sepik region, and from Tanna, in south Vanuatu. Comparing these Melanesian cases with each other and with the Australian ones, I will here try to locate the various forms and uses of ancestral tracks within what I have elsewhere described as an "economy of inscriptive and interpretive practices" (Rumsey 1994). There are three distinct but interrelated issues that I seek to address by way of this comparison.

First, I consider the relevant Australian and Melanesian forms of topographic inscription in relation to Deleuze and Guattari's model of the "rhizome" and their opposing notion of arborescence, which they associate with nomadic socioterritorial regimes and centralized, state-based ones, respectively. While this model has been around for some time now and has been much discussed in the fields of cultural studies and literary theory, it has not, to my knowledge, been addressed much by anthropologists. This is unfortunate, for while many anthropologists may not have read Deleuze and Guattari, Deleuze and Guattari have clearly read a good deal of anthropology, and have taken it seriously as a source of ideas and ethnographic evidence. In return, anthropologists ought to engage with their work—take it seriously as a possible source of theoretical insight, but bring to bear on it our specialist knowledge of the ethnography they draw upon and of the range of cross-cultural phenomena that they try to take account of.[1] Here I will do this with respect to some of the vast field they call "Oceania" and argue that their model is very revealing in some respects but that it is too dichotomous and must be further relativized in order to comprehend a wider range of difference than Deleuze and Guattari anticipate.

Second, I try to show that the emphasis anthropologists have given to tracks, traces, and the grounding of the sociocultural order in landscape has not been constant in the ethnography of this region but has increased in the recent past. Emerging first in some modernist Australianist ethnography of the 1940s, this emphasis has more recently found its way into some Melanesianist anthropology. This has happened at least in part as a matter of direct influence of the former upon the latter—contrary to the general tendency nowadays for Melanesianist anthropology to be a net exporter of theoretical capital and Australianist a rather more provincial power in the commerce among regional ethnographic traditions. Posing the question of why these changes of emphasis have taken place, I try to relate them to the more general shifts of intellectual orientation that have raised theorists such as Deleuze and Guattari to prominence over previously influential forms of structuralism.

Third, I point out that alongside these shifts of academic fashion there has been, in Australia and at least some areas of Melanesia, an increasingly self-conscious focus among the indigenous peoples themselves on the grounding of cosmology and social identity in landscape. Drawing on my own experience in northwestern Australia, and an ethnographic case from Vanuatu, I explore the historical conditions under which this development has taken place and offer some general conclusions about the relation between indigenous cosmologies and the politics of landedness in Third and Fourth World settings.

Before I turn to a discussion of the relevant ethnography, I will provide some background details concerning Deleuze and Guattari's "nomadology."

The Rhizome and the Tree

Deleuze and Guattari's well-known distinction between rhizomatic and arborescent models is part of more general framework to which they variously refer to as "schizoanalysis," "pragmatics," or "nomadology." Rejecting any a priori distinction between individual-psychological and sociopolitical levels of analysis, they distinguish instead among different types of libidinal-cum-social "machines," which are associated with specific types of "territorialization" or "deterritorialization." In their book *Anti-Oedipus* (1977), the three types are the "primitive territorial machine," the "barbarian despotic machine," and the "civilized capitalist machine." In their later book *A Thousand Plateaus* (1987), this three-way contrast largely collapses into a two-way one between sedentary state-based forms and "nomadic," anti-state ones. They see these not as evolutionary "stages" but as opposing tendencies that are equally primordial.[2] "The state" is not limited to a particular economic mode of production, but is "defined by the perpetuation or conservation of organs of power" (Deleuze and Guattari 1987:357). Following the ethnologist Pierre Clastres (1977), they see the potential for this as something that is present in all societies. Therefore, the "primitive" is characterized not by the mere absence of centralized organs of power but by the presence of mechanisms for inhibiting their development. One of these is what they call the "war machine" (Deleuze and Guattari 1987:351–423). Another is the "rhizome."

Deleuze and Guattari's notion of the rhizome can best be understood by starting with what they oppose it to—"the tree," which they claim has dominated "Western reality and all of Western thought" (Deleuze and Guattari 1987:18). For them, the most important characteristic of trees is that they are "centered systems," within which there is a fixed hierarchical ordering of units and subunits at successive levels of ramification. "Arborescent systems are hierarchical systems with centers of significance and subjectification . . . an element only receives information from a higher unit, and only receives a subjective affectation along preestablished paths" (Deleuze and Guattari 1987:16). By contrast, rhizomes (literally, rootstocks) are systems in which there is not only hierarchical ramification but also the possibility of reconnection:

> Unlike trees or their roots, the rhizome connects any point to any other point. . . . The rhizome is reducible neither to the One nor the multiple. It is not the One that becomes Two or even directly three, four, five, etc. It is not a multiple derived from the One, or to which One is added. . . . It has neither beginning nor end, but always a middle (milieu) from which it grows and which it overspills. (Deleuze and Guattari 1987:21)

As is apparent from my opening quote, Deleuze and Guattari themselves fall victim to the "arborescent" mode of thought insofar as they try to force such vast abstractions as "the West" and "the East" (or "Oceania") into a simple binary opposition between "tree" and "rhizome."[3] But their formulation is still useful in directing our attention to some important characteristics of all the forms of topographic inscription that I will be considering below and in giving us a handle on some of the ways in which these have been brought into *actual* "binary opposition" with the colonizing West, as we shall see later on in this chapter. I turn now to some relevant ethnography, beginning with the Australian case.

The Dreaming

As a classic example of what is entailed in the notion of "dreaming" in Australia I begin with an Aranda account of the awakening of Karora, the "Bandicoot Ancestor," as translated by T. G. H. Strehlow:

> In the very beginning everything was resting in perpetual darkness. . . . The *gurra* ancestor—his name was Karora—was lying asleep . . . at the very bottom of the soak of Ilbalintja; as yet there was no water in it, but all was dry ground.
>
> Then the *gurra* ancestor was minded to rise, now that the sun was mounting higher. He burst through the crust that had covered

> him: and the gaping hole that he left behind became the Ilbalintja Soak, filled with the sweet dark juice of the honeysuckle buds. (Strehlow 1947:7–8)

This one mythic fragment may stand for many, both from Aranda and from elsewhere in Australia. As Strehlow says, "The primeval landscape was transformed into its present shape through the labours of the great totemic ancestors" (25). Thus anchored in the enduring landscape, "every incident in the myth is firmly fixed" (6) and, conversely, "every feature of the landscape . . . in central Australia is . . . associated with one or the other of these myths" (6). The central Australian "does not regard the various physical objects in the landscape [merely as] . . . signposts that 'mark the spot' where the important events in the lives of his totemic ancestors took place at the beginning of time"; rather, he regards them as the "actual bodies of his ancestors" (28).

Many of these totemic ancestors did not merely emerge from the earth but moved across it, forming places that are thereby linked with each other in tracks, or through underground connections likened to the sinews and nerves that bind a living body beneath the skin. There is a kind of temporal paradox to the tracks, in that while they form an ordered series established by the totemic beings' movement from one to the next, the totemic being is nonetheless simultaneously present at all of them (25 ff.). This is related to a more general paradox: although the time of creation was before the present, it is also simultaneous with it.[4]

People who are currently living are linked to country through these creative acts, both in highly particular ways, through clan and conception, through dreamings that do not move, and more extensively through the connections among places that are established by the movements of the traveling dreamings. Knowledge of those creative acts, places, songs, and stories is itself localized, owned by the people for those places, as are the languages that were left in their country (Rumsey 1993).

In general, the relationships that were established among places and knowledges by the movements of the totemic beings are nonhierarchical ones: in Deleuze and Guattari's terms they were rhizome-like rather than "arborescent." Within small regions such as the clan countries created by Karora in the Aranda account above, there are originary centers such as the one at Ilbalintja, from which the bandicoot ancestor and his sons moved around the region and came back. But what they did there does not establish any relative priority or precedence as between that place and any of the many other Aranda clan centers and countries. The more far-traveled dreamings, such as the "Tjilpa" or the "Two Brothers," are generally of unknown origin, and nobody commands a knowledge of what they did along their entire route. Rather, people know the story for a particular segment of the journey within their own country. It cannot be otherwise, because in an important sense the country *is* the story (cf. Strehlow 1947:5–6, 159; Myers 1986:59; Rumsey 1994).

The relations among the places linked by dreaming tracks are rhizome-like in another respect, in that tracks cross each other, dreamings meet and interact in particular episodes identified with places where they meet. This pattern establishes a multitude of cross-cutting relations to places, in which connectedness and differentiation are necessary conditions for each other (cf. Sutton 1997). Figure 1-1, a drawing by the late David Mowaljarlai, a Ngarinyin man from the Kimberley region of Western Australia, shows this model rather speculatively applied at a global level to the whole of Australia, conceived as a single body that is literally "organized" by crosscutting ancestral tracks that are also sinews, bones, and internal organs.

Before moving on to the Melanesian examples, I will introduce some more Australian ethnography in order to provide a rather more detailed exemplification of the ways in which present-day social dispositions are grounded in the landscape by the actions of the totemic ancestors. The examples come from David Mowaljarlai's homeland in the far north of Western Australia, where I have been doing fieldwork on and off since 1975 (see also chapter 6 below, which deals with the same region).

Mowaljarlai spoke three Aboriginal languages (and English), but he was especially closely identified with one of them, Ngarinyin. This was not because he spoke it better than the others (he was in fact equally fluent in Worrorra). Rather it was because the land to which he had his main traditional links was within Ngarinyin country. But what is Ngarinyin country? Since *most* speakers of Aboriginal languages in the Kimberleys (and elsewhere) are and were multilingual like Mowaljarlai, such language areas cannot be identified by their being the homeland of a group of people who speak the language (as they are, for example, in the nationalist ideologies of Europe). Rather,

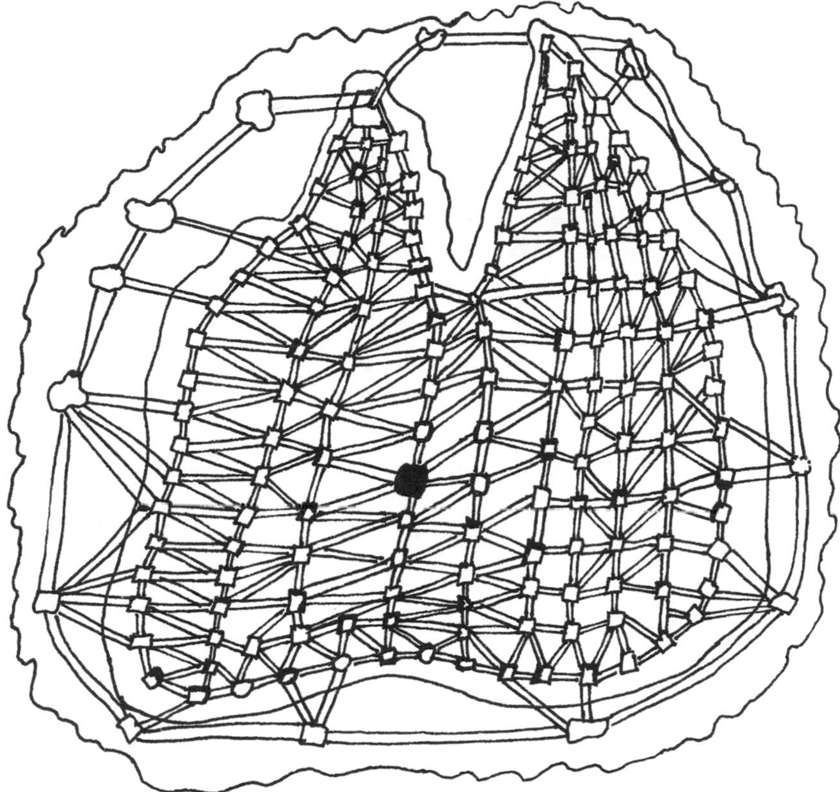

Figure 1-1. The Body of Australia, by David Mowaljarlai. Some details have been omitted for clarity. (From Mowaljarlai and Malnic 1993:205; redrawn for this publication by Doerte Sueberkrueb. Reproduced with the permission of Hannah Rachel Bell, executrix for the estate of David Mowaljarlai)

in this area, as elsewhere in Aboriginal Australia (Rumsey 1989, 1993), the link between language and country is a *direct* one, established by founding acts of the totemic ancestors: the Ngarinyin language was installed in the landscape by one of them who was called Andarri (Possum), who began speaking it at Gulemen (Beverley Springs) and then traversed a larger region. It was his propagation of the language throughout that region that established it as Ngarinyin country, and it will still be Ngarinyin country even if the language should cease to be spoken and be replaced by English (which seems likely to happen over the next generation or two).

Within Ngarinyin country, there are approximately sixty-five distinct named subregions known as *dambun,* which are associated with particular totemic species and with named creator figures called Wanjina, most of whom have "left themselves" as paintings found in rock shelters at one or more sites within the *dambun* (for further details, see Elkin 1932; Capell 1972; Crawford 1968; Redmond, chapter 6 below). The Wanjina are said to have formed the entire landscape and, in combination with the Wunggurr ("Rainbow Serpent"), to have deposited into it the immortal child-spirits, which successively animate the body of each living person down through the generations. People are linked to *dambun* in various ways. The most salient one for many purposes is the link through one's father. David Mowaljarlai, for example, was a *jirad* "Hybiscus" man, linked to the *Jirad dambun* in the western reaches of the Ngarinyin country, and therefore a member of the Jirad "clan" (Brrejirad), because his socially recognized father was (see Redmond, chapter 6 in this volume, for further examples). But there are other kinds of links to particular *dambun* that are established through other kin (-cum-affinal) relations: the *maanggarra* link through one's mother, *gaja* "mother's mother," *maga* "father's mother" (= "prescribed spouse" for a man), and so on. Indeed, the *dambun* "countries" themselves are said to be related to each other within these classificatory kin categories, and these relationships among countries persist even in the case of *dambun* for which there are no surviving clan members (people linked to them through their father). The countries are also linked to each other through another system of serial pathways called *wurnan,* in which sacred objects and esoteric knowledge are passed from one clan to another (Blundell and Layton 1978, Rumsey 1996). Here again, in both of these systems of relations among clan countries, as in the case of the language-land link, present-day social arrangements are seen to have been installed directly in the landscape by the world-forming acts of totemic ancestors.

Morehead River

Now let us consider some apparently similar forms of "totemic landscape" from Melanesia. One of the most striking examples comes from the Morehead River area, in what is known (from a Port Moresby–centric perspective) as the "Trans-Fly" region, about two hundred kilometers away from the northeastern tip of Australia. The Australia-like features of this region appear most clearly in the work of Mary Ayres, who did her fieldwork there during 1979–1981 as a University of Chicago doctoral student and submitted her dissertation in 1983 (cf. Knauft 1993:185). To a much greater extent than the previous ethnographer F. E. Williams (1936), Ayres emphasizes what she calls the "system of places" as the basis of Morehead cosmology and social structure. She says this system is "staggering in its elaboration" (Ayres 1983:38); there are "several thousand named places . . . all . . . made through the actions of the mythical beings [*meintj*]" as they moved across the landscape (Ayres 1983:44). The mythical age in which they did this, though only a few generations ago, was "qualitatively different" from the present, a "creative, formative time of events which have passed, irrevocably finished, never to reoccur; the present is a physical and cultural order fixed in meaning by the perceived reality of the mythical age. The land and landscape mediate the two ages" (Ayres 1983:48). As in Australia, knowledge of places and their stories is a highly valued and highly localized resource. To a perhaps greater extent than in Australia, the stories and especially the *names* in them are valued in abstraction from the places themselves: "The relationship of people to mythical places is based fundamentally on knowledge of the myths about the places, and in particular on knowledge of the proper names of the active beings who people the myths. A claim is made not so much on the site of the storyplace itself, but on the secret knowledge about it" (Ayres 1983:122; cf. 162).

Recounting the difficult time her guides had when trying to find an especially important storyplace, and their ultimate uncertainty as to whether they had found it, and citing a similar experience that Williams had reported having in 1927, Ayres comments that there is a "discrepancy between the awe in which storyplaces are held, and their [degree of] visible impressiveness" (326). She also claims that there is discrepancy between the amount of knowledge that people have of the places, "the content of the secret mythology" about them, and people's rather more tenuous knowledge of the "actual location of the places." Ayres says that the fact "that the places are real or actual is sufficient grounds to prove that what happened in the mythical times really and truly happened" (326).

Besides this apparently greater degree of possible abstraction of the currency of names and stories from the places in the landscape that underwrite them, Morehead cosmology also differs from Australian Aboriginal in the kind of relationships there are among the places and the social identities associated with them. Whereas there is in general no order of precedence among origin places in Australia, in Morehead there is quite an elaborate one. There is a single origin place for all the Morehead people, a place called Kwavar, now under the sea in Torres Strait. There is a second place, Tjuari, to which the survivors moved after the flood. From there they moved on to a number of other places, sometimes in linear series but often also in successive phases of proliferation out from common nodes, as shown in figure 1-2.

The word "branching" might seem appropriate for the latter mode, because the tree is indeed the main figure in terms of which Morehead people construe their segmentary social relationships and the mapping of these onto landscape (240). But unlike some dominant Western forms of arboreal metaphor, such as the one assumed by Deleuze and Guattari in contrast to the rhizome, the one used by Morehead people seems to focus not so much upon the tree as a fully formed object as upon the way it grows—what Ayres refers to as "the paradigm of differentiation." There are two variants of this paradigm, alternatively invoked by the Morehead people, based on two different sorts of trees: the *saker,* Black Palm, and *wasur,* a species that Ayres identifies only as "a type of *ficus* or fig tree" (100) but that from her description can be clearly identified as a strangler fig. As shown in figure 1-3, these trees are used as models of, respectively, "lineal segmentation from a unity" and "scattering or fragmentation from a starting point or center." While this process is irreversible in its temporal aspect, in its spatial aspect it is at least partially reversible in that nodal "center places" can be reconstituted by people moving back to them from the places to which they had dispersed (160). And no matter how many phases of differentiation may have occurred since the one at Kwavar, in a sense things remain in their originary state, since each episode of differentiation replicates the last. This, I take it, is one reason why Ayres can claim, despite the order of precedence established by the mythology, that "although places are different, they are non-hierarchically ordered" (178). There is also another, rather surprising, reason, based on specific attributes of the strangler fig, which I take up in the concluding section.

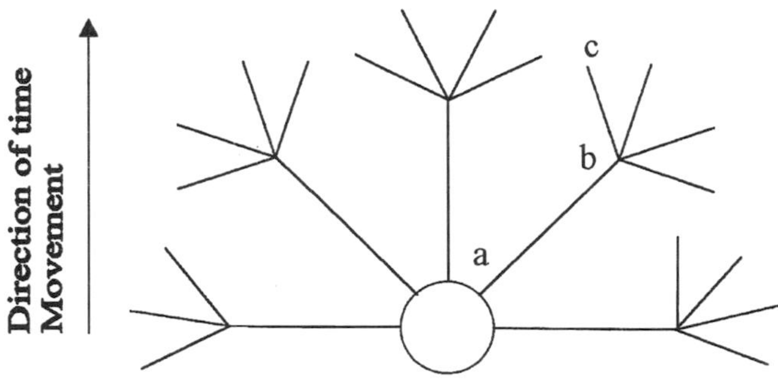

Scattering or fragmentation from
a "starting point" or "center"

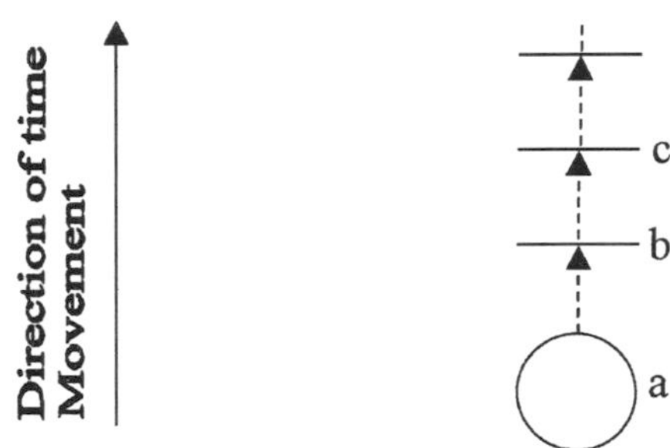

Lineal segmentation from a unity

Figure 1-2. Schematic representation of two paradigms of differentiation used in the Morehead River area of South Coast New Guinea. (From Ayres 1983:104; redrawn for this publicaiton by Doerte Sueberkrueb. Reproduced with the permission of Mary Ayers)

Iatmul

For the next example of Melanesian forms of "ancestral track" I turn to the Iatmul people of the middle Sepik, Papua New Guinea. I will be brief, referring the reader to the chapters by Wassmann and Silverman for fuller ethnographic details. Suffice it to say here that the

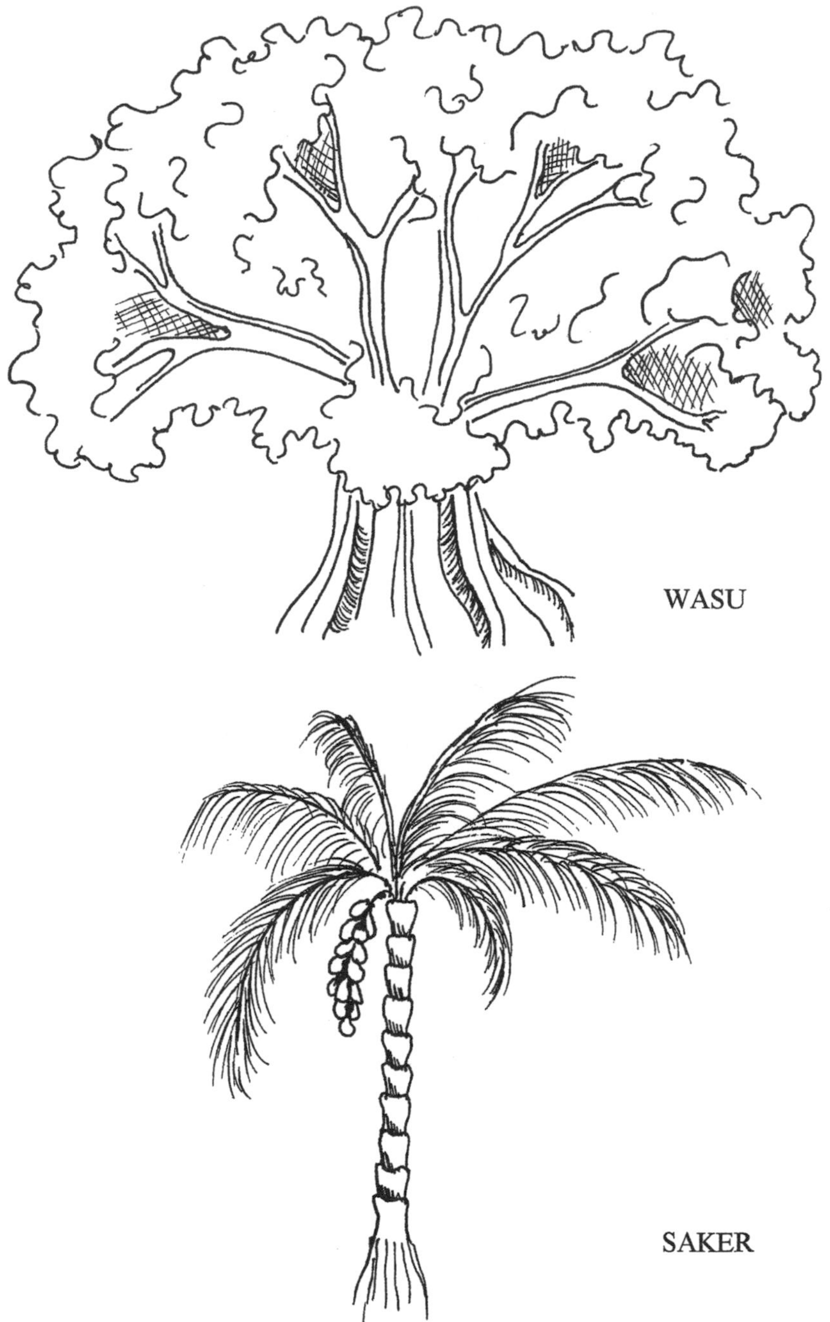

Figure 1-3. Two types of origin trees from the Morehead River area of South Coast New Guinea. (From Ayres 1983: 101; redrawn for this publication by Doerte Sueberkrueb. Reproduced with the permission of Mary Ayers)

Iatmul, in common with other people in this area, trace the origin of the world back to a time when all was flat, featureless, and aquatic. A pit then formed, out of which arose the totemic ancestors who moved around creating the various paths of named places and associated phenomena that are the property of each clan. These movements are reenacted by present-day clansmen through the recital of the esoteric paired names and the singing of totemic songs for each place along the path. Various kinds of mnemonic devices are used in this reenactment: the Eastern Iatmul use palm fronds, into which they insert a wooden peg for each pair of names; the Manambu use spears, arrows and sticks, and the Central and Western Iatmul a twine cord with a knot for each name, as shown in figure 2-3 of Wassmann's chapter.

I have already commented that the Morehead River cosmology, as compared to Australian forms of topographic inscription, shows a greater degree of possible abstraction of the power of names from the physical reality of actual places in the landscape. This is true to an even greater degree of these Middle Sepik practices. Here there seems to be little emphasis on the existence of the actual place as bearing witness to the veracity of the myth and a correspondingly greater emphasis on the proliferation of names for a single place or totem, which must nonetheless be recounted in the correct order. Indeed, most of steps in the sequence on the knotted cord are movements among multiple names for the same place or totem rather than among distinct places.

But notwithstanding this difference of emphasis, Middle Sepik cosmology shares with Australian Aboriginal a kind of radical particularism and sense of the localization of knowledges. As Silverman puts it: "Since each descent group has its own totemism, the Eastern Iatmul universe is plural, containing multiple histories and truths" (Silverman 1996:34). Similarly, Wassmann reports:

> Each "old crocodile" only controls part of the knowledge, since his clan group was responsible only for specific acts, ancestors, totems, and locations in ancient times. Correspondingly, today he is responsible for only a segment of the surrounding world; no clan group and no informant knows all the other knotted cords. Hence one's knowledge is always partial. (Wassmann, chapter 2 in this volume)

Tanna

My third Melanesian example comes not from New Guinea but from the island of Tanna, in southern Vanuatu, as described by Joel Bonnemaison. The Tannese creation accounts he recorded in the 1970s begin with a spirit called Wuhngin who "was here at the beginning of the world" (Bonnemaison 1994:115). Wuhngin created the land, which was originally "bare, lifeless and devoid of form" (115). He then sent a mob of stones, and "on the island's soft matrix, the stones created geographical shapes: mountains, capes, and headlands, ridges and crests" (115). For a long time the stones moved restlessly about. They created three great roads around and across the island and settled down along them (116). "When they settled down, they received names and turned into places" (122). Some turned into humans —the first men—and some turned into the first animals (123). Nowadays, says Bonnemaison, "on the island, there is hardly any mountain, spring or large rock that does not refer to a myth" (113). The myths are "replete with topographical details and place names" (114), and no Tannese questions them "because places and stones are there to corroborate the story" (113). As in Australia, "each local group protects the part of the myth that occurs on its territory and refers to the neighbouring group to know the next segment of the story. . . . The knowledge of myth-related toponymy is . . . perceived as locally owned" and "the fact that it has been committed to memory and transmitted from one generation to the next within the group" as "proof of both the authenticity of its origin and the legitimacy of the group's territorial rights" (114).

In comparison to the other cases I have reviewed so far, this Tanna creation story differs in beginning with a preexisting spirit, in the preeminence it gives to stones as agents of creation, and in the emphasis it gives to the opposition between random movement and fixedness, and the latter as the basis of the present moral order (though that theme figures in the Morehead River case as well). But notwithstanding these differences, there are striking similarities in the way the earth is interpreted as a surface of inscription, in the dense interconnectedness of named places along tracks established by the movements of the protean creator figures, in the localization of knowledge about those movements and the role that that knowledge plays in the reproduction and contestation of present-day people's rights in land.

Having compared four ethnographic accounts of the grounding of cosmology and social identity from Australia and three widely scattered places in Melanesia,[5] I now return to the three general issues outlined in the introduction.

Is Oceania to the West as Rhizome Is to Tree?

At several points in my discussion of the ethnography above, I have already referred in passing to Deleuze and Guattari's notions of rhizome and tree. The main problems that I think these examples present for their model are as follows:

First, the model is too restrictive in what it assumes about trees. As we have seen from the Morehead River example, it is not only in "the West" that the tree figures importantly in people's modeling of socioterritorial organization and social process. But the *way* in which it figures is underdetermined by the nature of trees themselves. Indeed, there are important differences among *kinds* of trees—for example, between deciduous trees, which only grow upward from the ground, and *ficus* species such as the banyan tree—a key symbol of life elsewhere in South and Southeast Asia (Bosch 1960; Giambelli 1998)—which also propagates from the aerial roots that grow out from the branches and hang down to the ground, where they can give rise to a new trunk. The strangler figs similarly propagate from aerial roots, except that they typically begin life not on the ground but on a host tree of another species, in which a seed has been left in the feces of a bird. Sprouting and taking root in the host tree, the strangler fig sends out aerial roots that grow downward until they reach the ground, thence giving rise to new trunklike growths that eventually surround and displace the host tree. In the developmental cycle of both the banyan tree and the strangler figs, there is a confounding of the one-way "hierarchical" relation between trunk and branch in that the aerial roots that grow from branches can give rise to new trunks, which themselves give rise to new branches, and so on. Furthermore, the aerial roots, after reaching the ground, can reconnect with the root system that is already in place and nourishing the branch from which they are growing. Thus, Deleuze and Guattari's "rhizomatic" mode, far from being opposed to the "tree," is a conspicuous property of these trees.[6] And, in the Morehead people's use of the strangler fig as a model for social process and socioterritorial relations, it is this rhizomatic mode of reproduction that is central (Fernandez 1998:99 and Linton 1959:v, regarding the banyan).[7]

The second problem lies not so much with the "rhizomatic model" itself as with what it assumes about associated forms of "territorialization." For Deleuze and Guattari, the state and the arborescent model are associated with what they call "striated space," and the opposing "nomadic," rhizome-based regimes with "smooth space." They see territoriality in the latter regimes as being "based on local, overlapping divisions. Codes and territories, clan lineages and tribal territorialities, form a fabric of relatively supple segmentarity [as opposed to the 'rigid segmentarity' of state regimes]" (Deleuze and Guattari 1987:209). It is difficult to know exactly what they mean by this because their use of actual examples is rather sparse,[8] but the overall impression they convey with words such as "smooth," "overlapping," "supple," and "nomadic" is that non-state-based forms of territoriality do not involve precise or elaborate differentiation of social space. All the ethnographic examples I have cited show otherwise. While few anthropologically informed readers will need any convincing on this score, the opposite assumption is still all too prevalent among even highly literate Westerners, and it is unfortunate that Deleuze and Guattari probably do more to promote that assumption than to dispel it—doubly unfortunate in that, as I shall argue below, the rhizome model is actually useful for countering that assumption and indeed plays an important part in at least some indigenous people's attempts to overturn it.

Why Now? Tracks and Traces in Ethnography and Elsewhere

Before discussing its role in the politics of land rights, I want to consider first how the groundedness of cosmology in landscape has emerged as an increasingly central focus in some Oceanic ethnography. In the discussion of the Morehead River case I mentioned that this emphasis was much stronger in the more recent ethnography by Ayres than in the earlier work of Williams (1936). This emphasis, and the view of landscape as mediating between the mythical age and the present, is no doubt at least partly attributable to the influence of

Nancy Munn, one of Ayres' academic supervisors. Ayres cites Munn (1970) as one of her main influences (Ayres 1983:49).

Joel Bonnemaison's account of Tanna ethnogeography would also seem to have been influenced by Australian ethnography, at least indirectly through the writings of Mircea Eliade. Bonnemaison's chapter "The Society of the Stones" begins with an epigraph from Eliade's book on Australian Aboriginal religions *(Religions australiennes)* (Bonnemaison 1994:130), and Bonnemaison uses the word "dreamtime" throughout his book in reference to the Tannese mythical period of creation. As he explains when first introducing the term (112 n, 333–334), this usage is modeled directly on the Australian Aboriginal one.

Granted that some kind of influence from Australian ethnography is evident here, is it appropriate to speak of it as a *theoretical* influence? Or is it just a case of ethnographers' reporting what is there in the indigenous cosmologies? I probably need not argue the point here that "cosmologies" or "cultures" never present themselves as such but are constructed in different ways, depending in part on the concepts one brings to bear on the fieldwork experience. In Williams' case, for example, it is clear that the absence of focus on totemic landscape is not attributable to any simple failure of observation. Ayres notes, for example, that Williams' recordings of myths in his field notebooks do include some of the same details she recorded about the location of events in them, but that he left them out of the published versions of the myths (Ayres 1983:67–68), apparently regarding them as unimportant, or as relevant mainly for questions concerning the actual origins and prehistoric movements of the Trans-Fly peoples, on which they did not provide good enough scientific evidence.

Likewise, other ethnographers of Tanna have mentioned the "society of stones" and the grounding of myth in landscape, but without giving them the centrality that Bonnemaison did (cf. Lindstrom 1990).

What might be some of the particular intellectual influences or political conditions under which the groundedness of cosmology or culture in landscape has or has not been emphasized?

Before saying anything more about its possible influence on Melanesian studies in this respect, I want to return to Australian ethnography per se and point out that however strong the emphasis on groundedness in landscape now is in the Australianist literature, it was not always so. Indeed, the main work I cited above, Strehlow's *Aranda Traditions,* written in 1934, was one of the very first works to place living, mythically inscribed landscape at the center of our understanding of Aboriginal culture (the other main pioneers in this respect being Stanner [1966]; Berndt [1951, 1952]; and Munn [1970, 1973b]). The earlier compendious Aranda ethnography by Spencer and Gillen (1899), which was, of course, for many years *the* paradigmatic Australian ethnography, contains a considerable amount of information about the movements of certain totemic ancestors, but in Spencer and Gillen's understanding, the bodies of those ancestors were thought to have died, the natural features then having arisen to "mark the spot" where it happened (Spencer and Gillen 1899:123; cf. Rumsey 1999b). Little or no sense is developed of the connectedness of places to each other or of the nexus among people, myth, and landscape. Again, this is not merely a failure of empirical observation. As evident in the monograph (Spencer and Gillen 1899:387–449), and from some of Gillen's comments in his correspondence to Spencer (e.g., Mulvaney, Morphy, and Petch 1997:166, 168), they did record a good deal of data on the localization of "totems" and ritual, and the mythical associations of particular places. But they do not accord landscape a central place in their account of Aranda social life.[9]

The same is true of Radcliffe-Brown, both in his own Australian ethnography (1913) and his comparative study of Australian social organization (1930–1931). The only kind of social relations he is interested in is the kind that yields discrete, non-overlapping groups and categories, or places persons in a uniform space of genealogically specifiable kintypes. In this respect, Lévi-Strauss in his analysis of Australian "totemism" runs true to Radcliffe-Brownian form. Declaring the genius of the system to lie in the abstract structure of logical oppositions among its categories, Lévi-Strauss treats its groundedness in landscape as a lesser aspect of Aboriginal culture:

> The totemic myths which solemnly relate futile incidents and sentimentalize over particular places are comparable to minor, lesser history: that of the dimmest chroniclers. Those same [Australian Aboriginal] societies, whose social organization and marriage rules require the efforts of mathematicians for their interpretation, and whose cosmology astonishes philosophers, recognize no break in the continuity between the lofty theorizing to which they devote themselves in those domains and a history which is not that of a

> Burckhardt or a Spengler, but of a Lenôtre and a La Force. (Lévi-Strauss 1966:243)

On the New Guinea side, a similar aversion to localized knowledge may have figured in the relatively lesser attention given to Iatmul mythic tracks by Gregory Bateson than in the more recent work of Wassmann and Silverman. Silverman suggests as much after the remark I quoted above about how "the Eastern Iatmul universe is plural, containing multiple histories and truths," to which he adds that Bateson was "seemingly unprepared for this plurality. Perhaps it conflicted with his own vision, borne of the natural and biological sciences . . . , in which the world conforms to a single structure" (Silverman 1996:34).

Nowadays, of course, we anthropologists are generally much less inclined to model cultures or societies as totalizing, internally coherent systems, and whereas Lévi-Strauss projected onto his ethnographic subjects the mentality of mathematicians and philosophers such as himself, anthropologists are now much more inclined to stress the partiality of their understandings—the plurality of knowledges—and to identify their ethnographic subjects as doing likewise. It is within the context of this general shift, I suggest, that the increased attention to the role of tracks and traces and the local groundedness of cosmology can best be understood. It is consistent with the general movement toward increased recognition of the importance of *place,* though predating that movement by many years in the work of the Australian ethnographers mentioned above.

Besides the currently fashionable rejection of structuralist forms of totalization, another reason for the recent revaluation of tracks and traces in the work of people with a postmodern or poststructuralist bent, such as Muecke (1992, 1997) or Dubinskas and Traweek (1984), is their rejection of reference-based or intellectualist theories of meaning in favor of notions of inscription, repetition, or mimesis. As against Lévi-Strauss' snide dismissal of Aborigines' "sentimentalizing over particular places" and his privileging of logical relations of homology among parallel series of differences, this view privileges relations of contiguity or identification, such as those between the founding acts of the bandicoot ancestor, the traces he thereby leaves of himself in the landscape, and the retracing or recovery of them by living people as they follow up his tracks. Or the relation between the original singing of a song by a totemic ancestor that is understood to have brought some particular animal species into being, and the re-singing of it by a living song-man that is thought to assure the species' continuing fecundity.

Traces, the Rhizome, and the Colonial Encounter

The increasing centrality of landscape in Australian Aboriginalist ethnography has not been an isolated development, confined within the walls of Academe, but has happened in close interaction with more popular forms of representation, including books such as Chatwin (1987) and Morgan (1988), exegesis of Aboriginal artworks, disputes about "sacred sites," and so on. It is surely no accident that all of the emphasis on landedness in this discourse began to emerge only after the long process of effective dispossession of Aboriginal land was nearly complete. But now that it has emerged, the objectification of social identity in landscape has taken on new force in that it not only provides particular Aboriginal people with a recognizable basis for claims to particular areas of land (however difficult these may now be) but also becomes a part of what it means to be an Aboriginal person in Australia.

It is instructive to compare these Australian developments with the way Tannese notions about tracks and traces have figured in the colonial encounter there. Unlike Australian Aborigines, the Tannese were never subject to large-scale dispossession, but they have had a long history of colonization and missionization, much of which they have actively resisted. There is a lively politics of *kastom,* and at several points in the island's history, such as at the turn of the century, when they all stood up against the Presbyterian mission, there have been wholesale, self-conscious reinventions of Tannese "Kastom." As Bonnemaison says about one such episode:

> Their intent was return to the equality of the "original" island community. . . . Countless meetings were organised [at which] they delved into the chants, narratives and myths of *kastom,* meticulously searching the lessons of the past in order to find new messages for the confrontations of the age. An entire population became the ethnologist of its own tradition and, in the process . . . found its identity anew.

> What came out was, in fact, a new *kastom*—partly rediscovered and partly re-created. (Bonnemaison 1994:112)

There is no way of knowing to what extent the Tannese ideas about tracks and places that I have summarized above were old convention or a new invention of the colonial period. The point to note is that in the present circumstances they have become a valued diacritic of the "*kastom*-ary" Tannese way of relating to land, and marking out the truly settled people of *kastom* in relation to it. I think there is every reason to believe that a more or less reconstituted set of ideas about ancestral tracks and traces will play a similar role in the emerging politics of Aboriginality in Australia, and in parts of postcolonial Papua New Guinea as well (Clark 1993; Wardlow, in press).

In Australia, this process has taken a new turn since the decision by the High Court in 1992 in the Mabo case, which overturned the two-hundred-year-old doctrine of *terra nullius,* whereby the entire continent was deemed to have been void of any indigenous system of rights in land that could qualify as a form of title recognizable at common law. Under the new disposition, now formalized by the Native Title Act of 1993 (amended in 1998), the potential existence of residual "native title" is recognized as a matter of law, but its actual existence remains to be demonstrated as a matter of fact in any given case that comes before the court. In principle this allows for the possible recognition of a far wider range of traditional links to land than had been recognized, for example, under the Northern Territory Land Rights Act of 1976, which requires Aboriginal claimants to establish that they comprise a "local descent group" with certain specified kinds of relations to the land under claim (Maddock 1980). But so far, very few claims have made their way successfully through the courts since 1992. No doubt this is partly the result of the strength of vested interests that are opposed to the claims, including the national and state governments and powerful financial interests such as the mining industry (Australia's largest). But it also seems to me to be partly attributable to inappropriate understanding of Aboriginal forms of territoriality even among those who are ostensibly working on the side of the claimants.

Here is where I think something like the notion of the "rhizome" can be of use. Perhaps influenced by the way claims have necessarily been framed and adjudicated under the Northern Territory Land

Rights Act, many lawyers and their advisers have assumed that Aboriginal customary law vests land in social "groups," and that what has to be determined in any particular case is what *kind* of group—patrilineal clan, language group, local cognatic stock or what-have-you—provides *the* central axis around which the system revolves; or in Deleuze and Guattari's terms, the trunk or taproot of the tree, of which all the other levels are ramifications.

From the Aranda and Ngarinyin examples discussed above, it can be seen that this is an inappropriately "arborescent" view of the matter and that the rhizomatic model is a more appropriate one. This does not mean (as opponents of their land claims would like to establish) that traditional Aranda or Ngarinyin spatiality is "smooth" or "nomadic." On the contrary, the earth is finely differentiated, in relatively fixed and stable ways. But places and countries are interconnected in multiple, crosscutting, nonhierarchical ways, and so are people and country (Keen 1994; Rumsey 1996). Deleuze and Guattari are right that this is a profoundly different form of socio-spatial organization than that which underwrites "the state." Even when the destruction of it as a total way of life has seemed most nearly complete, it is remarkable how strongly many Aboriginal people have resisted "arborescent" modes of consciousness (Povinelli 1995; Rose 1996 and chapter 5 below; Merlan 1998). Insofar as the Australian judiciary has opened the way for even a paltry form of recognition of Aboriginal land title "on its own terms," it must be prepared to listen to the case for a range of more rhizomatic relations to land than can be comprehended in terms of a model of tribes or clans as "proto-nations" (Rumsey 1993).

For example, in working with Ngarinyin people on the preparation of their case to be heard by the federal court of Australia, my collaborator Anthony Redmond and I have found them reluctant to single out any of the forms of linkage to country that I have discussed above as *the* sole basis for ownership of or rights in country, but still easily able to say, for any given place or region, who the "right" people are as determined by some combination of the relevant forms of linkage (Rumsey 1996). One consequence of this is that there are no areas of Ngarinyin country that are without people with links to them, notwithstanding the extinction of some Ngarinyin clans. Another consequence is that while in any given context, some people may be more important than others, there is nobody who is more important for the *whole* of Ngarinyin country. As in all the Melanesian cases I have discussed above, power and knowledge are profoundly *localized*. And here, as in Tanna, there is among the indigenes a well-developed sense of contrast in this respect between themselves as people who are "of the place" and their postcolonial overlords who are not (Stanner 1979). But contra Deleuze and Guattari, in these settings it is the latter—the "arborescent" Westerners rather than the "rhizomatic" indigenes of Oceania—who are positioned as "nomads." Such are the ironies of the colonial encounter, and of an avowedly critical theory of "difference," which is in this respect not so different after all.

Notes

1. I say "take account of" rather than "analyze" or "comprehend" because it is clear that Deleuze and Guattari's main aim is not to advance the understanding of "other" cultures or ways of life but to develop a critique of their own. Many anthropologists of course take this as one of their aims as well, but those of us who do are generally more concerned than Deleuze and Guattari are with trying to develop our critiques on the basis of close empirical investigation of the lifeways that provide us with our axes of comparison (cf. note 3 below).

2. "We are compelled to say that there has always been a State, quite perfect, quite complete. The more discoveries archaeologists make, the more empires they uncover. The hypothesis of the Urstaat seems to be verified: 'The State clearly dates back to the most remote ages of humanity'" (Deleuze and Guattari [1980] 1987:360; cf. 429–430).

3. Deleuze and Guattari themselves seem to acknowledge this problem when they say, "We invoke one dualism only in order to challenge another. We employ a dualism of models only in order to arrive at a process that challenges all models. Each time, mental correctives are necessary in order to undo the dualisms we had no wish to construct but through which we pass" (Deleuze and Guattari [1980] 1987:20). But in view of the ethnographically based conclusions I develop below, one has to ask whether such simplistic dualism as theirs was really necessary in order to found their critique.

4. As Central Australian Aboriginal leader Yami Lester has put it: "For Anungu [Aboriginal people], the time of the creation is real and it is here and it is now . . . when our ancestors were human beings who walked the earth the same as we do now, the land and its features were formed and our laws and our culture made for us to use and keep. For us the past and the present are part of the same thing" (Lester 1994).

5. Needless to say, the three Melanesian cases of topographic inscription

that I have adduced here in no way exhaust the field. Though I lack the space to develop another example here, it is worth mentioning that tracklike configurations figure prominently in the "sacred geography" of a congeries of peoples living about three hundred kilometers north of the Morehead and about as far west of the Iatmul, including the Huli, Duna, Duguba, Obena, and eastern Enga. For details, see Biersack (1995:16–19) and references cited therein, and Stewart and Strathern, chapter 4 below. By way of comparison with the Iatmul "knotted cord" and the Deleuze-Guatarrian "rhizome," it is interesting to note that sacred sites in this Highland system are thought of as "knots of the earth," which are "strung together in a subterranean network called 'the root of the earth' " (Biersack 1995:16).

6. This being the case, in the rest of this chapter I use the terms "arborescent" and "arborescence" for models that display the characteristics attributed by Deleuze and Guattari (in the quote above) to trees, but without assuming that trees are necessarily prototyical with respect to them.

7. I am indebted to James Fox for directing me to this possibility with respect to Ayres's paradigm of "fragmentation from a common source," which he thought might be based on the banyan tree.

8. To the extent that they support this distinction ethnographically, Deleuze and Guattari do it mainly in footnotes, with brief references to synthetic works such as Lévi-Strauss 1963 and Fortes and Evans-Pritchard 1978.

9. On this point I disagree with Howard Morphy, who claims that "the key concepts and themes that subsequently became associated with Aboriginal religion [including] the network of ancestral tracks that intersect the landscape . . . were all established in Spencer and Gillen's writings" (Morphy in Mulvaney, Morphy, and Petch 1997:37). While I agree that many aspects of later anthropological understandings of "the dreaming" were foreshadowed by Spencer and Gillen, the centrality of place in the people-totem-place nexus was not one of them (cf. Rumsey 1999b). They give far more attention to what is more specific to Central Australia: the role of Churinga sacred boards.

2
The Politics of Religious Secrecy

Jürg Wassmann

Every description of Iatmul culture feels like a simplification. Middle Sepik cultures in Papua New Guinea have obvious overall emphases: dual organization, a mythological stress on primeval events and totems, rituals of initiation marked by graded access to degrees of secret knowledge, sacred flutes, names as possessions of great significance. Yet the Nyaura (or Western Iatmul) are a society with their own actual theory of cultural interconnections, enabling them to mentally and emotionally connect various cultural phenomena in an explicit way. Their theory is, more precisely, a system of order constructed of numerous nodes of meaning that make it possible to interpret aspects of the culture that at first sight appear disparate and to show how they are linked. This "order out of chaos" is encapsulated in the knotted cord called *kirugu*. A cord is between six and seven meters long and has knots of different sizes at regular intervals. A *kirugu* represents an ancient migration; it *is* that migration. Each of the large knots in a *kirugu* represents a location along the migration route; the smaller knots contain the secret names of the "totem" associated with each spot (Wassmann 1988, 1991). The journeys across the topography seem to be the central topic for both Nyaura and Australian Aboriginal people, whereby the diverse places were created, as well as the present landscape and all living species including the ancestors of the present groups. However, identification between present and past people happens through names or by means of dreaming places. Differences exist in the ways in which Aborigines and the Nyaura perceive the landscape as interface between places and space, and this understanding is linked to a corresponding distinction between a more fluid versus a more fixed mode of sociality. But let's start at the beginning.

Formally, the Nyaura system has three characteristics:

1. It is related to *clan groups.* Clans are gathered together in groups of varying sizes. A primary distinction is made between the moieties, sky and earth; each moiety is divided into clan associations, each consisting of two clan groups of two, three, four, or more clans—in a definite hierarchical structure depending on the order of their mythological emergence. Each clan group has its own knotted cord or order, which differs from others in content but not in structure. But the two knotted cords of one association are always similar, the second one setting the example for the first.
2. It is *esoteric.* Knowledge of the links and ties is part of the secret knowledge of a small number of important men, the "old crocodiles" *(abuk waak),* whose influence is based precisely on this knowledge. There is a difference in principle between the multiplicity of the exoteric culture as it exists in a more or less pronounced form in the consciousness of most clan members and the fundamental cultural unity existing in the esoteric knowledge of certain "old crocodiles." On the one hand is the bewilderingly large number of totems, the thousands of names, the innumerable myths and fragments of myths that outwardly have no relationship to one another; on the other hand is the knowledge held by only a few men of the interconnections that simplify everything. It is therefore not so much the mythological tales themselves that are secret—some of them are even familiar to children as bedtime stories *(wapuksapuk)*—as their precise geographical locations and the true identities of their protagonists.
3. The secret interconnections form a *dynamic system,* although it is claimed that they represent an attempt to establish a static order. It follows that the praxis of this system—its daily application by the "old crocodiles"—is also dynamic. There is continuous rivalry among the influential men over the legitimate ownership (that is, ownership derived from the system) of names and totems (cf. Harrison 1990). The ownership of a name is equated with the power to dispose of the object designated. The climax of the disputes over the correct interpretation of the system is a public contest in which names are disputed at the ceremonial stool *(pabu).*

Gregory Bateson pointed out the existence of this system of relationship. He already perceived the link between the myth and the names by which things and people were addressed (1958:127). His writings also contain a description of the idea of a migration in primal times (1958:407). He made no reference to the existence of a knotted cord (the Central Iatmul among whom he worked do not possess any), and the system is described only fragmentarily. Bateson himself attributed this defect to the fact that he had succeeded neither in translating the totemic songs and names (1932:404) nor in establishing any kind of order in the whole system, which seemed to him a "dreadful muddle." "The system is in a terribly muddled state," he noted and found that there was a "fraudulent heraldry" and "tangle" (1958: 128). Today, decades later,[1] thanks to a much better knowledge of the *ndu* language and a kind of "collapse of pressure" in the social system such that secret knowledge is no longer so strongly protected, it is possible to collect data about the knotted cords and to translate the songs and the names, even though many uncertainties remain.

Establishing the Space

We have already outlined the formal characteristics of the system. In terms of content, each knotted cord revolves around two principal themes: the creation and the subsequent mythological migration of the ancient people. Implicit in the process of creation and the ancient migration is a space-time grid.

The stories of ancient times can be summarized as follows. Before creation, there was water everywhere. Then a crocodile appeared and split in two, its lower jaw becoming the earth, its upper jaw the sky. This cleavage explains the subsequent division of society into earth and sky moieties. Next, the first pair of brothers came into existence, and from them descended additional pairs of brothers by repeated processes. These pairs of brothers were the founders of the present clan associations. The first brother of the pair is the founder of the first clan group of an association, the second brother that of the second clan group. Their sons and grandsons founded the numerous individual clans one or two generations later.

The locale of these events is an area to the north of the Middle

Sepik near the village of Gaikorobi (figure 2-1). In the beginning, all the ancient people were gathered there. Then the founders of the clan groups and their relatives left the village, following in the tracks of crocodiles, which cleared the way for them. And thus came about the most important event of ancient times: the severance from the place of origin and the migration into the area of the present settlement. The paths of the migrations were through the bush around Gaikorobi to the Sepik River and across it through the district of the present Central Iatmul into villages now occupied by the Nyaura or Western Iatmul (figure 2-2). During this journey, always following the tracks of the crocodiles, which through their moves shaped the until-then-nondescript landscape, the people took possession of tracts of land, parts of the bush, lakes, and watercourses, and villages and hamlets were founded. The land taken and the villages founded at that time determine present claims of possession. The scraps of food and the excrement left behind on the migration were the origin of the water spirits *wanjimout*.

Two points are of crucial importance: the two brothers of a pair behaved in different ways, and the migrations of the various clan associations had their own typical patterns. The second brother of each pair was the dynamic one, the one who first crossed the Sepik. The first brother, by contrast, initially remained close to the bushland and the place of creation. This contrast is expressed with the fixed terms "by canoe" and "on foot," both brothers ultimately covering the same route—this is why the two knotted cords are also similar. A further point: the ground covered by the migration of a clan association (that is, of two brothers) centered on a particular area, in which it founded a particularly large number of villages, and that was either not touched at all by the other pairs of brothers or was explicitly used only as a "transit corridor." Each pair of brothers, and thus each clan association, had its own area. It is typical that the regions of the fraternal pairs of the earth moiety lay mainly above (to the west of) the Middle Sepik and those of the sky moiety mainly below (to the east). These two features explain the correspondence between the earth moieties and the upper course of the river and the sky moiety and the lower course and, ideally, that between the first clan groups and the areas on the left bank of the Sepik and the second groups and the areas on the right bank.

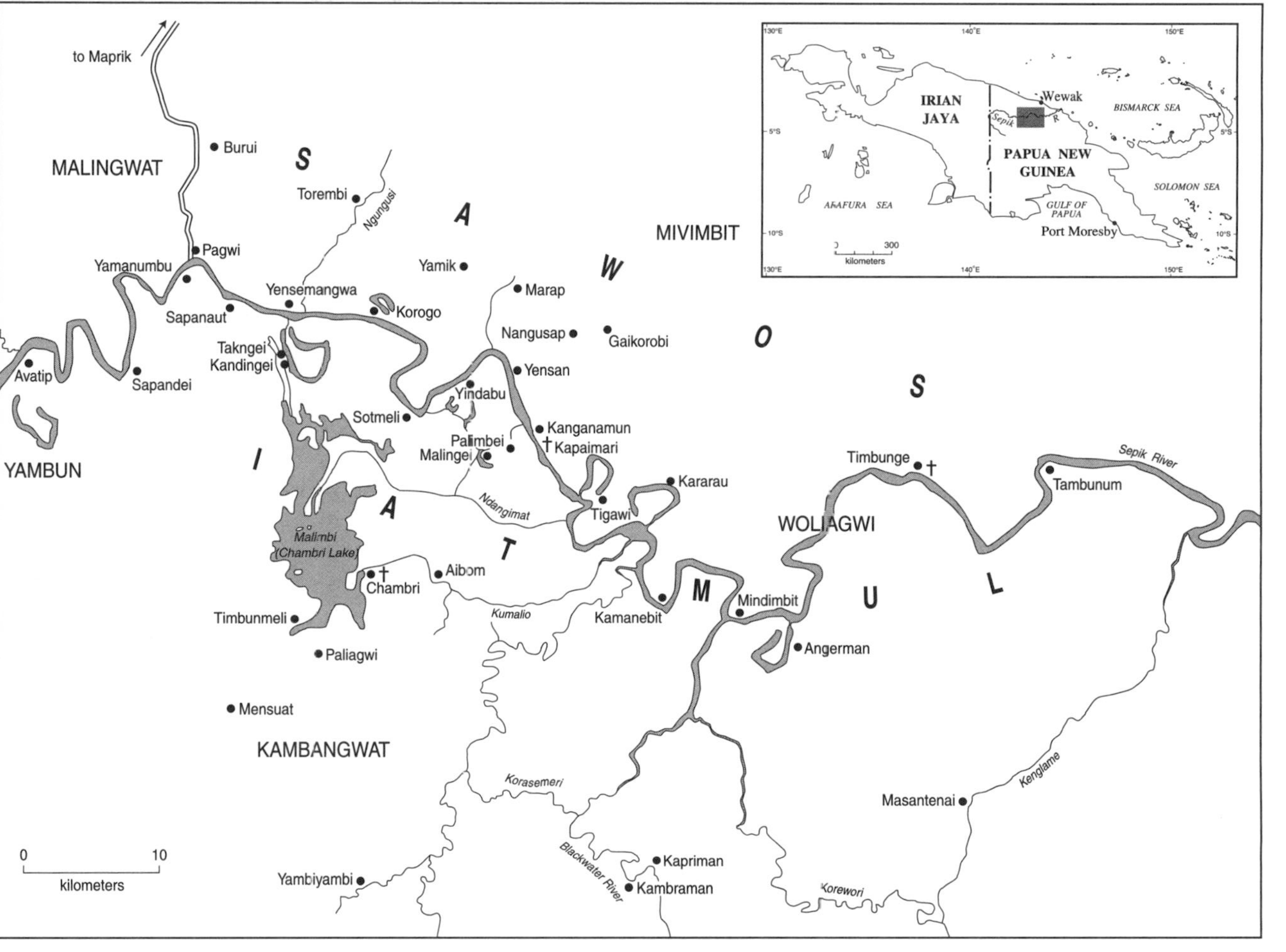

Figure 2-1. The area of the Iatmul. (Drawing by Verena Keck)

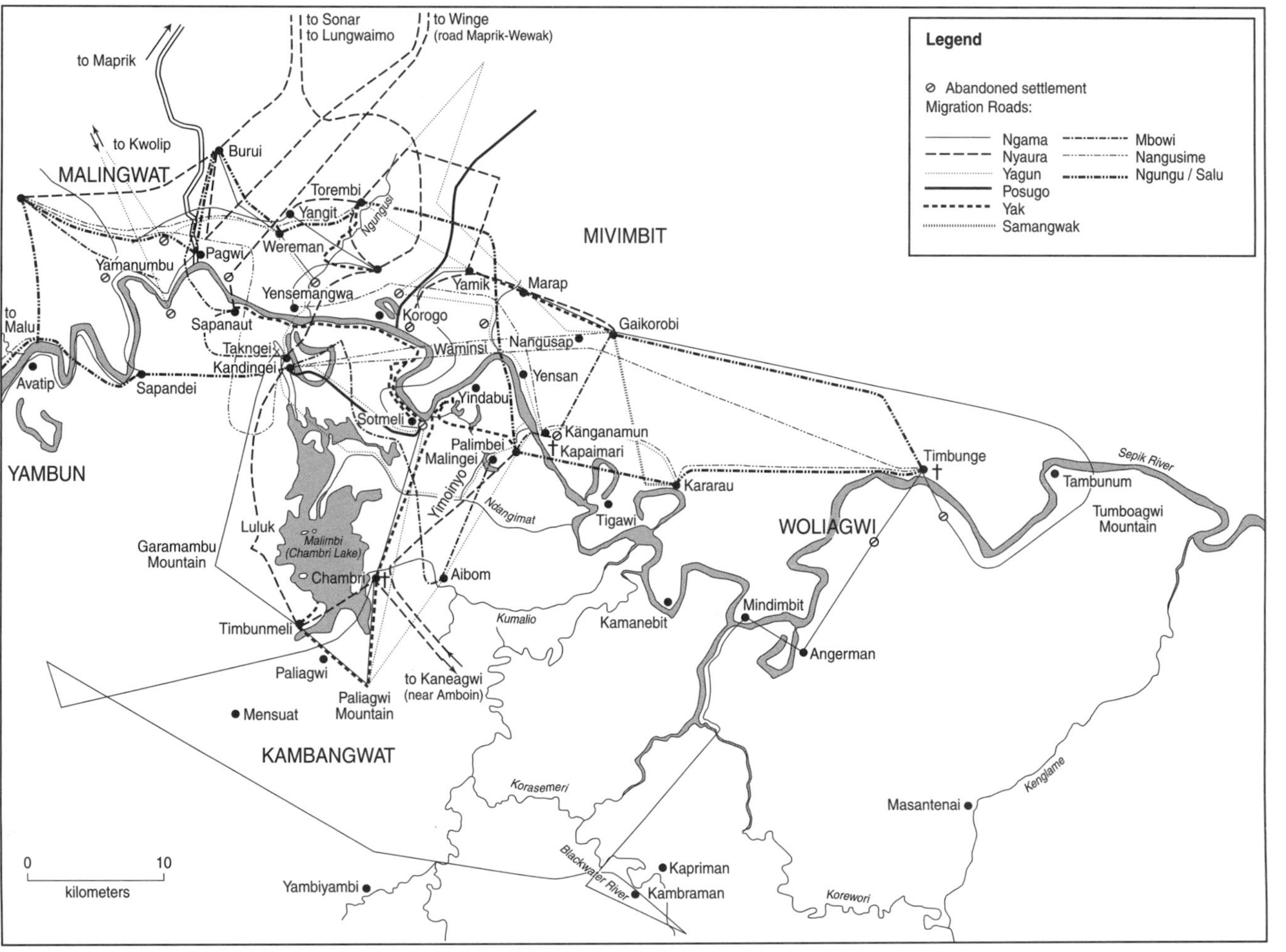

Figure 2-2. The routes of the ancient Iatmul migrations. (Drawing by Verena Keck)

On the Relevance of the Past

To what extent do the knotted cords have practical relevance? The question is whether all the land rights and claims can in fact be derived from the course of the migrations—as all informants vehemently assert—or whether the system is only a general frame of reference, its practice being infinitely more complicated. This point is particularly pertinent because one of the features of the system is, of course, its dynamic character; it is the locus of deliberate manipulations by the "old crocodiles" to provide retrospective legitimation for an existing state of affairs.

When the Nyaura visualize the area where they live in terms of space, the central feature is the Sepik River. In the central section of the river live the Nyaura *nimba* (the Nyaura people from Sapandei to Korogo; see figure 2-1), the Palimbei *nimba* (from Sotmeli to Kanganamun), and the Woliagwi *nimba* (from Kararau to Tambunum). These three groups feel that there are cultural, linguistic, and historical bonds among them. The space surrounding this middle section is divided into regions marked off to form individual districts (known as *ndimba,* "enclosures") inhabited by specific people. Each of these districts is occupied by *numungi* ("aliens" or "ignorant people"). To these must be added, as mythological regions, the area "under the water" *(ngungu ndimba)* and that of the stars *(singut ndimba)*. The fact that the lower course of the river begins at Kararau and that, consequently, the more remote Eastern Iatmul are actually "outside" shows how very much such divisions are determined by a particular geographical viewpoint. Each of these districts falls within the orbit of a clan association; they are the specific areas of the migrating pairs of brothers.

The system is of practical importance, however, only within the area belonging specifically to the Nyaura, that is, within their sphere of influence. When, early in my stay, I systematically recorded the haunts of the water spirits around Kandingei, asked about the names and owners of the districts, and investigated where particular women were allowed to fish, a picture emerged that could be interpreted only much later, when I had come to know the system. In the majority of cases, these places and specific areas of land were indeed located on the routes of the migrations.

If the relationship between the past, as the period of ancient migrations, and the present can be conceived as a spatial continuum, the following interrelationship can readily be visualized: in the past, the world and its people came into being; the latter gave themselves their specific social order. According to the system, the present is nothing but a precise reflection of the situation created at that time. In other words, the present social order and system of land ownership are legitimated simply and solely by the fact that they originated and were established in ancient times. All present members of the clans are direct progeny of the people of ancient times, and it is this genealogical link alone that confers on them the right to represent their ancestors in ceremonies and to narrate their actions in contemporary myth.

The Annulment of Time

A clear distinction exists between past and present time, but the flow of time within each period is not particularly important; interest is focused on the precise spatial (geographical), not the temporal, positions of events. For the past, in particular, actual duration plays hardly any part at all. Nor does the image of the succession of past and present, reasonable enough in our eyes, characterize their relationship in all respects. Inquiry into the historical accuracy of the system in its temporal aspects shows that there is no equivalence between the ancient migration and a postulated historical migration.[2] For example, the founding of the village of Kandingei (Nyaurangei) took place four generations ago; it was founded by ancestors whose actual names are still known and recorded in the genealogies. Yet its founding is also part of the mythological events. The distant past is, on the one hand, distinguished from the present, but, on the other, it is not only carried up to the present but carried into it as well. Mythological events are extended into the present.

If we look at names, we obtain a similar picture. At each place visited during migration (and, as I have explained, the places vary with the clan association), the clan group founder leaves behind a few men and women. He assigns to them an animal, plant, or some other object into which they can transform themselves; thus each place has its own "totem" or, more precisely, "mask" or "frame" into which they can slip. This totem and all the objects of the place receive proper names of their own, which are arranged in pairs in long strings. These name-strings can be either public or secret. The inhabitants of the village are also given names: the names of the totem of the village. The totems assigned in this way formed the basis of the present totem system. Most important of all, the names used at that time form the stock of present names. The whole stock of names from the past is used for the present; persons, men's houses, dwellings, canoes, dogs and pigs—all bear names drawn from this stock. Thus there is a close identification between all persons and things of the present with those of the past; furthermore, both are associated with specific places on the mythological tracks. The person of today is defined by his (ancient) name in the sense that he figures as a reincarnation—albeit a frail one —of the primal being of the same name (and place). He also has the responsibility for each totem into which his ancestor could change himself in the past. The use of same names causes the two periods to coincide and expunges the linear-genealogical succession.

To reiterate: The system of order is represented visually and, additionally, aurally. The visual representation takes the form of the *kirugu,* "knotted cords." Each cord is between six and seven meters long and has knots of different sizes at regular intervals. Each *kirugu* represents one of the ancient migrations; it *is* that migration and bears the name of the crocodile that cleared the path for the clan group founder. Each of the large knots in a *kirugu* represents a place along the migration route; the smaller knots contain the secret names of the totem associated with each spot. As a rule, in performing the system of order in a ceremony in which all the clans of an association participate, the responsible person for the aural representation in the songs is the leader of the first clan group (of that clan association), and the owner of the second, exemplary knotted cord and thus the paramount leader of the whole ceremony is the leader of the second clan group. Every time there is a change of place in the song cycle describing the primal migration, he seizes his cord suspended from the ceiling and runs his fingers over the small knots until he reaches the next large one representing a place and silently repeats to himself the secret names belonging to the totem of that next place. The relationship of the two leaders is one of complementarity and reflects, as would be expected, the role of the mythological two clan group founders, the two brothers with their distinctive characterization.

For example, the knotted cord of the Pulau clan group (the second clan group of Tipme Yagun association) is called Palingawi. Palingawi is the crocodile that cleared the way for the clan group founder, Wolin-

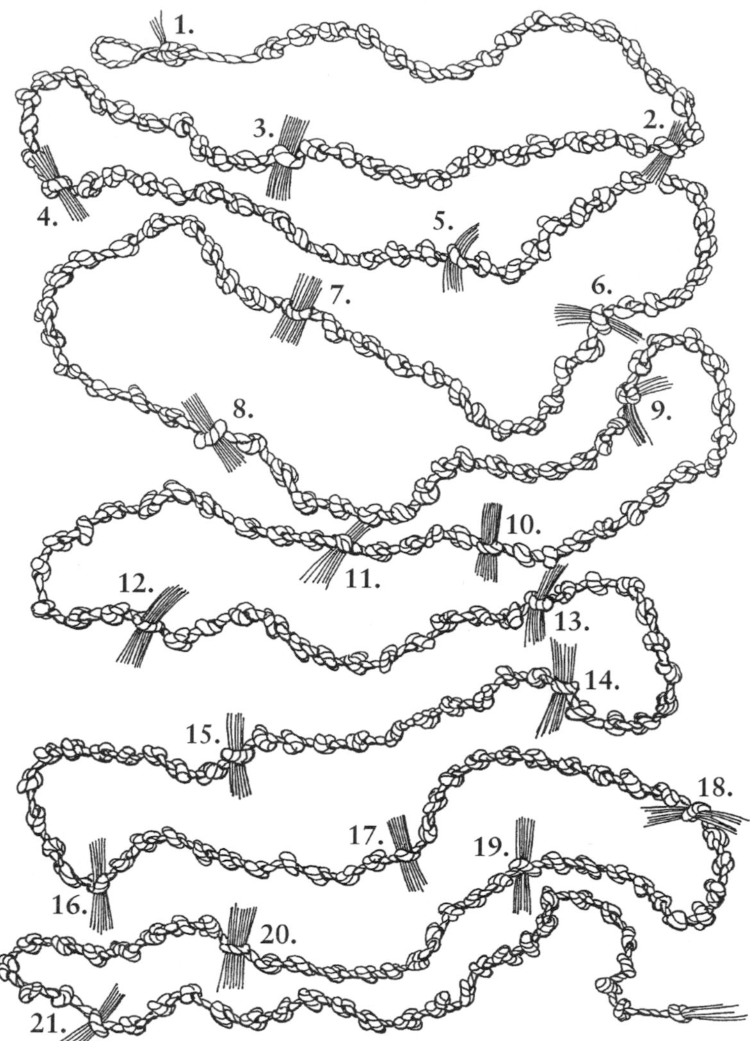

Figure 2-3. Palingawi knotted cord. The knots represent villages or other places visited on the Palingawi migration and the totems assigned to each village. Each of the twenty large knots on the cord corresponds to a village in the order shown below. Italics indicate the villages that were founded by the clan group in question; the others were just visited. Parentheses indicate the villages that were later abandoned.

1. Gaikorobi village: creation of the earth, crocodile, dog, first woman (kabi bird), clan group founder
2. Marap village: rooster and first men's house
3. *Silai village:* dove
4. Tugut village: leveling of the earth, crocodile

dambwi. This particular knotted cord has twenty large knots and on average ten smaller knots between every two large ones (figure 2-3).

The Song Cycles

Aurally, the parts of the knotted cord intended for the public are recited in song cycles *(sagi)*. Each cycle consists of a fixed sequence of songs and lasts between twelve and sixteen hours.[3] A cycle has three features: localities, names, and tales.

Localities. The cycle as a whole reproduces the course of the migration. Each individual song marks a place of the migration, with a few songs referring to the creation being sung before the first place (always Gaikorobi), and thus each song corresponds to a large knot in the knotted cord. For example, the song cycle of the Pulau follows the migration of this group (figure 2-2). The third song relates to the creation of the earth; later, the first place, Gaikorobi, came into existence.

Names. Each song revolves around a specific totem whose names are given in pairs in long strings. In each cycle, hundreds of names are mentioned—all in the correct sequences. These strings of names are regarded as public lists. The secret or "shadow strings" are those represented in the knotted cord by small knots.[4] Each public name is thus complemented by a secret name. The former is publicly voiced in the songs and used in everyday life, but the latter never is voiced: during the performance the owner of the knotted cord lets it run through his

---

5. Limangwa village: coconut tree, ant, blowfly
6. Torembi village: first initiation, wandering whistling duck
7. Yamik village: earth, dog
8. (Tirivuri village): kami fish
9. *Matsoon watercourse:* flying fox
10. *Yensan village:* ghost of dead men, white-crowned koel
11. *Palimbei village:* kwarip and kanambu trees
12. Aibom village: breadfruit tree
13. *Paliagwi mountain:* ancestress Wawawimangi
14. *Yamanangwa (Sotmeli) village:* primal woman, finery of Palingawi crocodile
15. *Solokwi (part of Kandingei village):* sister of clan group founder, water rail
16. (Mavaragwi village): fishing spear
17. *Wereman village:* big man and big women of men's house, dog
18. (Kongorobi village): burning the bush for new villages, smoke
19. (Kwolip village): kabi bird, wandering whistling duck
20. (Mansipambani village): pig, anchoring of the grass island

fingers like a rosary and calls to memory the corresponding shadow names of those who are publicly recited at the given moment. Every individual name is polysyllabic. It is composed of two, three, or even four common nouns strung together and followed by a suffix, an ending that is feminine or masculine. The nouns of a name pair in turn also form pairs. Etymology shows that the name in a general way refers to the totem it designates or gives detailed information about the primal events around that totem at its place. The nouns of which the name is composed form a semantic reference similar to that which occurs in the song texts. Each name "tells" a story in a sort of "telegraphese."

For example, the third song about the creation (at the subsequently created place Gaikorobi) mentions twenty-two public names for the primeval crocodile, twenty names for the first place to come into existence (Gaikorobi or Mivimbit), and eight names for the first woman of ancestral times. Let's look at some of the primeval crocodiles (equated with the primeval earth).

1. Andi-kabak-meli and 2. Kipma-kabak-meli (*andi:* old word for earth; *kipma:* earth; *kabak:* primeval crocodile; *meli:* masculine ending; meaning: The crocodile is the primeval crocodile, which is also the earth)
3. Lisi-nyo-mbu-ndemi and 4. Kasi-nyo-mbu-ndemi (*lisi:* shake, earthquake in one direction; *kasi:* shake, earthquake in the other direction; *nyo:* mother of pearl, seashell; *mbu:* break open or to pieces; *ndemi:* masculine ending; meaning: The crocodile or the earth has just emerged from the sea and is rocking to and fro)
5. Pat-nawi-gumbangi and 6. Nganga-nawi-gumbangi (*pat:* spittle; *nganga:* lower jaw; *nawi:* masculine ending; *gumbangi:* masculine ending; meaning: The crocodile has spittle in its throat)

Some of the names of the first place are:

7. Lili-lipma and 8. Kwakwa-lipma (*lili:* slip away; *kwakwa:* stand up and fall down; *lipma:* coconut palm, metaphor for place; meaning: The newly created place still rocks)
9. Man-mbo and 10. Tamba-mbo (*man:* foot, leg; *tamba:* hand, arm; *mbo:* dust, morning mist; meaning: The place is now dry and the dust settles on the hands and feet of the people of the first place)

Tales. Each song relates a short tale in which the totem of the place accomplishes a particular act. The texts recited in the song are simple, small, harmless extracts from the secret myths. For example, the third song about the creation (at the later first place) bears the title "The Song to the Crocodile That Split in Two." The contents revolve around the primeval crocodile rising to the surface of the water with a rotary motion, bringing with it a piece of earth, and later splitting in two, its upper jaw becoming the sky while its lower jaw becomes the earth. Extracts of the text of the song are as follows:

Father, your upper jaw,
Father, your upper jaw,
Ancestor, your lower jaw,
father, your jaw

Father, you Andikabakmeli,
Andikabakmeli, Kipmakabakmeli, O you,
my water spirit!
Father, in this place,
in the place Lililipma,
near the coconut palm Kwakwalipma,
you lay down,
and then your upper jaw became the sky

The total interconnected pattern can be understood only after the events that in the past took place at this subsequent first place are known. At present, they are described in the following myth (only extracts of which are presented here). The passages forming the background of the song are in *italics;* those relating to names are *<u>underlined</u>* as well.

> Once, there were no men, there were no women, there were no things of any kind on the earth, the earth had not yet come to be, there was only an endless empty stretch of water, only water. Only water, *ngu* (water), *kongu* (the water from which everything emerged). The stretch of water lay there and did not move. Suddenly the water foamed, it foamed for a long time, and a small thing was washed up, it was a tiny crocodile. Only a tiny thing, only rubbish. Some time passed and it grew legs, it grew arms, it grew a tail, it grew jaws, it grew eyes, it was a proper crocodile. There it lay, and its skin, its back and its legs were those of a crocodile, but its face was that of a man, its head was that of a man. . . . It wanted to be so and thus it happened: its *<u>spittle</u>* [cf. names 5 and 6] sank below, its spittle sank down, it did not drift upwards, no, its spittle sank below to the bottom of the sea, this spittle sank and sank and then rose again, rose up, rose and stuck to its breast, such a little thing. . . . Then [the crocodile] moved and *<u>together with the little thing it floated up,</u>* it floated up, it reached

the surface of the water, and there everything was lit up with the light of day. Day had dawned, it was bright daylight, and *the earth had come up, the earth had come up* (cf. names 1–4), only a little piece, it is true, but this little piece lay there.

The crocodile slid back into the water and it swam round it, it swam round this little piece of earth and circled round it, and *the earth grew in size*. And so it continued for a time and the earth became fairly big, like an island, a little island (cf. names 7–8). . . . The crocodile had come up together with the water, and, after a short time, it opened its jaws, the upper jaw rose up, the earth rose up, a man rose up, it was the sun Nyagonduma [which had come into being]. *It opened its jaws, 'Ahhhhh!' it went and split in two parts* [cf. song]; the sun Nyagonduma was thrown up, and it became light. It was Nyagonduma, and the day broke. And so it remained. Nyagonduma was the child of the water spirit Wanjimoutnagwan, *Kabak* [cf. names 1–2]. The crocodile looked around, around about it looked, and all the mountains, the parts of the bush, the grass, the plants, all things of the earth came into being. It went on looking, and the insects and all other things came into being and were there. *All things came into being and were there* [cf. names 9–10].

Reconstructing the Order

I stated at the beginning that the knotted cord has three formal features: it relates to clan groups, it is esoteric, and it is dynamic. All these features serve to safeguard the esoteric knowledge of the "old crocodiles."

Esoteric knowledge always remains specific to the clan groups, parts of it sometimes even to the individual clan, and the power derived from this knowledge is, in principle, therefore also restricted to the members of one's own clan group, with the boundaries between the two related clan groups being fluid. In actual fact, there are again and again "old crocodiles" who, because of their network of relationships, possess knowledge far exceeding that of their own clan group and even the clan association. But the esoteric knowledge of even a very influential man is never complete, for, at least in theory, it is always shared between two or three men, each of whom is specialized in a particular sphere.

Here I have to add a personal note. This kind of presentation of the system evidently has its limitations, because the secrecy of the knotted cords in principle applies to the anthropologist as well. What I am recording here is an attempt at a reconstruction proceeding on the basis of invariably incomplete information. It is incomplete because secrecy is still observed with regard to some areas and also because the anthropologist was—of course—not able to build a trusting relationship with all "old crocodiles." Esotericism in particular, and the concentration of the knowledge in the hands of few men that is its corollary, means that the field-worker must depend precisely on these influential men, who are the only possible informants he can enlist. But each "old crocodile" controls only part of the knowledge, since his clan group was responsible only for specific acts, ancestors, totems, and locations in ancient times. Correspondingly, today he is responsible for only a segment of the surrounding world; no clan group and no informant knows all the other knotted cords. Hence one's knowledge is always partial.

For the anthropologist, the methodological starting point is the comparison, first, of the complete (public and esoteric) series of names and, second—insofar as possible—their mythological background, which may possibly bring mutual relations to light. The first comparison is based on the habit of representing or deriving an existent mythological relationship between the totems by means of reciprocity in the quotations of the names. A relationship between totems that appears to be established through myths or fragments of myths or that is asserted by informants may, in certain cases, be verified with the aid of the name series of the totems mentioned insofar as one, two, or more names from one series occur in the other or even that all names correspond: in this case, we are dealing with two identical totems. Second, there are at the same time mythological interlinks that are not overtly represented and that cannot be read from the series of names. As I had expected, any attempt at obtaining an insight into these relationships proved to be difficult at times. Informants tended either to deny any relationship at all between the totems or to connect everything with everything. In sum, my attempt relied less on myths or fragments of myths than on diverse items of information that I was able to glean in long conversations with "old crocodiles." For the most part, they consist of a multitude of clues and fragments of information, a vast collection of bits of information that subsequently had to be fitted together.[5] The risk here is the assumption that the material possesses an internal consistency.

Safeguarding the Esoteric Knowledge

Let us imagine how a clan group performs the *sagi* cycle. The knotted cord is followed. All of the (say, one hundred) participants sitting in a men's house can see the owner of the knotted cord and observe how he takes the cord down from the roof beam at regular intervals, slips it through his fingers and murmurs something at each of the little knots; they can also see that when he comes to one of the big knots he hangs the cord up again. All present hear the solo songs and hear many little stories about the totems and a great number of names occurring in these tales. However, parts of the performance remain arcane to the majority of those present. The actual and efficacious names of the totem hidden in the knotted cord are secret—what are concealed are the connections between the various totems and their role in primal times and, most important, the places figuring in the migration of the clan founder made manifest only through the myth. To repeat: What is secret is not primarily knowledge about individual events in primal times but rather insight into the interconnections that actually make up the system. It is only the synoptic view of the pattern of primal events that gives the individual event its meaning and makes it available. Unless the real names of the primal protagonists and the place of the event are given, a myth is ineffectual; it is only the additional knowledge that makes it available for, say, magic or as ammunition in the name debates. The very core of the esoteric knowledge is the knowledge about the interconnections between the myths, the proper names, and the place names.

The vagueness and ambiguity of the content of the texts are also reflected at the linguistic level. Many words of the song texts are no longer used in the vernacular; such words are called "old words." In this connection, Bateson speaks of "shaman jargon" and of "standardized metaphors" (1932:404) or even of a "shaman language" (1932:417).

Another linguistic means of keeping the texts vague is to use only words or sentences of the simplest form, often without relational words and either without or with several personal pronouns. The indeterminate nature of the meaning of the sentence is intensified by a further and more general feature of the *ndu* language. Even in vernacular language, the meaning of the individual verbs is acquired only through their semantic environment—that is, by being placed between certain words or combined with other verbs. Isolated verbs often have only a general outline of meaning. An example is provided by the verbs *si* and *viya,* which often form a pair. Their outline of meaning is *si:* to shoot and *viya:* to beat, but, depending on the context, they may mean "displace water" (coming to the surface of the water), or "pushing open an opening," or "burn" (after rubbing a body part against the trunk of a tree). Thus additional information is needed for a proper understanding, very often information even above the linguistic level.

The principle of partial secrecy runs through all the various spheres of the culture. The confusing multiplicity is deliberately created. With regard to the performance, and hence particularly to the songs, the following technique is used: The individual items of information are torn out of the coherent whole, and all relation between the fragments of information uttered is deliberately veiled. What is of no importance is placed in the center and what is important is removed to the periphery. Instead of specific names general ones are used, the singer begins not with the first pair of names but with a later pair, totems are quoted from other clan groups, name strings are broken up and distributed, two name strings are coalesced into one, names are taken from other series and added to one's own, pseudonyms are used, "different" things are called by the same name (*kwarip* tree and clan founder, for example), and various names are used for the "same" thing (coconut and first ancestress).

Another example is Mivimbitwoligumbangi (mentioned in the third song, 1. place on the cord), meaning literally "the man of Mivimbit," a term that in a general manner refers to the first ancestor of the Pulau clan group but in the present context refers more specifically to the clan founder of the second clan group. His real name is Krugambo, the dove (present also as voice of flutes), who is mentioned in the songs (3. place on the cord), and sometimes replaced by his elder brother Wolindambwi. Wolindambwi is the founder of the first clan group and the brother of Kabiragwa (song, 5. place on the cord). Kabiragwa is the *kabi* bird and also the *nduba* duck and probably has connections with the white-crowned koel (the coconut palm is said to have originated from her skull). Primal man, Andigame, is the first name of the second pair of the strings, from the second pair onward both strings are the same. The *wundameli* fish (which is named only in myths) is thereby identified; he is the son of Wolindambwi. His name series in turn is the same as that of the rooster and also that of the *kwarip* tree (song, 11. place on the cord). But *kwarip* tree and the rooster "are" Wolindambwi.

In summary, one can maintain that a fundamental dilemma exists. The dilemma is that while as many of these clans' totems, ancient beings, and names as possible should be mentioned to enable clan members to identify with their clan intellectually and to emotionally justify to members of other clans their claim to their possession, at the same time, as little as possible of the secret knowledge of the relationships between the different parts should be revealed. However, the fundamental question of how much, what, and in what context a person really knows or in fact does not know cannot be answered: people enact roles (women have mythological knowledge but are not allowed to make it public), they play scenes, they conceal, show off, or mislead others. In any instance, the anthropologist is always more or less an outsider; is it really his task to document the extent of assumed nonknowledge among—for example—the younger Iatmul?

Debating the Ownership of a Name

If there is a fight about the rightful possession of a name, the opponents and their supporters meet in the men's house, in the center near the ceremonial stool, *pabu,* for the name debate. This is the highest social form of intellectual discussion. Given what has been reported so far, it seems understandable that the names are the crucial point of the ramified mythological system. Fights about land use or fishing rights or rights to names are always fights about names or fights at the level of mythology.

Leaves from a coconut palm frond are cut to the same length and put on the ceremonial stool. When a speaker makes his entrance, he takes up the bundle. He uses either the whole bundle or the single strips of leaves as a means for gesticulation; as the argument progresses, he puts the strips back onto the stool one after the other. As his train of thought comes to an end, the whole bundle is back on the stool.

Each speaker wants to prove that the name in dispute belongs to him or to his clan. He wants to prove in public to all the "old crocodiles" present that he knows the mythological background of the name. He therefore has to be able to mythologically "locate" the name. The location, however, is secret, and that is why the two litigating parties find themselves in a contradictory situation (which was already obvious in the performance of the song cycle): on the one hand, as proof, they have to point to a connection; on the other hand, they do not want to expose their mythological knowledge. As a consequence, only veiled hints are dropped, which test the participants' mythological knowledge. The result is an enigmatic and dynamic play of suggestions and interpretations, which are accepted or rejected. These mythological suggestions are not only presented verbally but are in part also staged and, perhaps in turn, interpreted with dramatic actions by the opposing party: by a speaker suddenly adorning himself with a red hibiscus flower (which may point to an ancestor) or by something being mimetically represented (a bird, the movement of a crocodile). The atmosphere is heated; the event takes place in a public arena, where moods are liable to change quickly, where political alliances and dependencies through kinship ties and social and financial debts, but also the prestige of the speakers, their rhetoric, and the ability to stage surprising changes, are decisive and may result in a specific opinion among the public—without necessarily having this effect every single time.

Here is an example taken from Stanek (1983:242–276): The issue is the dispute about the name Sisalabwan. The word *sisal* means to tease, to pull somebody's leg, and includes the hopeless and helpless situation of the person who is teased; *abwan* is a name-ending. The figure connected with it is the powerful and aggressive crocodile Wani, which teases people by bringing rain and causing wind and storms.

The two litigants, Kandim and Angrimbi, and their clan members are from two related clan groups whose mythology partly overlaps. Kandim believes that the name Sisalabwan belongs to the stock of names of his own clan. When Angrimbi's clan relatives hear Kandim's sister calling her son by this name, they protest. Angrimbi, the great mythologist, contests the claim that Kandim is the rightful owner: the latter intends to prove that the name belongs to him (which, however, in the end he cannot do).

Excerpts from a verbal exchange in the men's house (Stanek 1983:259–274):

Kandim: Now we are talking about Sisalabwan. . . . A crocodile moves in the swamp, its tail forcefully beats the surface of the water, a sound is heard—and the birds *wundan* and *mbarak*, which have their nests in the grass swamp, are crying: wa-la! wa-la! . . . It is about this *sisal*, this is what I am thinking about when I use the name Sisalabwan.

Angrimbi: So, you are using it?

Kandim: There is no other thing that could be connected with this name. This is enough! You cannot insist on having the sole right to this name.

Angrimbi: . . . If you cannot connect another thing with this name, your claim is lost, over, the end! You may soon stop using the name, brother! Because it is really about a truly big and important *sisal* [of the crocodile Wani]. . . . Do you know about its [mythical] dwelling place?

Angrimbi: . . . I now want to recite his string of names. . . . Yes, the string of names of the ancestor. Mevembitabwan, Kambiambitabwan; Wanimeri, Punsanmeri. . . .

Kandim: It is enough if you have recited the string of names; it is the same issue.

Angrimbi: No, not at all! My elder brother, you cannot talk like that. First you have to recite your line of names, first we want to hear it!

Kandim: It is enough if you have already recited Wani's string of names.

Angrimbi: No, not at all! Well then, your point is about the . . . this crocodile that lays eggs! He! Is this what you are going on about? . . .

Kandim: Indeed!

Angrimbi: . . . That is not enough! It is about the children who go swimming and when they jump into the water, there is a sound *pi pi?* . . . It is about this crocodile of yours that kills a snake and eats—what is it again it eats? . . . Is this your point?

Kandim: Hm. That is what it is about.

Angrimbi: No, not at all. . . . If you cannot state another point, your claim is lost. . . .

Angrimbi: Now I have listened to your string of names. Like a frog that every night clings to a different branch, you have put it together from different pieces! . . .

Angrimbi: He does not know anything! Come on, tell us the place where the *sisal* was! Name this place if you have learnt something about it from your fathers. . . . Come here and tell us this place where they will build a village. I will not define the ancestral being, I will not recite the list of names of this place, do not count on it that I will enlighten you. . . .

Kandim: Mevimbitandimangi, Kambiambitandimangi [Kandim lists the names of the village of Yamil or Yamik near Gaikorobi which is imagined as an ancestress; see figure 2-1 or 2-2].

Angrimbi: Let it be, leave my Yamil in peace. . . .

Angrimbi: So you wanted to talk about my Yamil? O, sorry, it is all wrong! . . . This is about a completely different village.

Discussion

After this very simplified survey of the inner order of the social and religious organization of the Western Iatmul has been presented, it becomes manifest that striking similarities, and some differences, exist between these and what we know about journeys, songs, and names in Aboriginal Australia, especially in Arnhem Land and the Central Desert.[6] We will discuss three central aspects.

Delimitations

The fate of general concepts such as "clan," "tribe," "boundary," "lineage," or "cultural pattern" in the Australian Aboriginal social context is uncertain, and there is growing evidence of the fuzziness of many traditional concepts taken for granted in anthropology. Numerous researchers have concentrated on narrative and interactive constructions of indigenous realities as equivalent and opposed to the hegemonic narration of Western history (Austin-Broos 1994; Beckett 1994; Morphy 1994). In his study of the Yolngu (Murngin, Wulamba, or Miwuyt), Keen, over the course of many chapters, describes the heterogeneity and fluidity of group relations, "connections among groups were not those of enclosing 'sets' but extendable strings of connectedness" (Keen 1994:63). Aborigines often insist on the immutability of the Dreaming and Law, both in general and often in specific instances as well. Myers (1986) discusses the negotiated quality of Pintupi social life against a background of assertions of the fixity of law. Merlan notes that it is widely observed and relevant that Aboriginal people often do see themselves, in land-related as well as other matters, "as acting most interestedly and directly on behalf of what they may call 'family,' usually some small- to middle-range grouping of kindred and consociates" (1997:3). But these compositions are shifting, and how such "families" are seen in respect to any larger-level and more inclusive identities varies considerably. "Tribe" has been reinterpreted as socioterritorial identity, crucially having a territorial aspect but connoting neither solidarity nor corporateness. Social delimitations cannot be understood as structural notions, but the general Aboriginal way of life involved greater or lesser impermanence of aggregation, limited in size and shifting in personnel, produced in and adapted to life situations of small scale shaped by forms of interaction over wider regions.

The kind of identity that inhered in such connections seems to be most aptly described in terms of belonging to country, rather than by the notion of containment within a solidary group. But this "belonging to country" as well does not necessarily imply spatial delimitations as we know them with their fixity, absoluteness, and systematicity; rather it means a substantial core of people who indisputably have rights to specific spatial fixed points in the topography (Peterson 1976; Sutton 1995, 1997). It is not social or spatial boundaries but cores that are central. In the Mabo case, the fact that the Meriam people live on an island clearly facilitated identifying a "people" and their "area" (Peterson 1995). However, the claimants were not asking for the whole of Murray/Mer Islands but only for small areas of the island that belonged specifically to them and their families (although the claimants were given Native Title rights over the whole island). Even the boundedness of the island is not as simple as it seems, since the Meriam do not recognize any clear distinction between land and sea.

In contrast, the Iatmul seem to be more definite in their social organization, more highly structured, and more stable, in a social organization that as a whole is legitimated through religion and cosmology and can also directly be seen in the large villages (for Papua New Guinea standards, up to eight hundred inhabitants) and their layout, with visibly separated moieties and separate living quarters for the individual clans. Of course, in the Middle Sepik as well there are clan scissions, and clans that are diminishing in size, but the strict social delimitations of the clans, moieties, and villages are more durable, and the assignment of the knotted cords—and hence of the abstract system of order—to the clan groups is definite. One might gain the impression that the "idea" of the system is constantly present, that people try to represent it in the social structure and in the outline of the villages. If, for example, a clan is in danger of becoming extinct, it is "topped up" again with adoptions from mythologically neighboring clans. Also definite is the delimitation of the Western Iatmul from the Central Iatmul (even though people are aware of the common ground). Proper names are attributed to clans or persons that can be named, and correspondingly—and this is comprehensible—they may only be used once the person is within the boundaries of the Nyaura; outside, however, these names may be used again. Combined with the fact that the Nyaura are settled and not nomadic, these Nyaura boundaries also mean that the places of the migrations, and thus the land rights, play a practical role only within the Nyaura's own region. What lies outside provides the background for mental and emotional ascriptions, yet the Nyaura do not have access to it (while the course of the mythological paths is definitely known outside the Iatmul as well—for example, to the neighboring groups of the Sawos, Abelam, or Blackwater).

Distributions

A further distinction may be that for Aboriginal Australia there is repeatedly talk about "basic myth," everyone knowing the same basic story. Not only are different versions of it read according to "party-interest," but different versions are also retold in each context anew, depending on the listeners as well as on the teller's personal experiences and the memory of the listeners (Keen 1994). The way a performance is enacted—which songs are sung and which parts of the "basic myth" retold and which body-design painted—depends on such things as the relationship between the groups attending, the prestige of the group of organizers, and the ownership of the sacred paraphernalia. In comparison, the Iatmul again appear to be the more accomplished systematists. (Or is it the data-collecting and -interpreting anthropologist?) All the ancestors of today's clans took part in the primeval events and, as a result, the individual clans "own" parts of these events, which they retell in the present-day myths or sing about in the songs, and they have the right to portray (in art) the transformation abilities of the ancestors of that time and the duty (vis-à-vis the other clans) to look after the well-being of their totems. In addition, the performances of the song cycles are strictly regulated, the sequence of the songs closely follows the knotted cord, the structure of the individual songs and pairs of names is highly formalized in detail.

The origin was the same for all the clans, but the subsequent migrations were different. The result is that all of the clans have a common first place (with a "common" first large knot on the cord, a common first song, a common name and totem of the first place). But then they went separate ways, and the totems, the names, and the mythological events became different even though interconnected, in part since the actors met or acted together. Virtually all the things of this world, whether the stars, winds, animals, plants, watercourses, or settlements, are distributed among the moieties, clan groups, clans, lineages, and individuals. They are mental ascriptions; the individual totems and their names are the property of individuals (who have a corresponding proper name). For example, the Ngama clan group (earth moiety) is in charge of the following totems (and of the corresponding hundreds of names and dozens of places): the *kwi* tree, the mango tree, the *yamboi* liana, the wrens, stilts, and coucal birds, the earth, and the night; the Smat clan group (sky moiety) is in charge of the rattan, the possum, the lizard, the sun, the moon, the morning star, lightning, thunder, the rain, and the sky. The two corresponding knotted cords are focused on these totems and supply their names. Yet no group of "mango tree people" or "sun people" exists (like there are "wild cat people" in Aboriginal Australia); these are segments of the world for which the respective clan groups are responsible, or rather their "old crocodiles," for they are the ones who distribute the *individual* totems among *individual* persons (again, the situation is much more complicated than this, partly because of demographic fluctuations). An individual Nyaura will bear the names of the sun and feel connected with this ancestor; during the performance of "his" song to the sun he may react very emotionally, jumping up and shouting, "I, I am Nyagalandemi" (the already mentioned first name of the sun ancestor). Identification happens through names, not through dreaming places or the mother's totem. The members of a clan group or a single clan belong together because they have a common ancestor who also attributed to them certain totems, names, and places during a specific migration. Unlike Aboriginal Australia, however, here there are no key sites that could define a social group.

Secrecies

Merlan describes a recent event from an area south of Katherine in the Northern Territory. People noticed a singularly shaped stone lying near the roadside, evidently as a result of some recent grader work.

> Not at all dismayed by the mundane immediate cause of revelation, their imagination was captured by the stone's unusual shape. It was shortly suggested that the stone was a dugong, this interpretation "co-constructed" in relation to the shared knowledge that some people residing locally at the camp came from the Gulf country, making this a socially meaningful and intelligible interpretation. (Merlan 1997:8)

Involved here, concludes Merlan, are practices of constant attention to the world around, to fashioning that world as one's home in familiar ways. In that process Aborigines—as would be expected—work largely from existing cultural material. It is plausible that explanations about the stone, where it comes from, and what other events it is related to, may soon constitute a new body of knowledge around that particular site. Such a new development may easily be misinterpreted as an "invention" of a new tradition in the sense of fabrication.

The journeys across the topography seem to be the central topic for both Aboriginal and Nyaura (Iatmul) people, whereby the diverse places were created, the present landscape as well as all living species including the ancestors of the present groups (although the Iatmul know no conception sites). Primal events, which are associated with an ordered succession of places (Fox [1997a] talks about topogeny), are then re-created through ceremonial or artistic activities for the maintenance of the cosmic and social order. The meaning of the names and the obsession about the exact location of the episodes in the group's area are also points held in common. A further strong similarity concerns the esoteric character of knowledge and the exclusion (albeit fluid) of younger men and maybe women (who have their own secret knowledge). The dilemma is how to preserve the secrets of the clan in public and at the same time represent the worldly part for which the clan is responsible, to captivate one's own clan relatives emotionally and intellectually. The irony is that the process of proving ownership through demonstrations of knowledge may become the context for the loss of control over knowledge. In a worst-case scenario, proof of ownership could become the opportunity for raids and thefts (Rose 1994).

The protection of secrecy is achieved through the ambiguity, condensation, metonymy, and metaphor of the visible "signs," through cryptic use of language and restricted access to information about the "true" meanings. A strict separation of knowledge into a public and a secret domain would be an oversimplification (Morphy 1991:76; Herdt 1990; Lattas 1989), and yet (official) access to knowledge is reserved for the men who pass through various stages of knowledge and competence from initiation on until old age and who are thereby able to manipulate and amass political power. Knowledge is organized as intellectual property that is not freely available to all. The social reproduction of the land tenure system depends precisely on the control and transmission of knowledge from generation to generation within demarcated groups in ways that are not open. In Aboriginal societies knowledge is land-based (Rose 1994:2); in Iatmul it is rather name-based, but in both societies personal authority, personal achievement, the authority of seniors, and the integrity and autonomy of local groups depend on the control of knowledge through restrictions on its dissemination. Performance of knowledge (through song, dance, story, debating names) is a performance of ownership: it identifies the person as one with rights and responsibilities to that totem or site.

Rose (1994:2) mentions an example of a dispute among Aborigines about land ownership. An old man, who claimed ownership, was asked by another claimant, "If it's your country, sing it." He failed to do so and lost the dispute (recall the dispute between Agrimbi and Kandim).

Such a body of knowledge, however, is neither complete nor fixed. There is an inevitability of leakage (see Weiner, chapter 7 in this volume). But what happens in the case of a failure of transmission? "Old crocodiles" are not isolated figures but people who act on the basis of shared knowledge. Myths are widely known as tales, like bedtime stories; what is secret are the links between the protagonists, which supply their true identity as well as their names and localization. These connecting links, however, can be redefined again and again. Also, no single "old crocodile" has the whole system in his head. Each one has only parts of it, mainly the parts that his own clan has charge of—but gaps can be filled, for example, by forcing revelation of names in debating contests.

Cognitive science draws our attention to a further point: it is impossible to store in one's memory long mythological texts and thousands of names as such, that is, propositionally. Rather, a person memorizes prototypes of sequences, from which the actual story is then built up, and names (which paraphrase myths in "telegraphese") then have to be reconstructed. It is as if one were to look upon the real events surrounding the ancestral wandering, as if one were to see images and those images can help one to verbalize what has been seen in texts, songs, and names.

Of the neighbors of the Nyaura, the Manambu, Harrison observes:

> Men claim that mythology never changes, and that someone who tried to alter myths or promulgate false ones would invite affliction by the totemic ancestors. But, in fact, myth is manipulated continually. On average, a completely new name-dispute breaks out in Avatip once a year, provoked by some group challenging a myth of another group with a newly-fabricated rival myth of its own. Mythology is therefore being constantly produced. Whether or not it gains currency depends on its proponents' success in the debating-arena. (1990:141)

Harrison's observation creates a connection to the above-mentioned incident among the Jawoyn, where new stones are interpreted as dugongs. New events or objects are integrated into already existing mental systems; traditions can therefore be quite recent. In everyday life, these mental systems are everywhere, constantly and intentionally manipulated and thus potentially changed. Secret knowledge continues to leak to the public and thereby becomes meaningless, new cognitive links are created and have meaning because they are (still) secret. What would actually have happened if not Angrimbi but Kandim had won the name debate? Of course he would have been allowed to continue using the disputed name Sisalabwan—but maybe a new localization of the crocodile Wanimeli would have had to be made and a reinterpretation of the Wanimeli songs. We do not know.

Notes

1. My fieldwork was done in 1972–1973 and 1983 in the village of Kandingei, West Iatmul, or, according to their self-ascription, Nyaura, with the financial support of the Swiss National Fund.

2. Geographically, the historical events could well be the nucleus of the mythological.

3. This is of course an enormous simplification. In every cycle of songs, three levels have to be distinguished: that of the songs with a mythological reference, that of the vocal hybrid forms that relate to the current purpose of the perfor-

mance (for example, in the case of a funeral, the accompaniment of the spirit soul downstream on the Sepik to the land of the dead), and that of additional recitative hybrid forms that cite specific totems. The cycle is performed in the case of deaths, at the inauguration of a men's house, a family house, or a canoe. All six independent song cycles have been published, in Ndu language and German translation (Wassmann 1988) or English translation, respectively (Wassmann 1991). (Three more knotted cords exist, but with "borrowed" songs.) For the musical part, see Spearritt 1979.

4. At the beginning of my *Song to the Flying Fox* (Wassmann 1991) there is a list of the secret knowledge I was allowed to publish according to the "old crocodiles." Secret names were not on that list.

5. The transmission of information in bits corresponds exactly to the way things are handled between "old crocodiles" and their younger successors.

6. See Ayres 1983; Wassmann 1988 and 1991; Weiner 1988; Guddemi 1992; Bonnemaison 1994; Goodale 1995 (for Melanesian examples of mythological tracks); or C. Strehlow 1910; Magowan 1994; Rumsey 1994; Borsboom 1998 (for Australian examples). What is lacking to a large degree is the publication of entire song cycles accompanying the mythological journeys.

3

Condensed Mapping

Myth and the Folding of Space / Space and the Folding of Myth

Roy Wagner

What has the shape of the earth to do with the shape of the story? More to the point, how did preliterate peoples, who knew the terrain on which they made their livelihood, take cognizance of the larger world around them, map the familiar on the oblique and vice versa? We always come to these problems, even locate them, in terms of our received knowledge of global and local geographies, and in fact presume geography before everything else. So a large part of the problem is going to be invisible to us at the outset. All of our stories about travel across the earth, exploration and research into its forms, are already frozen into place, and if we want to get back to the beginnings on this we must start map-first and then replot the journeys on which the map was made. Myth in reverse.

What if the tale of how the map itself was made were part of that map? In that case the principle of mapping itself, which is to condense a knowledge of a larger and more distant world within a smaller depictive plot in one-to-one correspondence, would be different, and perhaps anthropomorphic. The ancient Romans had maps of their Empire engraved and put up in public places. These maps were very practical and, like road maps or the depicted "tracks" of pre-European Australians, biased heavily toward the conditions and exigencies of travel. In such cases there is considerably more anthropomorphism, the shape of the person in the myth of space, than in a satellite photo or topographic survey. It comes, so to speak, with the territory.

But think, for the moment, of a whole world covered by apparently localized people, a world in which, whether they had maps or not, the folks were always living in two kinds of space. In other words, to make any kind of sense of their home terrain they would have to take account of its limits or boundaries, and therefore of what lay beyond them. But if the terrain they knew best provided their whole familiarity with space, they would always be plotting the distant and the cosmological down on the local, and the local out upon the distant and the cosmological. The shape of space itself, as well as of the human experiencing of that space, would be epicentric in a very fundamental sense.

Let me give an example. The portion of the upper Purari River known to the Daribi of Papua New Guinea as the Hawari, and to geographers as the Tua, loops around Karimui, first going west, then turning south and going back eastward before joining the Erave and forming the Purari, debouching again to the south. This is all very well known to the Daribi, who can explain it in better detail than I can. But when it comes to the cosmological significance of water and its flow, the plot is much simpler. Water, they say, tends naturally to the west, as do the spirits of the departed. Rivers are the roads of the ghosts, and when people die they wind up in a lake far to the west. Despite the rather contradictory turning of the big river itself, known but ignored, the more accessible portion of the river, as well as most of the tributaries that flow through Daribi lands, have a westward tendency, and that is what matters. To put it more bluntly, it does not matter so much where the river comes from or where it goes, it is how the flow of water comes into immediate appearance that counts most in its reckoning. Everyone knows that the sun and moon move from east to west, and there are lots of theories as to how and why they do. But what really matters is that the moon and sun move in and out of the surface of the sky, something that happens at sunrise and sunset, and it is their actual presence or absence that counts most at any given time.

The extreme localization of how the country, or the cosmos itself, comes into appearance for us, at this very moment, is apt to be very misleading, as is the content of myth itself. Unless one gets some clarity on the role of myth in the folding of space, the lore by which traditional folks knew the shape of the wider world is apt to cast them as extremely limited and parochial peoples. So perhaps the better example of how one might move through a world that is knowable by its "coming into appearance" would be the traditional Polynesian and Micronesian navigators. Before the work of Thomas Gladwyn and David Lewis in discovering their actual navigating techniques, it was commonly suspected that they came upon their oceanic landfalls by accident or random drift, more or less as myth was thought to "diffuse." They used many techniques—for example, observing how the stars or wave trains come into appearance. But they also used as a basic assumption —never mind for the moment whether it was "heuristic" or not—the idea that the vessel they were traveling on was stationary, with the sea and the islands moving past it. They also based much of their reckoning on a hypothetical island, also stationary, lying at a right angle to the direction of the prow. It made no real difference, all other things being relative, whether the vessel was moving and space was stationary or vice versa.

The intriguing thing is that these folk had a better grasp of the outlines of space beyond their immediate ken than did many of those that "discovered" them, and for all the fact that their knowledge was, so to speak, "stationary." By some accounts the Polynesian adage that "the sea closes upon itself" acknowledged the sphericity of the earth. We do not know, of course, how old that knowledge might be, nor, since it is also possible to travel great distances across the land, how much of the world's geography is folded into the myths that were supposed to have diffused across it.

A large part of the mystery of myths, what goes on within them or outside of them, is how suggestively analogous motifs, characters, and plots keep cropping up in distant times and places, forming chains across the earth. Do these themes, relations, and persons travel along trade and migration routes and map the strains of interethnic encounter like some sort of fantastic anthropology, or do they actually create them? It was the definitive insight of Lévi-Strauss' work on mythology that what goes on outside of myths is intrinsically related to what goes on inside of them, that there is a double twist to what used to be thought of as the diffusion of mythic lore. In large parts of Australia and New Guinea, and often in the Americas, the grafting of mythic content upon distinctive features of the terrain is definitive of "country" or landscape itself, as if the roles of diffusion were reversed so that landscape did the diffusing and myth itself were the agent of coalescence. It is almost as if the intimate features of locality formed a kind of prism through which the global facts of existence might be described.

Before I get to the core of this, mythic involution as spatial evolution, let me cite one more example of the folding of space, this time from England. We do not know the identities of the folk who built the henges and set up the lay lines in the British Isles; we may not know their myths or languages, or in any case could not identify them, and so we are obliged to make up our own myths about them. Doubtless, then, a great deal of astronomical lore—solstices, equinoxes, heliacal risings, and so forth—was folded back into the placement of stones in a henge that I visited in Cumbria. I did not check that, having a modern myth to go on. But I did notice that the respective heights of the standing stones in the circle formed an exact replica of the mountain skyline around them. Cosmos folded back into landscape; landscape itself folded back to form a model of its astronomical epicenter.

The story I have to tell is that of the origin of Genaa, the flood motif in Papua that is the same flood, and the same story, as Noah's flood in the Bible, and the one that the makers of the Bible borrowed from the older Epic of Gilgamesh in Mesopotamia. It is the story of the figure-ground reversal of land and water, not likely a real deluge across the earth but more probably a universalization of the myth that took its place.

In this version, for understandable reasons, it is a very localized phenomenon. In the region of Genaa, Lake Tebera, including the Mount Karimui area, a lake is always quite literally a "body" of water, the liquidity or effluvia of the person who died to make it so. The local knowledge is that water runs, like the course of life itself, and that when and where it stops, there is a body. Genaa people identify themselves with the lake and its liquidity in a uterine sense. They will not drink the lake water. When I stayed with them at Haiduru Island, where all the latrines were built flush at lake level, they sent canoes every afternoon to bring pure drinking water from higher-altitude springs along the shore.

The origin story of Genaa is a tale of pairs, pairs of same- and opposite-gendered people who reflect and refract each other, folding the space of human interaction more or less as the surface of the water redoubles the landscape around it. The lake is the people and the people are the lake. Here is how it goes in translation:

> Two male cross-cousins came to the valley before the lake existed. They were Genaa, who came from the northwest, and Mube, who came from the Pio River to the east. They made a small pool at the

base of a tree at the east end of the valley and went inside. Two men of the valley came there in search of *pa* grubs. They ate raw grubs with cooked sago, became thirsty, and looked for water. One found the pool and drank from it: when he looked into the pool he saw the face of Genaa. He told the other man about the pool, and when that one looked in to drink he saw the face of Mube. They filled bamboo tubes with grubs and also took packets of them home with them. When they got home they heard the water rumbling at the pool where they had drunk, and the water in their bellies also began to rumble. They cooked the grubs and distributed them; one man gave them to the women and children, and the other to the men. They asked if everyone had had enough, and everyone said that they had.

When they had finished, a young woman of the place went off to a menstruation hut, taking her younger sister along. While staying at the hut they saw Mube, with a cuscus tail around each arm, pointing out the rim of the lake-to-be. The girls went home and told their parents what they had seen. But their parents mistrusted them: "No, a man came, had intercourse with you, and mocked you." Now the girl took her small brother by the hand: "We saw something bad, but they wouldn't believe us. Let's go." They went to the top of the Mountain Misiro. Before dawn they heard a huge outcry from below: all the pigs, dogs, and people cried out, and they heard the trees and sago palms breaking. At sunrise they looked down and water, red with the blood of the dead, covered the land. They had a little food, and built a fire to cook sago. Mube saw the smoke and wanted to kill them. Genaa said, "You have killed enough people already; those are their successors." Mube was firm; he fought with Genaa. Mube said, "I am sick of the smell of urine and feces from the dead inside the lake; you can stay here, I will go away." Mube went off to the south; Genaa and his lake stayed here.

The young woman and her brother burned sago stalks to make charcoal; they put the charcoal in a bamboo tube and sprinkled it over the lake, coloring the water black, as it is now. They kept trying different trees to make a canoe; finally the *dogozo* floated, and they made their canoe of it. The boy took the canoe and hunted pythons and cuscus along the edges of the lake, and took them to his sister. Once when he was off in the canoe a *horabi* bird gave its cry: *ape we sa, ape we sa,* "cross-sex sibling wife-take." When her brother brought his canoe in and offered her his game, she didn't take it. She draped her bark-cloak across the middle of their hut, dividing it into two rooms. The boy thought she had taken a husband, but that night she embraced him in coitus; he struggled at first, then gave in. They had many children, the last two being twins, a boy and a girl. As the children grew up, they distributed them across the land, replacing those who had formerly lived in the various places.

When the Tebera people finished telling me this, they said that if you look down into the lake today, you can see the face of Genaa staring up at you. That is what they mean by the story. And they said that if you climb Mount Karimui on a clear day and look off to the south you can see the water of Mube stretching out to the horizon. That is what *I* mean by the story, for the water of Mube is the Papuan Gulf. *-Be* is a suffix meaning "named after" in the language of these people; *Mu-* is a cognate of the Orokolo *ma, maw* in some southern Polopa dialects, and it means simply "the sea." The Origin of Genaa is the tale of the enmity between Genaa and Mube as they divided space between them, as the water divided the land, and as the land itself now divides their two waters. It is also the tale of human survivorship—how the Genaa people got themselves a little piece of the sea and lived on it.

That is the map in the myth, how an infusion became a diffusion, a small pool at the base of a tree folded itself outward into an ocean. I had asked the Genaa if they knew the story of the man who cursed mankind with death. "No," they said, "if you want that one you will have to ask the Daribi, or the folks along the Erave or the Purari. Our story is different; it is the story of a flood." The huge complex of Papuan Hero Tales has many exact parallels, often noted, with the Gilgamesh Epic of ancient Mesopotamia. But as we know the different versions of the story from Papua, it includes a richer variational dynamic than what we have left from Mesopotamia. The tale of Sido that Gunnar Landtman recorded at Kiwai Island is the story, like Gilgamesh, of the first man who died. Olsame Jesus Christ, they said to Landtman. To the east, in the Purari catchment, the protagonist becomes the opposite sort of hero, a giver rather than a receiver of death. "You call him God," the Pawaiians told me at Iruo, in Karimui, "we call him Souw." They also call him the *tǫ nigare bidi,* "maker of the land."

The diffusional implications of just what might have diffused from where, when it might have done so, and why, are so difficult to imagine, let alone trace, that just thinking of them is enough to put one off of diffusion for good. What I find to be totally scary, so much so that I strongly expect that it is accidental, is the name of the mountain at Tebera. Misiro' is not a sound that fits well phonologically with any of the three languages spoken there. But it closely resembles Nisir, the name of the mountain on which Utnapishtim's ark grounded after the flood in the Epic of Gilgamesh.

So I suspect that, instead of diffusion or its traces, we are dealing here with a kind of relativistic spacetime truth; myth moving across the surface of the globe as, in order that, or perhaps even because, the land moves and folds itself within the surface of myth. What I mean by this is that if myth predates rather than presupposes geography as a primary vector of land knowledge, how it got from one very distant place to another may be less important than how a single myth pulls the two places together. Misiro' may be exactly the same mountain as Nisir, plotting the same sense down on two different localities.

The Daribi knowledge of the flood story may be a good example of this. Daribi know the story of Genaa in bare outline and tell it to one another as someone else's story. But they also have a lake of their own, one that they sometimes recommend to visitors as a convenient alternative to making the difficult trek down to Tebera. A pond, really, it lies in a limestone valley of the same size, shape, and direction as the Tebera one, and if it flooded, it would give us another Tebera and take many of the Daribi out.

Seen in an aerial photograph, or sketched closely, the Hagani lake is a bit of limestone pornography. It has two extensions, called the *bidi sigi* or "man-lake" and the *ari sigi* or "woman-lake," shaped and positioned to suggest a coupling in the characteristic seated coital posture, with a small swampy conduit connecting them at just the right place. The myth that connects and explains them develops from water rumbling in the ground through drinking, water rumbling in the belly, sexual intercourse, subsequent urination, more rumbling, to a general flooding of the valley. The man and the woman became one in their union and their fluids engorged the whole Hweabi karst formation. It is said that the creator Souw appeared on the mountain rim and told the man and woman to separate and subside, and thus they may be seen today, their sex reduced to a mere trickle.

Would Lévi-Strauss want to tell us that the Deluge is menstrual with coital after-effects at Tebera, but the reverse of this, coital with subsequent runoff, at Karimui? Actually there is some more evidence for this. Daribi say that the lake "explodes" from time to time, and though I do not know exactly what this might mean, I have sometimes heard its roar through the trees. It explodes furtively, as the Daribi have sex, and despite the fact that my house was situated right above it, and despite the hours I spent sitting next to it with my camera, I never caught it in flagrante.

There is more, too. The lake is dangerous, like Daribi sex, much of it adulterous for added spice. It has what Australianists might call a resident *bunyip,* a Medusa-like reptilian with a brilliant erectile crest, called the *bidi taurabo haza,* or "human ripe-making animal." Anyone who catches sight of it becomes "ripe" like a fruit, yellow-skinned and engorged with juices, and drops off soon afterward.

The lake imagery in all of these instances used an experience of liquidity that is over-familiar in the human body—the engorgement of fluids in sexual intercourse or human ripening, liquid rumbling in the belly as it rumbles outside, the explosion of liquid or its disengorgement in menstruation or urination—to make an all-too-acute sense of the sensible terrain around it. Condensed mapping recondensed in the body, liquid space folded in and out of the body as the reflective surface of the lake folds and unfolds the figures and distances around it. The lacustrine body, liquid corporality, is the animate vector of the middle ground between the too-close-for-comfort and the very very distant—water rumbling in the belly and the water of Mube stretching out infinitely, merged with the horizon. So no wonder the deluge, an accident that happened in the past and is always waiting to happen.

An incisive interpreter of symbols and legends might want to ask what *is* the connection between the world-covering flood of the Old Testament and the Gilgamesh Epic, and the immortality sought by Gilgamesh and more or less promised in the New Testament. The familiar terrain was made to disappear beneath an enfolding, reflecting surface and then appear again as it now lies. But there is the mountain. Ararat or Nisir-Misiro', standing like a pillar above the flood, and in the lore of the Middle Eastern peoples, Judaic as well as Islamic, the lone male survivor, Noah or Utnapishtim, is known as the Pillar of God, an immortal being in mortal form. Utnapishtim becomes the mentor of Gilgamesh, instructing him in the procedures for attaining immortality. A body, once again, about whom the waters of space have folded and unfolded.

Is geography the artifice of Mube, "named for the sea," that would-be killer of humankind? We lose the sense of body and its liquid bid for immortality in a world of spaces plotted geographically and understood geologically as if they could just as well belong somewhere else. And we lose that funny little map in our heads of the Original Terrain that we all grew up with. Reconfiguring it to match new locales has become so much of a habit or necessity that we know our own ground from elsewhere, and know elsewhere from where we are.

4

Origins versus Creative Powers

The Interplay of Movement and Fixity

Pamela J. Stewart and Andrew Strathern

Stories that relate to "origins," seen as events that lay down a permanent state of affairs, can be contrasted with stories that deal with "creations," seen as events that initiate a new state of affairs in historical terms. Of course, each origin is a creation, and each creation in this sense also becomes an origin-point for a phase of history, but the phases are open-ended, leaving room in principle for further creations later, whereas origins in the sense outlined here define history in a closed manner from the outset.

We argue that when this distinction is applied to mythic narratives having to do with the connections between people and the land, it reveals differences in the ways that people conceptualize their claims in circumstances of change. An emphasis on origins leads to a tenacity of self-identification, while an emphasis on creation leads to a more fluid sense of identity. In looking at specific examples where elements of these two tendencies can be found mingled together, we will find that this simple contrast does not quite hold in practice because of cross-cutting complications. We use it, however, as a means of gaining perspective on a comparison between materials on the Hagen area in the Western Highlands of Papua New Guinea, where we find an emphasis on "creations," and on the Yolngu people of northeastern Arnhem Land in northern Australia, among whom there is a stress on "origins." We make it clear in this chapter that this contrast is one of nuances, not absolute differences. We are also well aware that Aboriginal cosmologies in practice allow for flexibility and change while giving an appearance of fixity, just as New Guinea ones provide certain points of fixture while giving an appearance of much fluidity (see Maddock 1972:111; R. Tonkinson 1978:14–17 and 1974:71).

It is important to note at the outset that such a contrast can proceed only against a background of basic similarity, and in keeping with the basic theme of this volume we recognize that the similarity here has to do with an overall strong identification of people with land, through notions of ancestrality, substance, revealed power, and the need to renew fertility by ritualized access to power. The effect of such an array of ideas is to saturate the perceived landscape with values and meanings that provide a rich material network of associations for identity constructions, from the personal and emotional to the social and politico-legal. In other words, when we inspect the ethnography for differences, we can make our "cross-regional" comparison with some confidence because at another level we are implicitly constructing a wider "region" of similarity to which the data belong. Many statements about ethnographic facts can therefore be selected from Australian contexts that would apply equally well to Melanesian ones, and vice versa. For example, there is the "subordination of time to space" referred to by Howard Morphy for the Yolngu (Morphy 1995: 188), and there is the theme of transformations or "turnings" of ancestral beings into humans on the one hand and creatures or features of topography on the other, also referred to by Morphy and others (e.g., Keen 1994:44) on the Yolngu. Both themes are familiar in Melanesian contexts. And these two factors are ones that are integral to the specific topic of identity constructions, which is to be explored here. Our subtitle also specifies that the powers of origin-making and creation constitute images of movement and fixity. In the Yolngu case, mobile ancestral beings transformed themselves into fixed features or created these as they moved. In Hagen, ancestors are portrayed as travelers who discover features of a landscape or have events revealed to them that then create a fixity of their identification for a period of time. In both cases it is the interplay between movement and fixity that creates power. In recent years a cross-fertilization of topics has occurred between Australianist and Melanesianist ethnographies, in which the "Australian" feature of "sacred trackways" of power has been discovered in Melanesian contexts and highlighted more than previously—for example, for the Duna people (Stewart 1998; Stewart and

Strathern 1997) and also for Hagen (Strathern and Stewart 1997 and 1999; see also generally Rumsey, chapter 1 above).

The accounts of these trackways and their cosmological underpinnings indicate very clearly that the relationship of people to land and its resources was complexly mediated in terms of a double ideology, linking people to particular ritual sites and linking these sites further in long, connected pathways putatively based on the primordial passage of an ancestral figure, reenacted in the ritual transference of bodily substances and parts from site to site as a means of replenishing the fertility of the earth. The Duna *hambua hatia* and *kirao hatia* trackways were examples of these ritual passages or pilgrimages seen as culminating at the place Gelote or Kelokili in the territory of the Huli. Central ritual sites of what the Duna called *rindi kiniya* and the Huli called *dindi gamu* were places where the "root of the earth," described as a python with a liana twined around it, could be accessed and rituals performed to renew its power on behalf of the wider coethnic region. The regional scope of these notions is clearly comparable to the traditions of Dreaming trackways among Australian Aboriginal peoples. They are also clear examples of the movement/fixity interplay, which is central to our argument here.

In terms of regional connections and the ritual interdependence that exists across landscapes, we may take note of the Huli myth of Hela, the common ancestor of the Huli, the Duna (the people to the northwest of the Huli), Obena (the Enga, Ipili, and Paiela peoples to the northeast of the Huli), and the Duguba (this includes all the peoples of the Papuan Plateau, for example, the Etoro, Onabasulu, Kaluli, Tsinali, and Bedamini) (Frankel 1986:16; Biersack 1995:14–16). These groups were thought to have migrated to their present localities from a common origin site. The groups represent linguistic clusterings: Obena corresponds roughly to speakers of the Enga language family —the Ipili, Enga, and Mendi; Duguba includes speakers of Kaluli, Onabasalu, Etoro, and Bedamini; and Duna is the language of the Duna (Ballard 1994:135; Haley 1996:279–281). This representation of linguistic difference and unity can be compared with the Yolngu stories discussed by Sutton (1997:222–225) in which *wangarr* spirits allot languages to peoples as they travel in a landscape. The Huli narrative exhibits a particular view of languages, related to geography and trade, though not to the lexico-statistics of linguists (Ballard 1994: 135; Haley 1996:279–281). All of these people were in trading relationships with the Huli for an array of goods ranging from stone axe blades to tree oil used in decoration and ritual enactments. Through these trade partnerships, in which the Huli served also as intermediaries between Obena and Duguba people, ritual notions, practices, and paraphernalia flowed.

Ballard explains this integration of the regional sacred geography in terms of the underground python bound with cane and capped with stone. Rocky outcrops are interpreted as the python's stone cap and caves as its mouth. Whenever the "root" surfaces, there is a major ritual site of the earth. Moreover, the flow of power in the root is from the Papuan Plateau northward, reversing the direction of river drainage and the passage of spirits of the dead. Further, the ritual sites (*gebeanda* in Huli and *auwinda* in Duna) are sometimes places where mineral oil seeps to the surface. Torches soaked in this oil were lit by ritual leaders entering caves, and the ability of oil to produce fire is linked to the idea that the sun by night travels back along the earth's root before rising again. The *dindi gamu* rituals aimed at renewing fertility thus were bound up in the sun's own ritual "death" and rebirth in the diurnal/nocturnal cycle. Ballard points out that the sun is the python and the python is oil and this oil is a latent flame, or the sun by night (Ballard 1998). Likewise, among the Duna oil is seen by some informants as the "eggs" of the python, which she protects. It is also seen as the transformed "grease" of the dead, which generates fertility in the soil, and if the oil is taken from the ground it is thought that it will become "dry" and infertile (Strathern and Stewart 1999).

These trackway narratives have to do with both the general creation and the renewal of powers of fertility and increase in the material and social cosmos. The "Dreamtime" pathways of ancestral beings in Australian mythology thus become similar in overall function to the mythical trajectories of spirit beings in Melanesia, as well as to the historical pathways of particular cult performances from place to place by means of which the sacred landscape is periodically reinfused with power. The permeability of these narratives to historical events is also clear. Yolngu mythology includes the Macassans and Whites; Mount Hagen stories become inflected with references to God as well as the ancestors and are adapted to issues having to do with land shortage and cultural property, as we will show. First, however, we look at some examples of Hagen narratives relating to groups.

Hagen Narratives of "The Creative Event"

Hermann Strauss' accounts of the mythical origins of individual Hagen groups are here analyzed for components that stress origin site, sacrificial elements, connection with Sky Beings, movement of people, and the repetition of the creative event (Strauss and Tischner 1962:24–65). The stories sometimes trace the actual first origins of group ancestors, but sometimes they are more concerned with showing the ritual association of empowerment between an ancestor and spiritual powers that lies also at the heart of the narratives couched in terms of origins.

The features of particular importance for our purposes in these narratives are (1) the act of "revelation" of a place of creation, (2) the way that this discovery "fixes" a group's identity in time and space, and (3) the fact that the creative event of revelation can be "repeated" and thus renewed over time.

The Myth of the Muntka

In this myth a young girl finds an egg lying in a bed of *munt* bush leaves while walking through the forest. She accidentally breaks the eggshell and eats the contents raw. On her return home she finds that she is pregnant and subsequently gives birth to a son, whom she names Munt-Ka, after the bush where the egg was found. Upon growing up, Munt-Ka takes a wife and makes sacrifices at the *munt* bush where his mother found the egg. Munt-Ka and his wife have four sons whose descendants are the Muntka Kâwudl-önggidl, Muntka Temboka-önggidl, Tedlaka-Muntka, and Mönts-Muntka.

The Muntka recognize *munt* twigs as the group's Mi. The Mi is a central symbol in Hagen culture (Strauss and Tischner 1962:passim). It is a sacred plant or object, connected with a group's origins, and is a sign of the creative powers granted to ancestors of the group by the Sky Beings (Strathern and Stewart n.d.). The Mi has a protective and legal function in that it can give warning of impending dangers or failure, provide protection against false accusations and unfounded demands of atonement in legal cases, act as a guarantee of peace, and consume the life force of any miscreant who denies his sins and refuses to atone. The Mi substance is one that requires sacrifice, since it provides life force while at the same time serving as a sign of land/property ownership. The place where the girl found the egg at the *munt* bush is called the *kona wingndi* of the Muntka. *Kona wingndi* is the origin place for the original Muntka Mi-group and thus a place where sacrifices should be offered by the group living there. *Kona wingndi* is also the place(s) to which one of the descendants has moved and where specific knowledge has been revealed and hidden powers have been bestowed as "creative gifts." The word *wingndi* means "to do something skillfully" or "to be the first to do something," that is, being creative. The term *kona* here means "place." Thus *kona wingndi* is the "extraordinary, creative place" or where something extraordinary, new, or creative happened. The content of this creative event is revealed in the origin myths. In the Muntka myth, the main feature of the place of the creative event is the bird egg. Likewise, when descendants of one subgroup of the Munt-Ka (the Muntka Temboka-önggidl) dispersed out on their wandering, they came to a place where, after they had killed a marsupial, a *rapa* lizard suddenly appeared. This event was taken to be a sign that their new *kona wingndi* had been revealed to them. In the myth the wandering group had asked, "Where shall I go to next?" and had set out on the journey without knowing where it would lead. The appearance of the Mi, the *rapa* lizard, marked the place where sacrifices should be made and where the group could settle and establish their cult sites, since the powers that had previously been hidden in the place had now been revealed to them and were available for their use if appropriate sacrifices were made. The point here is that the group now has two "creative places," one a place of first origins and the other a place where power was again revealed to them in a creative way.

The Myth of the Mineimbi

As in the story of the Muntka, the principal ancestor is a bird (here an eagle). In this story a girl finds an egg at a place called Mineimb and puts it in her netbag to be cooked. Later, when she opens her bag, she finds a boy where the egg had previously been. An eagle comes and brings the boy bits of pork until he grows big and strong. The boy was called Mineimb-i-köi (bird from Mineimb). He took a wife and had revealed to him the *kona wingndi* of the group when he went to Mount Aeng and found that a cooking pit was prepared with hot stones in an isolated, uninhabited site. He declared that this extraordinary event marked the place as the group *kona wingndi* and the cooking stone was revealed to be the Mi of the Mineimbi group.

Myth of the Kentipi

In this story, a Sky Being who was light-skinned came down to earth, bringing a dog with him. The dog was left on earth and told to direct the people whom he first encountered that they had discovered their Mi and *kona wingndi.* The Kentipi had this revealed to them when they arrived at the place, and they made pork sacrifices there at the site.

Myth of the Olt-Pöi

Here also, a Sky Being brought a dog to earth to reveal to the people their Mi, *kona wingndi,* and cult site for making appropriate sacrifices.

Myth of the Nöglkö

The ancestor of the group, Nögl, was wandering in search of a home place when he was surprised to see an unusual clump of *neng* —trees in the middle of a grassy, swampy area at Ep, north of a hill that rose sharply from the plain. He realized that this was the Mi and *kona wingndi* for his people. Later, the group increased in number and thought that they would like to move away from the grasslands and live in the nearby hills, where there would be wood for making fires and building. One day the group's leader heard a dove cooing *(ku-wök, ku-wök),* and he thought that the bird was expressing his desire to live closer to the Ku ("rock"/stone) forested area. Thus he moved to the area where the group now lives, and he saw the dove fly across and hide near Muri-Ku, which he realized was now the *kona wingndi* for the group and that is where they now made their sacrifices. Here,

	Sky-Beings	First Origin	Sacrifice-Claim	Migrations	Second Creative Event
Muntka	–	+	+	+	+
Mineimbi	–	+	+	–	–
Kentipi	+	+	+	–	–
Olt-Pöi	+	+	+	–	–
Nöglkö	–	+	+	+	+
Kungurnkö	–	+	+	–	–

Figure 4–1. Narrative elements in group creation stories by Strauss. The two cases recording migrations also record a second creative event, and their profile of elements is identical (Muntka and Nöglkö). Mineimbi and Kungurnkö patterns are also identical, as are Kentipi and Olt-Pöi. (Figure by authors)

then, there is again a duplication of "creative places," such as we found for the Munt-ka and as we will find also in the case of the Kawelka, who live to the southern side of the Ep mountain ridge.

MYTH OF THE KUNGURNKÖ

In the story the founder comes to a site that is revealed to be the *kona wingndi* after he has killed marsupials and is preparing them in the cooking pit. The circular rope of a cordyline plant falls down and encircles the cooking pit. Later he makes sacrifices at this site and puts a fence around the specific site to prohibit entrance to others. In the area just around the cult site the group settled and recognized the cordyline as their Mi. (The cordyline is also the Kawelka Mi). The distribution of elements in these stories is shown in figure 4-1.

Mul Temb and the Ulga

Thomas Nakinch has given us a study of origins, creations, and contemporary relations among the Ulga people of the Nebilyer Valley south of Mount Hagen township, as seen in accounts given to him in the 1970s along with his coworkers Michael Kunjil and Gabriel

Pil (Nakinch 1977). His account of the Ulga shows several illuminating variations on the themes we have seen in the narratives compiled by Hermann Strauss. His chief informant was a leading man of one branch of the Ulga, Ugl El, to which Nakinch himself belongs. Ugl attributed Ulga origins in the first place to a being called Mul Temb (which can also refer to a kind of forest form of greenery), also seen as the founder of a neighboring tribe, the Penambe, who were nevertheless enemies of the Ulga. Ugl argued that Mul Temb was an overall founder and guardian of the clans in the Nebilyer but had concentrated his attentions most closely on the Ulga. Ugl also declared that Mul Temb was sent by God to guide the Nebilyer people, a notion compared by Nakinch to the story of Moses in the Bible. Mul Temb also appeared only to special big-men, especially Ugl, in order to give them advice, partly through the medium of dreams. Ugl recounted how Mul Temb had appeared to him on the Aundula mountain with which he is associated, and also in a dream, advising the Ulga to sacrifice pigs to him before entering into a war with another tribe in 1971. Ugl followed Mul Temb's advice, but other Ulga did not, and the Ulga as a whole lost in the fighting. Mul Temb, however, is thought to be immortal and to continue to look after the Ulga through his chosen leader.

The details appear as an interesting 1970s inflection of the pattern of stories found in Strauss. Thomas Nakinch later stood for Parliament in the Tambul-Nebilyer electorate and became an M.P., a position he held for many years, strengthened by his cross-cousin tie with Paias Wingti, a Hagen politician who was twice Papua New Guinea's prime minister, then was defeated in 1992 through a split in the Ulga vote. His narrative makes Ugl and his lineage central in the Ulga group and in the Nebilyer via the association with Mul Temb, and Mul Temb in turn is said to have been sent by God, making the Ulga into a "chosen people." Mul Temb is akin to the Sky Beings found in some of Strauss' narratives, but he is fitted into a Christian scheme on the one hand and contemporary politics on the other via the notion that he advises the leader Ugl by privileged visions (appearances) and dreams. We can see that the elements in narratives of ties with powerful beings at the "creative places" (*kona wingndi*) have here been expanded to encompass a widening world of ideology and action. The same potentials exist in the Kawelka narrative.

The elements that appear in the Ulga story overall are as follows:

1. Mul Temb lived, and lives, in Ulga territory on the top of the high Aundula mountain, at a place whose name means "one stone" (Ku Tilipela), where sacrifices of pigs were brought in early times. The association with the mountain suggests he is a "man of the above," a Sky Being. Aundula is therefore a "first" *kona wingndi* where Mul Temb's sacrifice claim was recognized.
2. The first Ulga man as such was called Aundula Nining, who lived peacefully with the Penambe founders. Later the two groups fought and separated. At this time the Ulga ancestors were called Namala. They saw the Ulga River and believed that by following it they could escape from the dangers of their conflict with the Penambe. In thanks for doing so, they called themselves Ulga. This, then, is the migration and resettlement story.
3. The Ulga settled at a place called Kapiya Kola, where there was a magnificent *kapiya* tree in front of a men's house they built (this kind of tree is often found in the Nebilyer planted as a *pokla mbo,* a sacred marker of ancestral power at a ceremonial ground used for exchanges and cult dances). From Kapiya they discovered a sacred place at Arua where they offered pigs and made sacrifices to the Male Spirit (*Kur Waup* in Nakinch's rendering equals *Kor Wöp* in the Melpa language, spoken to the north of the Nebilyer). At the same time they continued to offer sacrifices to Mul Temb at Aundula. This element stands in place of a discovery of a second *kona wingndi,* and is of the greatest interest because it shares a clear parallelism between the "creative place" idea and the establishment of cult sites to spirits such as the *Wöp,* the Female Spirit (Amb Kor) and the *Eimb* fertility spirit. In other words, the *kona wingndi* notion is of a piece with general ideas of the arrival, perception, capturing, and tending of flows of power issuing from spirit agencies that inform the ritual trackways of cult transmissions that crisscross the Hagen landscape. Nakinch again tied the idea of spirit power into politics by noting (1977:16) that only Ugl El knew the details about the *Kur Waup,* passed on to him by his father and grandfather, and hence he was the leader in *Waup* sacrifices. This is a very strong corroboration of the idea that the big-man system in Hagen was actually underpinned by notions of ritual power (Strathern 1993).
4. Further elements of expansion and separation between subgroups are explained by conflicts and denials of solidarity between men, declared in retrospect to have been instigated by Mul Temb so as to make the group grow and expand. We see here an element of "destiny" that is productive in the creation of meaning. Whenever ancestors are said to have "found" places, this means that the places were intentionally "revealed" to them by spirit powers, who then can be seen as directing the larger-term trajectory of the group as such. Such an idea can easily shift into a contempo-

rary Christian notion that things happen according to "God's plan." They then also strengthen the sense of authenticity of claims that groups have over resources and the tenacity with which they are prepared to assert these claims.

The Kawelka: A Narrative in Four Parts (given by Ongka in 1969)

1. *At Kimbapukl.* This is a small hill in the Nebilyer Valley. An old man who lived there, at the *kona wingndi,* cooked bush rats as a sacrifice for the sickness of his son. The son saw an old man crawling down a tall palm tree, headfirst, like a *konda* snake, and the old man told him to cook pigs in the future, not rats, and if a cordyline leaf fell on the cooking pit, the sacrifice would be heeded. He tapped the boy on the forehead with his stone axe. The boy told his father, who would not listen, and the son died. The father cooked a large female pig and offered it to the spirit. A cordyline leaf fell on the sacrifice. He saw this, however, as a sign of ancestral displeasure and left. [The event appears to recapitulate some original appearance of power at Kimbapukl. It marks the cordyline as the Kawelka Mi, and it explains why the ancestor moved on.]
2. *At Kim.* The ancestor and his wife moved north, to Kim in the Wahgi Valley, and there the Kawelka expanded and spread out in different directions. [Carrying with them the power of reproduction from their original *kona wingndi,* they grow and segment.]
3. *At Kuk.* One place they spread into was Kuk, and there they fell into conflict with old allies of theirs, the Mokei. They were chased into the swamp, where many died by drowning or were killed as they waded in it. [Kawelka bones thus entered the swamp.] A big-man, Koi, was killed, and the Kawelka thought: "We can't stay here. Koi is dead and we are no longer strong." Kaepa, Ongka's father, sacrificed a pig to the land, saying he was sorry for it because they had to leave it now. Then they fled northward to relatives at the places Mbukl and Mbakla. [Warfare causes a further migration. Koi is identified with the group's strength. They reaffirm their tie with the land by a sacrifice.]
4. Mbakla was a place with which the Kawelka already had ties. A separate narrative tells how an ancestor called Kipilya or Uip went hunting and came to a place where he looked down and saw an isolated clump of trees at Mbakla Eimb Manga (Mbakla Fertility House) amid gardens. He went down there, caught mar-

> supials, and cooked them with wild greens. He met a woman of the Tipuka group there who was also collecting greens and they married and had children, ancestors of Kawelka subgroups. [This section appears to restart the myth and to stitch it on to parts 1–3. It makes Mbakla the equivalent of a new *kona wingndi* for the Kawelka who live near it. It is in fact a place of water springs, and the Eimb cult was performed there. It functions in the Kawelka story as Arua does for the Ulga. For the full narrative, see Strathern 1972:36–39.]

These four parts of the narrative can be further reduced as follows:

1. Original settlement at *kona wingndi*. Sign of the Mi. Reason for migration.
2. Second settlement. No *kona wingndi*. Expansion of the group at Kim.
3. Warfare. Loss of big-man Koi. Sacrifice to land and departure from Kuk.
4. Discovery of the second *kona wingndi* at Mbakla.

The Kawelka have subsequently returned to Kuk, where most of them now live, and have refashioned a story centered on Koi that inserts the equivalent of a *tertium quid* in their history, a "creative event" that gives them special ties with Kuk through the actions of Koi. It is notable that in Ongka's 1969 version Koi was said to be the source of the Kawelka's strength, but the ritual underpinning of this was not expressed. This underpinning is given in the story of the Kuk stone stela (Strathern and Stewart 1998).

Very briefly, the ancestor Koi is said to have found this stela on the hillside of the Ep ridge at Ropri when he was hunting marsupials. The long slab of stone "spoke" to him by making guttural sounds. He took it and (presumably with the help of others, for it was long and heavy) set it up near where he lived and instituted the performance of sacrifices to it in times of need. This story was current in the 1960s, but not greatly stressed. By 1995 it had come much into prominence, owing to the Kawelka's need to assert their land claims vis-à-vis other groups, including the Mokei, and in relation to the former swamplands, drained to make a government agricultural research station and now being informally recognized by the Kawelka themselves in a situation of abandonment by the government and their own shortage of land for planting coffee. In this context the story of Koi's discovery of the stone and its erection on Kawelka land came to function as an equivalent to a *kona wingndi* theme. Significantly, when the Kawelka performed a Female Spirit cult ritual in 1983–1984, the cult site was very close to the stone stela. Both stela and cult thus reinforced Kawelka land claims. We see here a clear example of the reshaping of narrative elements in contemporary situations, facilitated by the open-endedness of the concept of "creative event." In the account of Kawelka history given by Ongka in 1969, Kimbapukl was a *kona wingndi* but of no contemporary importance and no claim was made to it (Strathern 1972:36–39). Kim was not a *kona wingndi,* neither was any claim made to it. Claims were made to Kuk by virtue of burial places, deaths, and sacrificial invocations, but it had no *kona wingndi.* Mbukl and Mbakla were the sites both of contemporary claims and of another "creative event." By 1995 Kuk had also been equipped with an investiture of power and claims to land functionally similar to the "creative place" idea: a creative progression of narratives and knowledge.

Of these narratives the story of the Kawelka shows most clearly the pattern of shift in recognition of creative places over time, but this feature shows also clearly for the Muntka and Nöglkö stories given by Strauss (see figure 4-1). The creative forces are perpetually present. They can re-manifest themselves to ancestors at different times and in different places, creating history as they do so.

We turn now to "origins" among the Yolngu, leaping over the Sahul shelf into Australia on the trackway of our discussion.

The Yolngu: Origins, Turnings, Perfusions

For this discussion, we draw on the work of Lloyd Warner (1937), Ian Keen (1994), Howard Morphy (1995), and Nancy Williams (1986). The accounts of these authors essentially fit well together, though they may differ in details. The themes we wish to pick out here have to do with (1) ancestral shapings and creations along trackways; (2) forms of identification of persons with localities; (3) the concept of "turning" or transformation/metamorphosis that underlies (1) and (2); and (4) the idea of mixing or perfusion, which lends both closure and openness (in different ways) to person-land identifications. It is the combination of closure and opening that gives rise to possibilities of disputes, whereas the notion of ancestral shapings gives a firm foundation for permanent claims to landscape and its resources.

SHAPINGS

Yolngu ancestral beings known as *wangarr* (Keen 1994:43) were credited with moving around in early times and creating features of the earth and sky. They were beings with a human form, but also had some of the properties of the beings whose names they took (e.g., Rock or Honeybee), and they had extraordinary powers, including powers of self-transformation. Some *wangarr* also engendered the human ancestors of groups. Others engaged in conflicts with categories of outsiders such as the Macassans; for example, Honeybee is said to "sting" a Macassan, which can be interpreted as a "spearing" in human terms. Shaping the environment could take the form of creating or giving things to people or of turning into things such as rocks. In a key passage, Keen notes: "*Wangarr* ancestors existed and were active long ago; their traces and power remained and people explained some of the *wangarr* were still alive and active beneath the waters and earth" (Keen 1994:43). Examples of the *wangarr* were the Djang'kawu sisters, who carried dilly bags containing *rangga* or sacred objects and saw and named "places, plants, animals, birds, fish and other creatures." They created freshwater springs as they went. They also bore the first members of the Dhuwa moiety (49). These *wangarr* thus laid down aspects of the environment and founded one of the two main Yolngu regional moieties. Hagen mythology does not have a real equivalent of this category of being. It tends to begin rather with a specific human ancestor who encounters/discovers an originary power, as we have seen. The notion of originary power is present, but not elaborated as it is in the Yolngu case.

Howard Morphy's account parallels that of Keen. Taking a phenomenological approach, he argues that landscape was taken as "evidence" of ancestral action. "The ancestral presence was there and immutable" (1995:186). Landscape is therefore "integral to the message" (186). The land today is also the land the ancestors used, the land they experienced (188). Thus, "the ancestral beings, fixed in the land, become a timeless reference point outside the politics of daily life" (188). Furthermore, their actions "can be re-performed through ritual and represented through sacred objects and paintings" (189). Such ideas present us with myth as charter indeed and belong strongly to the category of thinking in "origin" terms as we have defined it.

Morphy also notes that individually acquired mythic knowledge "attaches the person in a particular way to a structure of places" (189). We can compare this with Lloyd Warner's account of local identifications.

Forms of Identification of Persons with Localities

Lloyd Warner (1937) details in his ethnography of the Yolngu that the people's myths and folktales secure a record of territorial ownership and boundary maintenance and that each clan possesses its land by immemorial tradition. He states that for the Yolngu, "land and water, people and clan are an act of the creator totem and the mythological ancestors, who always announce in myths and ceremony that this is the country of such and such a clan; to expropriate this land as a conscious act would be impossible. Just as the totem, the creator, and the members are a permanent and inextricable part of the culture, so is the clan's ownership of the land" (19). A Yolngu's identity, from birth to death, is linked to the land and the sacred wells that each clan identifies with and that serve as a core for the spiritual life of the group. The water holes found in the territory of a clan are divided into two classes: *garma* wells are totemic but not sacred, while *narra* wells are sacred and can be seen only by the initiated young men after the age of puberty. The symbol of the well is painted on a man after his initiation, when he receives his totemic name, and also when a small boy is to be circumcised (26). All clan totems are thought to be beneath the surface of the water holes in subterranean waters. The life force that produces a child comes from the spirits living in these wells (20–21). The names of the wells throughout the Yolngu show the totemic affiliations of the clans.

Warner's account explains, then, the specific ties of clan members to a localized territory, partly in terms of ideas of local spirit-conception and partly in terms of initiation. The clan water hole also represents a point of fixity in counterpoint to the wide-ranging movements of the *wangarr* spirits and their far-flung residues.

Nancy Williams (1986) also states that the Yolngu "take the most important aspects of their identity from the spirit-beings with whom they are associated, through their mothers and fathers. These spirit-beings in turn assume the characteristics, particular activities and appurtenances by which Yolngu know them in relation to particular lands" (27). She goes on to say that Yolngu assume that all of the land of Australia is owned by one or another Aboriginal group, since in the past the spirit-beings moved across the land and put names to places and put spirits and the people in the land (30).

TURNINGS

Stories of shifts of shape or of being are perhaps universally found in the mythologies of Melanesia and Australia alike, so to note this as a fact does not take us far. More important is the question of what such shifts signify. Keen, for example, points out that shape-shifting is linked to ambiguity, polysemy, and richness of meaning (1994:44). Morphy notes that the scheme of mythological knowledge is also a scheme of ecological knowledge, which makes an association between the tracks of particular ancestral beings and particular ecological zones (1995:193). The encoding of this knowledge is consistent with the idea that ancestral beings "have no set form but transform from animate or inanimate form to human form and back" again in different myth sequences (193). This identification of human with other forms is a heightened instance of the "perfusive" relationship between people and land, we may suggest. If ancestral beings could "sit down" and "become" places, in a lesser way humans can do the same by continuous residence, especially since individuals over time may become like spirit-beings (Williams 1986:31).

Williams also gives a good account of how meaning is condensed in certain phrases. For example, "Mosquito thrust his proboscis into the ground where a mound now is" carries eight implications, linking Mosquito's actions to the future ownership of land around the places where he thrust in his proboscis, to the creation of the mound, and to the fact that humans identified with Mosquito would show courage in ways by meditating on his proboscis/spear (Williams 1986:23–24). The power of Mosquito enters the places and the people with whom he is linked in a continuous transformation and replication.

"Turnings" also feature in Hagen myth and folktale. In the narratives of the founding of groups, eagles or dogs may be the aspects taken on by the powers of the sky, or an ancestor may appear as a snake. But the notion of originary beings who become places is more strongly marked among the Yolngu, supporting the idea of their stress on "origins."

Perfusion

Williams (1986:31), Keen (1994:45), and Morphy (1995:197) all give indications of the very close feelings of identification with land or country that characterize Yolngu thinking. Morphy refers to this as charting "their own unique course through the ancestral grid" (1995:197). He adds further on: "It is through individual lives that the ancestral past is both renewed and transformed. The ancestral past is continuously recreated by the sedimenting of past and present experiences" (204), and he points out that new identifications are constantly being made. The ancestral past is thus fixed, but the present has a fluidity in it, leading to the resedimentation of relationships into place. It is this that we call "perfusion." Since it continues, and replicates ancestral actions, it simultaneously represents both continuity and change. We see here an approximation to the openness of the Hagen idea of "creative events," held within the framework of an "origin-dominated" cosmos. In both instances, therefore, there is room for contestation and conflict, especially in circumstances of contemporary change and development. In such cases rival "perfusions" and rival narrative "creations" may spring into being.

In summary, Yolngu ideas about ancestrality and land do correspond strongly to the "origins" model, but through the concept of perfusion they are also open to degrees of "creation." When Yolngu/Hagen mythology is examined further, it is striking that the scope of Yolngu ideas on "creation" is wider, laying down accounts of the development of languages through naming practices, establishing multiple totemic sites, and themselves shaping or becoming environmental features. Such a scope seems appropriate to the facts of interdependence for trading and ritual purposes of interspersed language groups occupying large stretches of land. The regional focus, however, is shared with the Huli-Duna complex of peoples in the "Papuan borderlands" (Biersack 1995), as we have seen, for whom Ballard also points out the connections with trade (Ballard 1994). In the Yolngu narratives the *wangarr* spirits lay down the regional preconditions for groups and languages to emerge in particular areas, establishing also wider interconnections between peoples. In Hagen such a regional focus is absent. Trade routes and the passages of circulating cults tend not to be worked into group creation stories. Instead of the agency of the collective Dreaming figures, we find the agency of an individual human ancestor sharply delineated. The ancestor is traveling and *finds* a place, *recognizes* it as a significant point of access to power, *holds* on to it, and *names* it for his group (the Melpa terms are *kandepa ti, tepa mindi, ömbögli,* and *mbi tei*). The ancestor is, of course, privileged to come into contact with an underlying power that has prepared the situation to be discovered, but it is still human creativity that is stressed, in conjunction with ancestral power, and this creativity relates only to local, not regional, claims. In the Hagen narratives, the nearest character to a Dreaming *wangarr* is Mul Temb, of whom Thomas Nakinch writes that he is immortal and still guides the Ulga, having also a more shadowy tie with other groups in the Nebilyer region (and here it is possible that the portrait of Mul Temb has been colored a little with ideas about God conveyed by the Catholic mission among the Ulga). Mul Temb seems to be a figure cognate with the Sky Beings *(Tei Wamb),* who are thought of as the ultimate sources of power, fertility, and knowledge and who, as we have seen, feature in Hagen "origin stories" generally, so we could argue that the Hagen/Yolngu local/regional contrast is modified if we think of the Sky Beings as backgrounded Hagen counterparts of the foregrounded *wangarr* among the Yolngu.

Conclusion

Our Yolngu/Hagen comparison has not been intended as a typifying exercise. We do not claim that Hagen "stands for" a whole region or that Yolngu "stands for" all of Australia. We do think, however, that the two cases exemplify well instances of an interplay between a stress on "origins" as against a stress on "creations," which is likely to be found widely in both Melanesia and Australia. Somewhat paradoxically, perhaps, hunter-gatherer societies like the Yolngu seem to have placed a more intrinsic and enduring relationship of ancestrality on land than did the horticultural, relatively high-density population found in Hagen. But this paradox makes sense. The Yolngu need to be able to claim access to areas along their own seasonal trackways, as well as in defined localities. Hageners, as horticulturists, were more likely to abandon claims on areas they had left and could no longer defend or use. Their notion of the *kona wingndi* appears to encapsulate an ideology of fixity. But when we realize that the myth can replicate itself and that a new *kona wingndi* can be found, we have to conclude that this means "creation," not "origin" at that point.

The relevance of this argument to contemporary life in Hagen has already been pointed out. The Kuk stone site is becoming the equivalent of a new *kona wingndi* under the pressure of competing land claims, land shortage, and possible disputes over former government station land. An open-ended "creation" ideology makes this a very easy shift to make. In such circumstances, the stone becomes a resource for "evidence" in a new, legal sense, or as one man put it, it becomes a "witness" for the Kawelka. And just as it "shows" their authentic claim to the land they use for subsistence and cash-cropping, so also it might be held to show their "claim" to the prehistoric archaeological findings that have been made in the Kuk swamp, where Kawelka men died in precolonial warfare, since a valid claim has a form of "predestination" built into it. A claim through a "creative event" need not depend on a notion of ancestral connection by "origins." Origin narratives, on the other hand, such as the Yolngu have, can also be used as evidence in legal claims once they are accepted as historical stories about events represented in polysemic terms. That this is so can be illustrated by an example from another region of the world, Canada, and the issue of Native American rights there. Recently the Gitxsan tribe of British Columbia, Canada, have cited an origin story that can be used to support Gitxsan land claims, and the narrative has been deemed to be legally binding evidence by the Supreme Court of Canada. Opposition to this decision states that indigenous claims to the land were extinguished when British Columbia became a province in 1871. One of the main worries is how the uncertainty over who legally controls the land will undermine land-use decisions and potentially threaten British Columbia's timber and mining industries. The Gitsxan argue that they want not only rights to hunt and fish in "traditional" ways but also to be able to participate in decisions on granting timber licenses and mining concessions.

The court's decision stated: "The law of evidence must be adapted in order that this type of evidence [oral histories] can be accommodated and placed on an equal footing with the types of historical evidence the courts are familiar with" (*New York Times,* February 9, 1998). When asked what evidence the group could put forward to support land claims, one of its leaders said, "There are the names of the territory, the names of the streams, the names of the mountain pools. This took thousands and thousands of years. These are our boundaries. You could not fake them."

In this example we see not only the declarative force of naming but also a willingness to adopt new forms of evidence, since the tribe employed geologists to bore holes and discover mudslides at a certain prehistoric depth within the range of their own mythology, which represents such slides as the result of a huge grizzly bear churning up river waters. The Yolngu would appreciate this mode of argumentation. As for the Kawelka, their stories do not make them autochthonous to Kuk, so they cannot claim to be the direct descendants of the prehistoric swamp dwellers, but their "creative event" ideology could, as we have noted, allow them to claim that they were destined to be the custodians of the residues that were left by those forerunners and that Koi's stone marks this destiny as well as their contemporary land rights vis-à-vis the government and others. Both "origins"-oriented and "creations"-oriented forms of ideology then lend themselves well enough to being transformed into arguments about "evidence" in contemporary conflicts. Finally, in terms of the theme of movement and fixity, we can summarize by saying that "movement fixes" in the Yolngu case, while in Hagen it is "fixity" that "moves." Yolngu originary beings fixed elements in a landscape across which they moved, giving identity to their descendants. In Hagen the power of the Sky Beings is fixed, or perpetual, but their power is capable of moving and re-creating its presence over time and space. At the highest level of generality, the notions of creative power in the two cases are the same.

Note

We thank the government of Papua New Guinea for permission to carry out research in the country. We also wish to thank an anonymous reviewer of our chapter for some perceptive comments and suggestions, not all of which could be pursued because of lack of space. We also want to thank James Weiner and Alan Rumsey for their support.

5
Sacred Site, Ancestral Clearing, and Environmental Ethics

Deborah Bird Rose

This chapter moves toward issues of environmental ethics through an examination of geographies of generative space. My focus is on what I call the work of the world: the work that generates and regenerates living things. I look first to an Australian case study: "sacred sites" and country in the Victoria River District of the Northern Territory (map 1). I then look at the clearing and forest among the Kaulong people of New Britain as represented by Jane Goodale (1995) in her recent ethnography *To Sing with Pigs Is Human.* In contrast to the work of scholars of religious studies, who see the sacred as the product of ritual work, my analysis is in confluence with that of scholars such as Povinelli (1993) in Australia and Goodale (1995) in Papua New Guinea in showing how relationships between enduring sources and ephemeral life are sustained through the everyday work of the world. I conclude by examining some comparative issues between hunter-gatherer and shifting horticultural modes of subsistence in the context of global development.

I am using the term "environmental ethics" in a loose sense rather than in a technical sense, taking it to refer to a system of responsibilities that humans hold in relation to nonhumans. In the past few decades discussions of the environmental ethics of non-Western people have increased exponentially. As in so many other discussions that contrast the West and its chosen others, while any given author usually refers to specific peoples, there is a generalized lumping together of indigenous peoples in contrast to people of the West (see Fajans 1998 and Jorgensen 1998 for deconstructions of homogenizing views of "others"). And yet, the ways in which people conceptualize the generative structure of their world and their own place in that structure are fundamental to any analysis of how they construe human responsibility and accountability. Different understandings implicate humans in different relationships of responsibility toward their world, and the quality of difference has a great bearing on how they define and target human responsibilities toward nonhumans.

Peter Dwyer's (1996) brilliant essay "The Invention of Nature" is a recent link in the distinguished lineage of anthropological studies in Papua New Guinea that engage with and destabilize Western concepts of "nature" and "culture" (for example, Strathern 1980 and Wagner 1981). Dwyer examines the relationships between people and landscapes in three Papua New Guinea societies: Kubo, Etolo, and Siane. He finds degrees of separation such that at one end of his transect Kubo people engage in small amounts of gardening and large amounts of hunting/gathering. Human activity permeates the whole landscape, and the whole landscape is humanized (168). At the other end of the transect, Siane people expend most of their energy and time in gardening. Their actions generate a distinction between a humanized area and its periphery. Dwyer contends that this "created periphery of the visible world, increasingly divorced from human contact and understanding, emerges as 'nature' " (178). In contrast, among the Kubo the world is all "cultural"; there is "no 'nature' " (178). Dwyer suggests that hunter-gatherer peoples (and in an evolutionary sense, primal peoples whoever they may have been) like the Kubo inhabit a world that is all culture rather than all nature.

My work with Aboriginal Australians indicates this to be the case (see Rose 1996). Like Dwyer, I am concerned with "the ways people live within" their landscape, and "with the impress of them upon it and of it upon them" (162). An impress is a set of traces of productive activity. How, then, is production understood? What are the sources of life, and how are human actions toward those sources evaluated and enjoined? These questions take us to environmental ethics via a path through generative sources and the responsible actions of living things.

Hunter-Gatherer Land Management

The analysis I pursue here depends on a body of very recent knowledge that is in the process of reconfiguring most of what once stood as conventional wisdom concerning Aboriginal hunter-gatherers. I can present my case study most coherently if I first summarize this new knowledge.

Western thought pervasively and profoundly has contrasted those who cultivate the soil with those who do not. Many of the differences between cultivation and hunter-gatherer modes of subsistence have been conceptualized in Western thought by reference to human intentional action in the world. According to Ingold (1996:148), "the producer is seen to intervene in natural processes, from a position at least partially outside them; the forager is supposed never to have extricated him or herself from nature in the first place." The nature-culture dichotomy, although now destabilized in many contexts, continues to situate hunter-gatherer people ambiguously. Ingold (1996:147), for example, notes that contemporary usage that replaces the term "hunter-gatherer" with the term "forager" perpetuates both the dichotomy and the slippage: like animals, foragers graze across a landscape.

Contemporaneously, a revolution in anthropological thought is quietly taking place in Australia concerning the relationships between Indigenous people and their country. In recent years, issues of indigenous land management have come to be understood as questions for research. In Australia the long-term lack of research, like the lack of general public awareness of these issues, is connected with the settler view that Aboriginal people were parasites on nature. Elkin (1954: 15) gave the mark of scientific authority to this view in a book first published in 1938: "The food-gathering life is parasitical; the Aborigines are absolutely dependent on what nature produces without any practical assistance on their part." This view of parasitism was intricately connected to the view of *terra nullius*: the idea that the land was untransformed underpinned the idea that the land was unowned. By this logic, Aboriginal "parasites" were excluded from forms of ownership by reason of their own nature (lack of culture).

An important corollary was that hunter-gatherers did not shape the landscape, or, that the landscape was shaped by them only as a by-product of their foraging actions. Williams and Hunn's (1982) publication *Resource Managers* marks a key moment in shifting the accepted conventions surrounding these issues (see also Williams and Baines 1993). The start of the demolition of the parasite view, however, dates to Rhys Jones' (1969) work on the use of fire in a system of land management. He called this system fire-stick farming, and his use of the term "farming" was deliberate (Jones 1995). Inaccurate as it is in attributing the culture of cultivation to Aboriginal people, it provocatively struck an intellectual and political nerve. Since Jones' original work, numerous studies have shown Aboriginal people's proactive care of Australian fauna, flora, and ecosystems. It is becoming increasingly evident that both the distribution and the diversity of Australian biota across the continent are artifacts of Aboriginal people's intentional actions. This is not to say that Aboriginal people have always and only managed ecosystems well; knowledge and practice are not always in synchrony for Aboriginal people any more than for others (Lewis 1993:10). This new knowledge indicates that when Europeans arrived here the continent was an artifact of Aboriginal people's active and intentional management (R. Jones 1969, 1985).

The implications of this new knowledge are enormous. Research is in a very early stage; it is interdisciplinary and has yet to be fully accepted within any mainstream discipline. It has been assimilated unevenly, and often crudely. A little more than a decade ago there was debate about whether Aboriginal people actually did engage in fire-stick farming (Horton 1982); today it is almost universally accepted that they consciously managed large portions of the continent through the use of fire, and contemporary Anglo-Australian land managers now seek to use fire to manage landscapes in North Australia. In addition, there are studies that deal with the aesthetics of burnt country (Head 1994) and the spiritual and emotional meanings of fire (Bradley 1995).

Looking at the continent as a whole, it is now evident that the actions of Indigenous people are clearly responsible for maintaining the open grasslands that covered much of the continent (R. Jones 1969), for the preservation of specific stands of fire-sensitive vegetation such as acacia (Kimber 1983), cypress (Bowman 1995, Bowman and Panton 1993), and remnant rain forests (Russell-Smith and Bowman 1992), for the protection of refugia including breeding sanctuaries (Newsome 1980), and the preservation of sources of permanent water in arid environments (Latz 1995; a brief summary of many of these issues is found in Rose 1996). In addition, their actions are directly responsible for the distribution of many plants (Hynes and Chase 1982; Kimber 1976; Kimber and Smith 1987), and probably for the distribution of some fauna, such as freshwater crayfish (Horwitz and Knott 1995). If research continues to produce new knowledge at this current rate, it is probable that I am discussing only the tip of the iceberg. As conquerors we are able to understand Aboriginal organization of country only retrospectively, and undoubtedly much of the evidence we would want to examine has been obliterated. Yet, while there are many open questions, there is no doubt that indigenous people's care of country has shaped and sustained the biota of this continent.[1]

This new knowledge has yet to make a significant impact upon anthropological thought. I believe that when it does it will require major rethinking about how we understand the history of our species, how we understand differences between modes of subsistence, how we understand philosophical issues of being and becoming in the world. I believe that there are major implications for how we Westerners understand our own dichotomized thinking and for how we impose our knowledge systems on others (see Dwyer 1996).

Sacred Sites: Law and Responsibility

My analysis is alert to both the poetics and the politics of the sacred (Chidester and Linenthal 1995:1–42), but I emphasize the architectonics of sacred space. Nancy Munn's (1996) essay "Excluded Spaces" detours around conventions that reproduce static separations of space and time, and thus is able to provide the outline of a theory that links space and time through human action; my work here continues this project. I use the term "sacred" in this Australian Aboriginal context with the intention of encompassing both the substantival concept of world creative powers and the situational practices through which people bring that power forth into the world in the form of living things.

In Aboriginal Australia, the living world is a created world, brought into being as a world of form, difference, and connection by creative beings called Dreamings (see Morphy 1996 for a discussion of the term). The Australian continent is crisscrossed with the tracks of the

Dreamings: walking, slithering, crawling, flying, chasing, hunting, weeping, dying, birthing. They were performing rituals, distributing the plants, making the landforms and water, establishing things in their own places, making the relationships between one place and another. They left parts of themselves, looked back and looked ahead, and still traveled, changing languages, changing songs, changing skin.[2] They were changing shape from animal to human and back to animal and human again, becoming ancestral to particular animals and humans. Through their creative actions they demarcated a world of difference and of relationships that crosscut difference. Victoria River people articulate the view that in their part of the world everything came into being by Dreaming, and every ephemeral thing exists because of and through relationships established by Dreaming.

The places where Dreamings traveled, where they stopped, and where they lived the events of their lives and deaths, these tracks and sites make up the sacred geography of Australia. Sacred geography defines the structures of embeddedness that are the sources of ephemeral life, human and nonhuman. These structures are characterized by intersections, overlap, and crosscuttings; there is thus a web of relatedness in which everything is connected to something that is connected to something, and so forth. It is not the case that everything is connected to every other thing, but rather that nothing is without connection, and "there is no alien world of mere things" or of things with no meaning (Sutton 1988:13).

Sites and tracks, origins and connections—Dreaming creation is the source and template for a "dynamic jurisprudence of duty" (Jacobson 1992) that is called Law in Aboriginal English. The dynamism in this system derives from the fact that sentience and agency are located all through the system: in human and nonhuman persons, in trees, rocks, stones, and hills; wherever Dreamings are, there sentience is. Wherever the dead people are, there sentience is. Rainbows, wild women, and all manner of extra-ordinary beings along with the more "ordinary" beings pervade the world, imbuing it with sentience. Crucially, the conditions for being are exactly that—conditions. Life in all its transience is a continuous bringing forth. This process, the coming forth of it all, happens through intentional action on the part of sentient beings. Daily life is lived on the "threshold of unfolding events," to borrow Scott's (1996:73) eloquent phrase; it happens because sentient beings discharge the responsibilities that are theirs by law.

In this created world, life is embedded within sites and relationships. The bringing forth of life and law is what life is—an unfolding of relationships, a bringing forth of life in its embedded complexity. The process can be examined through several lenses: country, totems, and individuals. The life and law that are contained in sites unfold out into the world in a dynamic system of interdependent units, each of which is called "country" in Aboriginal English. Country is an organizing unit of life, sustained in mutual interdependence with other equivalent units; clusters of mutually interdependent countries constitute systems that are roughly congruent with ecological zones (Peterson 1976).

Life and law also, and equally, unfold out into the world in a dynamic system of totemic consubstantialities. Most totems are both living species and Dreaming figures. Like the structure of tracks and sites, the structure of totemic categories is built on intersections and overlaps. Totemic consubstantiality is exclusive, but it is also massively crosscut. Matrilineal totems cut across patrilineal ones, for example, and subsection totems cut across both. Different categories intersect each other, and the people who are related in one context are differentiated in another context. Every difference is crosscut by some other difference, and intersubjectivity is embedded in multicentered systems.

Dreaming action unfolds out into the world in the bodies of specific human beings through processes of conception, birth, and growth. With conception, Dreaming propels itself into a child-to-be. Characteristically, "spirit" enters a food resource that is killed by the father of the child-to-be, is eaten by the mother, and is born into the world as a new person (Povinelli 1993:137–139; Rose 1992:59). Throughout childhood, people are nourished by the food of the country. Victoria River people say that country gives them body, and having the body of the country generates responsibilities toward the nurturing country (Rose 1992:61, 107–110).

In sum, relatedness is the meat of life, situating people's bodily presence in shared projects that link human and nonhuman interests around intersecting and crosscutting contexts of tracks, countries, totems, and sites. Every discrete category is linked to other discrete categories through kinship, and is crosscut by other discrete categories; thus the concept of exclusivity is both sustained (because categories are discrete) and demolished (because they are crosscut). This system links species, places, and regions, and leaves no region, place, species, or individual standing outside creation, life processes, and responsibilities.

The action that brings life forth from its source is the work of the world. Dreamings changed over into living things that grow, mature, and die. In the monsoonal tropics of the Victoria River District, the transience of this kind of everyday life is expressed by reference to seasons and growth. The rain annually washes the marks of the actions of people, plants, and animals away from the face of the earth; human and animal tracks are washed out, plants die. The kind of life that ends in death is spoken of in these kinds of ways, and it is understood that people quite literally will be washed away, although current mortuary practices are disabling this system.

Dreaming bodies endure as sites; their life continues to happen in the world precisely through the ephemeral. Through actions of knowledgeable living things (a category that is not exclusively human) the enduring life of the source is brought into ephemeral existence. It is not just that the power of a site is located at a center "from which a space with uncertain or ambiguously defined limits stretches out" (Munn 1996:453). Rather, it is also the case that the site is unfolded out into the country in the lives of the living things who belong there, and through the actions of the living things who are responsible there. Dreaming is thus actualized transiently in the present, and the perduring life of the world is carried by ephemeral life-forms. All living things are held to have an interest in the life of the living things with whom they are connected because their own life is dependent upon them. Care requires presence, not absence, and a fundamental proposition of contemporary Victoria River people is that those who destroy their country destroy themselves.

Organizing the Country

To be connected is thus to be in a relation of mutual care. My friend and teacher Hobbles Danayarra offered a succinct explanation of his people's responsibilities toward land, stating that "before white people, Aboriginal people were just walking around organizing the country." As I have indicated, research into how Aboriginal people organize the country is still very new. My interest here is with the connections of embeddedness entailed in this created world. A major context for care is country, as I have indicated. Country is a nourishing terrain (Rose 1996); it is the place where ephemeral bodies, time, and sentience come into being and carry on the work of the world that makes further unfolding possible. We have a good literature to help us understand ritual practice (Strehlow 1970 is excellent), but bringing forth is equally a product of everyday life. As Povinelli (1993:139) states, "All hunting trips interact with the sentient landscape, and the sentient landscape most commonly encounters humans engaged in economic, not ritual, activity." It is a matter of presence: you put your body in the country to do the work of the country, and the country gives you body.

The main technology for the organization of country is and was knowledge. Knowledge is country-specific, and virtually the whole body of knowledge for any given country is related to the generation of life in and around that country. Countries are interdependent, so it is not the case that one person's knowledge is restricted only to one country, or that countries are self-sufficient in their knowledge, but it is the case that each country has its own specificities, the knowledge of which belongs to some people and not to others: where resources are located, where permanent water is to be found, which ecological events signal other ecological events, weather signs and patterns, where the sacred and dangerous places are and what restrictions apply to them, how to address the sentient land, water, trees, and stones, and what kinds of fires to light in particular land-forms at particular times of day and year. The most publicly secret knowledge is linked to sacred sites, but all knowledge—of land-forms, resource locations, water sources, seasonal markers, environmental history, medicinal plants, animal behavior, floristics, plant phenology, and much more—belongs to the people of the country and is shared among people who have a range of responsibilities there.

Human beings are not the only sentient beings who organize the country. I know less about the responsibilities of nonhuman animals, but some points are formally articulated. Flying foxes, for example, are linked to the Rainbow Snake, and in the Victoria River District they go to the riverside during the late dry season, and they tell the Rainbow Snake to bring rain. Through the system of totemic consubstantialities, some human beings are also flying foxes, and some human beings are linked to rain (light and dark rain) in various ways. The knowledge of the organization of these connections between different segments of the living world is held to be powerful, and a lifetime of learning promotes ever greater understandings of connections.

Responsibilities of care are organized along connections. They thus overlap and crosscut. Nothing is responsible for every other thing, and every thing has responsibilities of care and is the subject of care from others. For humans this means knowing where your responsibilities lie and respecting the limits of your responsibilities. Practices of care cluster around three main projects: practices of memory and education that enable the knowledge gained in one generation to be coded and transmitted to new generations; practices that ensure that resources are not overused; and care of habitats. The first goes beyond my purposes here, other than to note that stories, songs, and other forms of site-based knowledge are major vehicles for ecological memory. The second includes practices such as replanting portions of yams for next year, localized and temporary hunting prohibitions, temporary food taboos, prohibitions on hunting in breeding season, and prohibitions against waste (see, for example, Baker 1993:139). The third project includes practices such as burning firebreaks around the rain forests where the yams grow. The use of fire is well documented compared to other practices,[3] but the most important consideration, and the most urgent area for further research at this time, is the convergence of practices. Thus, to take one example, Latz, a botanist who has carried out extensive work in Central Australia, notes that the most sacred/protected places are likely to be places where a number of Dreamings meet up or cross over. He describes them this way: "There's a lot of dreaming trails which cross over, these are really important places. They are so sacred you can't kill animals or even pick plants. And of course you don't burn them. You might burn around them in order to look after them" (Latz 1995:70).

It is urgent to keep at the fore a key aspect of this paradigm: you cannot bring forth yourself. Humans are embedded in the habitats or ecosystems that nurture them. In the Victoria River District, people say that their country gives them body. The relationship is reciprocal: you take care of the country, the country takes care of you. You come into being only through relationships. Not only your origin but your ability to keep on living from day to day is embedded within the relations that nurture you. The generation of life is the process by which life is unfolded by the actions of transient living things in interaction with Dreaming presence. The process rests on subject-subject reciprocity: an intersubjectivity of bringing forth. Persons are immanent in those portions of the world that are theirs, and those portions of their world are immanent in them (see also Ingold 1986:139). Ephemeral persons are embedded in the world, and by the work of their lives as they "walk around organising the country," they bring forth the life of the world.

The conventional Western division between pragmatic action and mythico-religious action breaks down completely in practices of care, as Ingold (1996) recently argued, and as Huber (1980) demonstrated in a Melanesian case study. All practices are understood to affect the life of the country, and thus to engage in care is to engage in bringing forth the life of the country while making oneself available also to be brought forth. An "increase" ritual is just as pertinent as a well-organized fire; indeed, these dimensions are simply not separate. For example, Nanikiya Munungurritj, an Aboriginal traditional owner in eastern Arnhem Land, and a ranger with the Dhimurru Land Management organization, spoke about burning his country, saying that you sing the country before you burn it. In your mind you see the fire, you know where it is going, and you know where it will stop. Only then do you light the fire (personal communication).[4]

Is this production? Ingold argues (1996:148) that the term "production" invokes a Western view: "planned intervention in nature, launched from the separate platform of society." He endorses Bird-David's (1992:40) suggestion of the appropriateness of the term "procurement" in its connotative range of "management, contrivance, acquisition, getting, gaining." In my view, neither "production" nor "procurement" does justice to the mutuality of Aboriginal Australian ecological interactions. The practices I have discussed here involve knowledgeable care based on mutual engagement among mutually embedded living things. I use the term "generation of life" to refer to this matrix of connection and mutual care.

It is probable that the current environmental devastations that many Victoria River people see and have experienced have heightened their awareness of the fragile contingency of the living world, but the relationship of mutual unfolding that exists between the enduring and the ephemeral speaks to a world that is ever emergent and ever contingent. The concept of congealed action, it seems to me, must be balanced by an analysis that links the daily and ephemeral with current and ancestral labor. Ingold's (1996:139) examination of Myers' (1986) Pintupi ethnography, for example, follows a train of logic that holds human action within landscape rather than positioning it as external, and reaches the conclusion that "the landscape . . . is . . . life's enduring monument." The landscape of linked sites and tracks is well understood in this way. But if we regard landscape in the more proactive and living sense of country—the webs of ephemeral life—then we see a continuously becoming, or a continuously coming into being, process. It is not held fixed by cultural reproduction but is nurtured and sustained through cultural procreation. Flourishing life is evidence of current and ancestral labor, but it is not a monument in any enduring sense, for it all comes undone when the organization fails.[5]

Life is thus an ever emergent becoming, carried by the ephemeral beings whose work is to keep life happening. The sacred is actualized through the everyday work of the world, and Dreaming continues to happen for as long as ephemeral beings do the work of the world. I believe that the structure of relationships of responsible care can be glossed as a system of environmental ethics for purposes of comparison and dialogue. In brief, the system I have been describing is one of multicentered subjectivities embedded in overlapping and crosscutting relationships of care that encompass, or are believed to involve, whole ecosystems. The system of connection is sustained through actions of mutual bringing forth exercised by the living things whose ephemeral lives actualize the perduring possibilities and conditions of life.

Ancestral Clearing

In this section I draw most particularly on Jane Goodale's (1995) study of the Kaulong people of New Britain (map 1). I will suggest that for Kaulong people the work of the world consists in sustaining a managed system of continuity that is parallel to and differentiated from the self-sustaining system of the forest. In comparison with the system of embedded connections and mutual bringing forth that characterizes the Aboriginal case, the Kaulong case indicates a gradient of disembedding.

Goodale's analysis focuses on the work of differentiation:

- to differentiate the clearing from the forest, and thus to demarcate a specifically human space

- to differentiate humans from forest animals, through the production of gardens
- to differentiate one human from another through competitive knowledge and exchange.

Kaulong people are gardeners as well as hunter-gatherers. The taro they grow in their shifting agricultural plots is regarded as the foundational food for humans, but forest resources constitute 40 percent to 60 percent of the people's food consumption (69). Gardens are cut out of the forest. They last for a bit more than a year before being left to revert to forest, and they are constantly at risk from pigs (81).

Sacred space is modeled as sites of origin: the hole in the ground from which came taro (78), the site (hole or tree) from which came the ancestor of a contemporary descent group, and the clearing or hamlet *(bi)* that is the unambiguously human place (117). Human origin myths relate how the founding ancestor(s), a man or a brother and sister, emerged from their source in the forest. The brother worked to make a clearing, planted a ficus (fig) tree in the center and fruit trees around the periphery, and built a main house. Brother and sister, or father and daughter, are the generative ancestors; the woman got a husband elsewhere, and the man and woman of the clearing founded a group of cognates who are consubstantial not only with each other but also with the foundational place and its resources (113).

Within the clearing are located the ficus tree of the ancestor; the fruit trees, which are consistently cared for and replaced as they die; the main house, beneath which members of the group for the place were buried in times past; and the sites of former main houses, which were abandoned when there was no more room for burials (117). The open ground of the clearing is "*the* unambiguous human place" (117). It is where all the activities of intergroup sociality, exchange, singing, and pig killing take place. The blood of pigs is in the soil of the clearing along with the bones of ancestors (117).

Cognatic groups of people who link themselves to a foundational place are not exclusive groups but rather overlapping kindreds. A given person maintains links to three or four ancestral places. These places "are far more than mere points of reference. They symbolize the core meaning of kinship and of being. Coming from the same place is the essence of sharing an identity not only with other people, but also with all the non-human resources of the place as well" (115).

Goodale's work on concepts of replacement is well known. In her view, the generation of human lives through time is managed by the Kaulong according to a cultural model of replacement that links humanity to domesticated plants. Taro is the key model of human replacement. Like humans, taro has its origins in the ground; it is brought out of its source and into the gardens of human beings with physical labor and magical words (78–80). Taro stalks are kept and replanted from one period of growth to the next, and thus from one garden to the next. The corms are the key food for humans, and managed properly they are not destroyed in the eating. Rather, stalks are saved and replanted, so that a single taro ancestor has a continuous life of growth, replanting, growth and replanting. The plant grows and is consumed, and grows again, while the substance remains identical. This taro life cycle serves as an ideal for humans. Children are understood to be replacements for their parents, and human life is devoted to the twin projects of personal growth and replacement for the future.

Goodale proposes that forest and clearing are complementary and opposing kinds of space:

> In the Kaulong world, the forest and the garden are two contrasting spaces in which to live and work and become human. The forest is quite clearly the preferred place of the two, but it is equally clear that it is a place where humans are just another creature, occupying the same space as animals, insects, birds and spirits. But while both men and women spoke of the forest with an emotional attachment quite unlike the way they spoke of a garden, it was in the gardens that they worked to become differentiated and human (Goodale 1995:85)

Kaulong Ephemera

According to Goodale, the cycle of life begins and ends in the forest (1995:234), and the forest is self-sustaining. Differentiation is a process of disembedding; it seems to be accomplished by human intentional action on three scales. The clearing is brought out of an enduring forest, is maintained for generations as the major site for public human achievement, and subsequently returns to forest. Gardens are on another scale: they, too, are carved out of the forest, but they are worked for only a year or two before being left to recede back into the forest. Human life constitutes a third scale; it is brought out of the forest and into the garden and clearing, where it is sustained through human action, until at death it moves back into the forest (235). Personal labor in making gardens, maintaining clearings, and achieving personal renown and replacement thus establishes a human figure differentiated from the forest ground. Taro gardens are human-generated space. Past and future for garden space is the forest, while the taro itself is managed continuously from one garden to the next. The Kaulong are explicit: they walk the taro from place to place, and the histories of their travels constitute tracks through the forest. A human, like a garden, is brought out of the forest and reverts to forest at death (245). Transgenerational lines of humans are like taro: substance is carried from garden to garden, and from adult to child across generations.

Using Weiner's (1988:9) theoretical framework, we could say that the forest is the given cosmic flow that human moral action halts and channels into distinctions for socially important purposes. What is "precipitated" out of human labor as it diverts the forest flow is a kind of space and a kind of production for replacement, both of which are differentiated from the space and reproduction of the forest.

Kaulong people know themselves to be animals, and thus "of the forest," according to Goodale, yet they strive to differentiate themselves and to become humans "of the clearing." The work of differentiating humans from other animals, and of differentiating the gardens and clearings from the forest, is captured and expressed in the endings of the songs to commemorate the dead (243). Song endings speak to that margin where the forest meets the clearing, and to the cold fires of abandoned clearings. The work of the Kaulong world is to ensure the continuity of clearing, taro, and generations, so that while the ephemeral comes from and returns to the forest, human labor channels certain forms of life into a parallel and disembedded system of continuous and identical substance and discontinuous space.

Thus, Kaulong people have not separated culture from nature so much as they have generated a geographical and cultural divide that runs through the domains that Westerners generally refer to as culture and nature. The Kaulong divide turns on humanized and nonhumanized worlds. Aspects of humanity, and types of nonhuman life, are included within each "world." Thus, within the nonhuman world there is the self-sustaining forest and those aspects of human beings that are most properly thought of as "of the forest." Within the humanized world there are taro humans, pig humans, and human humans. This distinction is similar to, and finds ethnographic parallels with, that made by Biersack (1996) in relation to Paiela gardens. In her understanding of Paiela metaphysics, "animals are inherently social and political, *not* natural" (4). The fence marks a "boundary between a receding and largely irrelevant mere nature . . . and a worked-on or worked-up crafted nature" (4). Kaulong and Paiela devote cultural attention to a threshold site (edge of clearing, fence) that marks the achievement of differentiation, and labor becomes visible within the clearing.

The action of differentiation is a disembedding of the unambiguously human world from the ambiguous world of the forest. For the Kaulong, the generation of life reproduces differentiation by sustaining discontinuity. The Kaulong distinction between different kinds of processes for the generation of life is a corollary to the division between forest and garden. The forest is self-sustaining, while only humans can and do manage lines of continuity (human and taro) across discontinuous sites of differentiation. The site of a garden is cleared from the forest, but the source is not of the forest: the source of gardens is other gardens. Differentiation thus interrupts the pervasive mutuality that characterizes the Aboriginal system and introduces gradients of connection.

Site and Clearing: Environmental Ethics

The Kaulong division of ecosystems into those that are understood to be self-sustaining and those that are sustained by humans makes a separation into ground and figure and thus articulates human action as an interruption of the given ground. The organization of human responsibility toward the world is thus diminished in comparison with the Aboriginal Australian system I have described. In respect of taro, human responsibility remains essential, but the greater part of the landscape has become an environment for which humans are not responsible. Thus, responsibility for a few demarcated "human" species is accompanied by diminished responsibility for a large number of "nonhuman" species. Greater responsibility for the small-scale ecologies of the garden and the clearing are accompanied by greatly diminished responsibility for the large-scale ecology of the forest. The contrast between humans and pigs can be thought to say something about responsibility: if pigs are what humans would be if they were not human, then the implication is that if humans were to revert to the forest they would revert to a world of no responsibility. It would be a world of all ground and no figure.

The shrinking of responsibilities suggests a shift not only in focus but also in reciprocities and connectedness. Victoria River Aboriginal people assert that humans are just one of the species with law for country; others share responsibilities in ritual and in everyday practice. In asserting that other species take responsibilities, they do not seek to devalue or evade their own human obligations; rather such assertions stress co-action in a world of connection. Consubstantialities overlap and crosscut each other so that most of the living world is brought into relationships of shared substance and mutual responsibility. By contrast, it does not appear that the Kaulong expect that anyone, or any living things, have a responsibility for them. Goodale's analysis of the Kaulong people's passionate pursuit of individuation and differentiation seems to point to a worldview in which nonhuman living things neither share responsibilities nor reciprocate them. If responsibilities are taken as the figure, then the world of Victoria River people's responsibilities is all figure; there is no given ground.

This line of thought leads me back to the issue of human culture being progressively extracted from nature (Ingold 1994:3). According to the logic I have developed here, it appears that human "culture" may indeed loosen its embeddedness in the world. The Kaulong case suggests, and Biersack's and Dwyer's analyses lend credence to the idea, that a disengagement of human activity from the world happens as an outcome of conceptual divisions that separate the world into domains for which humans bear a responsibility and domains for which they do not. Kaulong people, of course, are surrounded by forest, are knowledgeable in respect to the forest, and clearly hold it to be a valuable zone not only for resource use but for restfulness. To the extent, however, that they see themselves as part of the forest, they hold that to be a condition to be overcome. The result is a diminution of human responsibility in the living world, a cline in the organization of responsibilities toward other living things across a gradient of cultural/ecological zones, and a loss of complexity. As Dwyer (1996) argues so lucidly, the practice of cultivation is not the causal factor in the "invention of nature." And yet, the intensification of labor toward processes of differentiation detaches human responsibilities from portions of the world and turns cultural attention toward sites of differentiation and processes of disembedding. There is thus a major contrast with the Aboriginal case, where cultural attention is turned toward sustaining relationships of mutual embeddedness.

Environmental Politics

When Aldo Leopold (1976) kicked off the current round of interest in environmental ethics in his 1949 book *A Sand County Almanac,* he contended that a new domain of ethics must evolve. His argument was that human ethics have evolved in a sequence, and that the direction of change is toward ever widening circles of responsibility: "The land ethic simply enlarges the boundaries of the community to include soils, waters, plants and animals" (1949:202–203). While I agree completely with the view that our current global culture of exploitation is in urgent need of an expanded ethic of responsibility, it is clear that Aboriginal "caring for country" embodies both an ethic and a structure of responsibility that answers Leopold's call in many important respects.[6]

From an evolutionary perspective it would seem that intensification of labor and production entails a diminution of connection and responsibility, and it follows from that proposition that the diminution works both ways. That is, as humans define themselves as ever less responsible to and for the world, they find themselves ever less cared for by other living things. My ethnographic endeavor does not lie in the field of evolution, however, and for me the most interesting possibilities in this analysis center on the inescapably brutal facts of our contemporaneous lives.

Wagner has written that "the dangers of working out our own problems on the soils and in the hearts and minds of other peoples should not be overlooked" (quoted in Dwyer 1996:182). It is not possible to talk about "sacred sites" in Australia today without acknowledging the concerted effort on the part of many politicians and developers to contest concepts of the sacred, and especially to marginalize or eliminate Aboriginal people's participation in the ongoing management and development of the continent. The shadow of these issues has hovered around my analysis. When Hobbles spoke of organizing the country, his further implication, of course, was that colonization was disorganizing the country in the most destructive fashion.

I address these issues directly, albeit briefly, in order to link the ephemeral and the sacred to current politics. Near the Aboriginal community of Pigeon Hole on Victoria River Downs station there is a Dreaming site for lilies. There is a stone at the site, which is the source for water lilies (Nymphae spp). The lilies at this billabong are believed to have been placed here by the Nanganarri Dreaming Women, and the stone contains the life and law of lilies. When I accompanied Anzac Munnganyi there in 1989 he struck the stone with green leaves; this is his country, and it is his work to perform this ritual. In this case, however, his action was simply a demonstration with the purpose of proofing of evidence for a claim to land under the *Aboriginal Land Rights (NT) Act* of 1976. At the site there was by then only a murky billabong surrounded by trampled mud, with not a single lily to be seen. This is country that has been grazed by cattle for more than one hundred years. The lilies disappeared in the 1930s, as near as I can determine. There are two closely related billabongs, and Hobbles Danayarra explained that the traditional owners had been able to bring the lilies back to the other billabong, but not to this one. Rituals for lilies for this billabong are no longer performed, as it is believed to be a hopeless case under current land use patterns.

Europeans label this type of land use "developing the North." It was the driving ideology even before Anglo-Australians got here. Responsibilities toward living things are organized so differently in systems driven by conquest and its development counterpart, and the destruction of species and systems is so massive, that Indigenous people like Hobbles end up saying that white people must be mad.

In 1986 I pulled up at the side of the road to film some of the most spectacular erosion in the Victoria River District. I asked another teacher/friend, Daly Pulkara, what he called this country. He looked at it long and heavily before he said: "It's the wild. Just the wild." He then went on to speak of quiet country—the country in which all the care of generations of his people is evident to those who know how to see it. Quiet country stands in contrast to the wild: we were looking at a wilderness, man-made and cattle-made. This wild was a place where the life of the country was falling down into the gullies and washing away with the rains (see also Rose 1988).

Life was washing away, and so was the possibility of life. I have suggested that in this indigenous system labor is made visible in the ephemeral. In quiet country Daly could see the action of his forebears as they had worked to bring forth life; he could see this because he knew the difference between organized country and entropic country. His history, and the ancestral labor, accrued not only in the enduring geomorphology but in ephemeral living systems. And, as he said, the damage was killing both life and time: "We'll run out of history," he said, "because *kartiya* [Europeans] fuck the Law up and [they're] knocking all the power out of this country" (Rose 1992:234).

In sum, the politics of sacred sites is not separable from the politics of environmental ethics, and both are undergoing a tortured refinement in the globalizing activities known as development. The deep issue is not about protecting sites, species, or geographical/ecological zones in isolation but about enabling ephemeral life (including our own) to flourish. Political, social, and spiritual life thus converges on contested lands, and on questions of which soils will sustain life, which rivers will flow, which species will live or die, which forests will grow, and which peoples will exercise responsibility.

Notes

The "Myths to Minerals" conference was a stimulating event; I am grateful to Alan Rumsey and Jimmy Weiner for organizing it, and for their subsequent comments on my presentation, as well as for the discussion that took place throughout the conference. Peter Dwyer read a draft of this chapter and offered detailed and constructive comments. It will be clear that my thinking has been strongly influenced by my friend and professor Jane Goodale. It was a privilege to work comparatively with her Melanesian ethnography. Errors and oddities are all mine.

1. At its most basic, this fact has been known for a long time. The Australian explorer Major Mitchell described the interrelationship between Aboriginal people, their fires, kangaroos, and grass: "Fire, grass, kangaroos, and human inhabitants, seem all dependent on each other for existence in Australia, for any one of these being wanting, the others could no longer continue. . . . But for this simple process, the Australian woods had probably contained as thick a jungle as those of New Zealand or America, instead of the open forests in which the white men now find grass for their cattle. . . ." (quoted in Rolls 1981:249).

2. Minimally this term "skin" refers to social categories the English technical terms for which are "section," "subsection," "semimoiety," and the like (depending on the precise organization of the skins).

3. The logic of care is based in long-term interests that include humans and nonhumans, regions as well as countries. The actual enforcement of practices of care is social and is based on immediate interest. To harm the country, or to harm a particular species, is to harm the people of that country or that species (see Rose 1992 for an example of the social consequences of harm) and is treated as an act of aggression. For example, starting a fire that burns out of control and goes into someone else's country is an act of aggression for which the punishment, in the Victoria River district, is asserted to have been death. Law surrounding the use and misuse of fire is in decline all over Australia, as the contexts of practice decline. Bradley (1995) discusses this issue; see also Bright (1995) for a brief discussion of misuse of fire.

4. Talk presented to the Bushfire '97 conference, Darwin, July 8–10, 1997.

5. I will have to leave for another publication the important question of how Aboriginal people conceptualize and evaluate loss, especially extinctions.

6. "Caring for country" also answers many of the criticisms that are directed toward an ethic of care in relation to environmental ethics, and in other contexts. In several recent papers I discuss this and the ethics of dialogue around environmental issues (for example, Rose 1999).

6
Places That Move

Anthony Redmond

A full mobilization of human imaginative resources is required to grapple with the world, regardless of the "prepackaged" cultural forms that are available to the human subject. Neither the physical landscape nor the constellations of affect that are offered with it in the form of stories are a fait accompli. Here I take issue with a theoretical paradigm that has construed Aborigines' experience of the landscape as set in stone by ancestral action.[1] This paradigm denies the extent of bodily imagery in expressions about country and has the effect of obscuring the sense of agency that the human subject brings to the interpretation of the lifeworld. I propose that mythopoeic feelings of "everlastingness" exist not in opposition to bodily experience but as enteroceptions of a core continuity of being enveloped within a mobile sense of self. This position necessitates the dissolution of received notions of what is "inside" and "outside" the body and landscape in which it moves.

When an older Ngarinyin person asserts that "we humans didn't make the world with our own hands," this simultaneously asserts an awareness of ever-present primary processes that shape the sense of self in the world, and indeed shape the world itself, and a recognition that these processes are not reducible to either the practical consciousness or the physical capabilities of individual human beings. These primary processes are, however, believed to be active and accessible in each living subject, and this becomes clear in the explicit identifications that a person makes with his or her Wanjina, totemic species, conception spirits, places, and specific deceased relations.

John Morton in his critical analysis of Nancy Munn's now classic (1970) paper, argued that while there are strong tendencies to conservatism in Aboriginal religions, he was not convinced that such "characterisations . . . tell the whole story" (1987:111). He argued—correctly, I think—that creative interaction with the world is no less intense because the process involves reproducing exactly a design, song, or track that is preestablished. Furthermore, a human subject "will create songs . . . and designs in response to his own visions and dreams" (111). This is quite clearly the case in the material that I am about to discuss from my recent fieldwork in the north Kimberley, where new songs are seen to be given to the composer in a complete form from a deceased person. A composer has to be particularly gifted to withstand the psychical fragmentation necessary to the song-dreaming process. I will discuss how older versions of a particular story intersect with a version composed in the 1960s. I also hope to be in a position in the near future to situate these versions amid a new *balga* (a north Kimberley song genre) about the same country, which is still in the process of being dreamed at the community in which I have been living.

My current work centers around a cluster of phenomena associated by the common thread of places that move, features in the landscape that travel, shake, tremble, and split. These places range from cave sites that were said to be transported on the shoulders of Wanjina during the *lalan* (Dreaming), to giant stones with soft centers that were carried from one mountain range to another by personages assimilating historically known persons with originary beings, to stone formations that are said to teeter, sway, move, and sing in a permanent state of unstable equilibrium. Many land formations in the eroded, glaciated, and crumbling stone-scape of the north Kimberley readily lend themselves to imagery of a precarious and momentary balance, far removed from the static, timeless images of land that non-Aboriginal Australians are inclined to imagine.

The principal site that I will discuss is a hill on the central Kimberley plateau known as Winjagin and is in the patrilineal estate *(dambun)* of the Garnjingarri clan. My own visits there with the traditional owners and the stories I was told about the place are supplemented by two published versions of the stories, one by the late David Mowaljarlai and one transcribed by Capell in the 1940s (1972:49).

For the older Ngarinyin people with whom I have worked, images of land and body are interpenetrating, polymorphic, shifting and metamorphosing sediments of experience that establish a foundational identity *(boror)*. Stories of moving places explore the tensions and overlaps between the living, active, moving, changing body and the resting, sleeping, dreaming, dying, and dead body. This creative tension also exists between the bodies of ancestral beings and the human bodies that fill the contemporary social universe. It is apparent in the Ngarinyin world that the ability and desire for mobility or fluidity forms the foundational common ground between animal, plant, human, mineral, and heavenly bodies. This is the primary quality that all bodies share. It is also primary to the mythopoeia and everyday practices of Ngarinyin people who matter-of-factly point out nonhuman species and even what non-Aborigines would classify as "non-sentient" entities as "my granny that one," "my uncle that one," or "that me that one."

Before I launch into the Winjagin story itself, it would probably be useful to provide a very brief introduction to a few of those elements of Ngarinyin cosmology that are most relevant to this theme of movement.

First, the actions of moving and lying down are best understood as processual moments in the continual reanimation of Dreaming forces, which works toward everything in the country becoming Yorro Yorro, "everything standing up alive" (Mowaljarlai and Malnic 1993).

Ngarinyin use the image *we awani* for the "lying down" of the Wanjina, the ancestral creators whose lower bodies are composed of falling rain, whose wanderings shaped the country before they lay down and pressed themselves into the soft jellylike surface of the earth in the primordial period known as Lalan. Living people are those who have emerged, "been pulled" from the Wanjina body (in the father's conception dream), and thus brought forth into the world through the reflective surface of the water hole through which the Wanjina originally gave birth to itself as a reflected image. It was explained to me that the Ngarinyin verb *bun* means "pushing up like a sprout. We *bun* the country, *dambun,* live in it, sexy place . . . like baby opening up vagina . . . where we come out." Rumsey (1994:128) has followed the trajectory of the word *ngarr-arin,* which overlays concepts of "clan country" with "body/being/person/presence/self" (also Coate and Elkin 1974:45).

The recurrent imagery of ancestral beings lying themselves down in the caves draws power from the lying-down position of the painter who retouched these paintings at the beginning of each wet season. Ngarinyin people see these rock caves as actually being cloud formations, stating unequivocally "that rock there—it's a cloud" (see also Mowaljarlai and Malnic 1993 and Mowaljarlai and Vinnicombe 1995). Indeed, the convoluted shapes of the white and gray sandstone and quartzite rocks standing out from the flat surface of the land readily yield up such an interpretation with their whorled and hollowed morphology. In some of them, there are curving struts, spars, wind tunnels, and long, narrow light shafts that are also plainly visible in the biomorphic cloud structures above. Ngarinyin country is said to be made of "greasy *(mil)* rocks not dry one." The quartzite fragments scattered around the cave living sites are said to be hailstones, petrified water, transfixed between watery and stony states and capable of becoming soft again in the hands of healers. Large white "bailer shells," paper thin, almost transparent, and shaped like an elongated skull, are left filled with water among the bones of deceased relatives in these same caves.

A common expression that Ngarinyin people use for the time before they were born is "me still longa water yet." The spirit children, *anguma,* which are said to be about the size of a finger, are attached to the long green weed, *jala,* which grows in the water holes. They will leap out onto men who look into the water and lodge themselves initially in the hollow between the collarbone *anganda* (see also Lommel 1969:33). In running water this green weed fans out and moves like hair. After the father has dreamed of the child and been told its name by the *anguma,* he will often carry the spirit-child wrapped up in his own hair for up to a couple of years before the child actually gets conceived. People have pointed out to me the tiny pulsing veins in the translucent bodies of a small gecko associated with rainclouds. This pulse is also pointed out in the fontanel of newborn babies (membranous space between the parietal bones before they weld together). This gecko, *delwa,* with its throbbing pulse, and newborn babies are both regarded as forms of the Wanjina. Newborn babies with their almost visible internal structures and only semi-shaped external shell are the closest human form to the Wanjina, an identity that is underscored by their inability to talk, their reclining, pliable, soft, and watery bodies, and the oscillating continuity between their dreaming and waking states. Baby-talk or *jebelerr* is regarded as being particularly good for attracting fish, since a baby's connections with the creatures of the water are still only partially severed. Strong associations are made between the inarticulate sounds of babies and the thunder sounds that are produced by the mouthless Wanjina through its nose. These sounds are onomatopoetically reproduced as either a low, long *mmmmmmmmmm* or a percussive gurgling noise like *gugugugugugugow.* These notions of embodiment proved to be important to the Winjagin story.

The principal figure associated with the mountain Winjagin is Damalarrngarri, the black-headed python. Native Cat, Wijingarri, the first of the composers or *barnman,* was the husband of this black-headed python. He traveled down from the country called Wudmenggu, where he had conducted the first circumcisions on the flying foxes, which, as people point out, show the marks of the operation on their penes. Wijingarri then traveled on to Burranjini, where he circumcised all the other people/animals. After this he became sick (the spots on Native Cat's body are the sores from his illness, *wijin* = sore) and died in that place. Wijingarri's widow came down to Winjagin after the funeral ceremony for her husband at Burranjini. The clan country around Winjagin belongs to people of the Jun.gun moiety and thus forms part of the grouped clan countries collectively known as *mamaladba.* The *gi* (totem) for the neighboring country to the southeast around Mejurrin is Wargali (wattle), another Jun.gun moiety estate.

After moving down to Winjagin, the widow was surprised some time later to find that Wijingarri had got out from his grave and followed her down there. She was extremely annoyed and turned around to him and told him that it was too late to return to her now since she had already gone through all the mourning ceremonies. She was already wearing the charcoal that is smeared over the head after the hair is burned off. This is the origin of the characteristic black head of this particular python. She told him to go back to his grave and lie down there forever, calling out "*buuuuuu, buuuuu!*" Thus death of the body came into existence for the first time, though a child will often bear the marks of a returning ancestral body on its own skin.

Nowadays people continue to assert that the mountain itself gets up and walks in the night and that dreams of its doing so are a portent of an approaching death. The strong association with night is underscored by the activities of the two beings, Wijingarri and Damalarrngarri, both of whom belong to the group of creatures that move about in the night and are strongly identified as "law people."

At Winjagin the black-headed python raises her head from her position entwined around the rock toward the rising sun, looking for daybreak to dispel her sorrow, but another aspect of her faces west "looking for *wurnan*" (objects in the exchange system), for the pearl shell *(jaguli),* which passes along the *wurnan* line. The bright, scintillating qualities of pearl shell were lighting up the world from this direction, leading the widow to believe that the sun was actually rising from the west, the direction of the island of the dead. Her mourning had predisposed her to expect the sparks of life to come from that direction.

Just a little to the east of Winjagin is another hill containing the cave of the Wanjina named Branggun, "calling out for daylight," or Brad Wodenngarri, "daylight lay down and painted himself." Here Damalarrngarri is also represented, with her forked tongue flicking out like a projectile. *Damala* is a Ngarinyin word that can be used in swearing and means "to throw out the tongue, lick the lips." In this image there is a suggestion of inappropriate carnal appetite in a recent widow, which compounds the already ambivalent nature of this figure. She reaches with her tongue beyond her now taboo and internalized body, seeking solace and company. She reaches as far as she can, with all its implicit senses of limits and constraint. She has abandoned her dead husband's camp and returned to her father's country, to the confinement that accompanies this return to a celibate state. The widow longs for both a reentry into the flux and carnal joys of everyday life, and she tries to internalize the lost object, the bones of her husband, the eternal part of him that will survive in her feelings for him.

Having mourned her late husband, the widow-python becomes open again to the vital potentialities that find their incarnation in the transactional social exchange, *wurnan,* which animates the fabric of Kimberley societies. Powerful objects come from the east (Kununurra and Daly River) and the widow-python casts her regard in this direction. The raised head of the python coiled around Winjagin (which itself juts with startling suddenness out of the plateau), embodies the strong consciousness of the Ngarinyin of themselves as "hill people," and the joy in this is succinctly expressed in the phrase *liny ngiyadi wal ngawan-ngarri,* "your spirit flows out as far as the eye can see." By looking out from the high points in the landscape a person "expands" *(wal)* into the country before them, one becomes "satisfied or pleased" with oneself.

During the 1960s, a highly regarded Worrorra composer "dreamt" a new song based upon the story about Damalarrngarri. In this song the python travels from Winjagin, which already had the powerful Ngarinyin story about her, to a pair of twin peaks some distance to the south called Mejurrin (which can be translated as "two-ness"). The widows become split into a pair of sisters, with one wrapped around each peak. An ambiguous quality of dual-unity had characterized the Ngarinyin image. This quality is embodied in the two contemporary owner-sisters, who share responsibility for the smoking of the country and dialogically narrate the story in situ.

According to the Ngarinyin stories, in the creation time, the local clan, Garnjingarri, had devised a plan to move their mountain Winjagin down to Mejurrin, where the two peaks are, in order to "box up the gap" between them. As in some of the other examples of this genre, there is a strong sense that people wanted to share out geomythic resources, giving presents of land features that others were seen to lack, sometimes in response to strong appeals from those relations who were pitied for not having "high places" or other such desirable features. The transmission of songs into the exclusive possession of a group related in the exchange network seems to be working with a similar dynamic, given that most songs are evocations of places. The Mejurrin songs themselves were passed or "sold on," to exchange partners on a remote cattle station after the death of the composer in the 1970s.

Under the pressure of the Garnjingarri people pulling on the hair ropes, the mountain became unstable and started to shake and wobble, pieces flying off in all directions. This unstable, floating quality is known as *ngaraj,* a word that can be used to describe the quality of "being desirable or fascinating (if dangerous)" when referring to a person walking with a sensuous style. This attempt to move the mountain was made at night, the paradigmatic time for the activities of Law people, closely associated as they are with nocturnal animals. But daybreak came before the move could be effected, the hair belts snapped, and the attempt had to be abandoned. The widow-python wrapped herself forever around the mountain in order to hold it together. The hair belts, which are woven by widows, were also wrapped around the mountain in order to stabilize it, much in the manner that the *wulun* or paperbark "skin" (again strongly identified with feminine forces: *wulun nyindi* = woman) is wrapped around the anointed bones of the dead in order to hold them all together.

The scene from the song about Mejurrin is one of the three places depicted in a spectacular mural in the hall of the settlement of Mowanjum, to which many Worrorra, Ngarinyin, and Wunambal people were relocated, first in 1956 and then to the present site in 1976. It was painted by some young men of mixed Ngarinyin-Worrorra affiliation who are locally revered contemporary composers in a country/blues genre and the nephews of the original composer. The other scenes are of Mount Trafalgar, a Worrorra place that was also split and moved in the Lalan, and Gandiwal, a Wunambal country to the north from where Mount Trafalgar was shifted. Gandiwal is also the place where Native Cat, Wijingarri, originated. Obviously the theme of moving places exerts a strong hold on the people who dwell in this displaced community, itself subject to innumerable moves in recent decades at the demand of government and missionary agencies. Traditional stories of moving places may well have come into a sharper focus as the displaced attempted to make sense of their dislocation.

Whether this was empirically true or not in the two decades from 1956 to 1976, the new song cycle seems to have been regarded locally as being unprecedented in its wide-ranging scope, linking places and songs across a vast breadth of country. This was regarded as an ambitious project with an uneasy potential for overlaying different stories upon each other. Some of the senior Ngarinyin people I have spoken with say "they are both right, those different stories but we don't know." The new song constellates places and person with new emphases that may sit a little uneasily with some of the older people's versions. One old man who belongs to Winjagin through his mother believes that the composer could have "got it wrong . . . might be."

This is a case of the creativity of mythic thought in process. The poetics of Ngarinyin/Worrorra song are employed to overlay the imagery of the mountain being unsuccessfully moved, imagery of the continually restless nature of the mountain and the version in which Winjagin, as widow-python, moves on to Mejurrin, as though flung there by the fragmenting force of python/widow/hair belts as they snapped. It seems to me a good example of the process in which relationships to land and the interpretation of those relationships are articulated and extrapolated. In this instance the song-transformative process carries strong resonances with Ngarinyin land-tenure law, which requires the same moiety adjacent clan to assume responsibility for deceased clan estates. The Mejurrin song seems to be following a cultural shape or trajectory that also appears in other contexts involving the interdependency of person and country.

The mythic treatment of a theme of entropy, dissolution, and death and the narcissistic resistance to, and social patterning of, these forces in the exchange network lies at the heart of the powerful images animating the widow-python stories. It is hardly surprising that L———, someone who calls Winjagin "mother," should be one to most definitively resist the idea that the embracing python moved on to Mejurrin. This man has no problem with the idea that Damalarrngarri traveled across the length and breadth of the continent, and he proudly announces that they have stories about the same python right across into the "Northern Territory, Alice Springs and South Australia." When it comes to the more localized sphere though, he is extremely attached to the image of the sustaining presence of Damalarrngarri wrapped around the crumbling edifice of his maternal place at Winjagin. This particular man has narrated to me a recurring dream he has had of climbing this mountain as he used to do in the years after World War II. "It's easy to get up but when I look back behind it all worn away, fallen away. I can't get down, can't get back, one-way trip." The mountain shakes and trembles, shedding stones and becoming hollowed out from within and then he wakes up.

L——— identifies himself in a fundamental way with Winjagin. He says, "When people dream of that stone moving then they get signal that I coming up [approaching]." Such signals and their interpretations are well known and widely experienced among Ngarinyin people. Dreams of particular places and also a range of almost imperceptible pulses or flutterings in various muscle groups correspond to an extrasensory contact with a codified order of relatives.

L———'s dream begins with the image of "climbing up, easy to get up." Referring again to pulsations in the body corresponding to particular relations, a fluttering in the buttocks *(nyimala)* is indicative of the approach of a person's mother because "mummy carry me lift'em up me" *(ngaji marnu marnu nganmindarrn)*. The characteristic way for the mother or sister to carry the young child is on the shoulders (on the hip for very small children), and the point of contact between the two bodies is obviously buttocks to shoulders or hip. Height, elevation, safety, and the joy of effortless transport are the result for the child.[2]

L———'s sudden terror of then being stuck is extremely eloquent despite its characteristically oneiric abbreviation. On one level, an elderly man is casting a dreaming glance back over irrecoverable years, but from an island of maternal safety that is itself falling away beneath his feet and from which he will eventually be catapulted into the inside space of his maternal place. His maternal introject, his "me," is itself shedding and disheveling despite the crystalline qualities of being that he has consciously nurtured as desirable and useful human attributes. His laugh as much as his chest cicatrices mark out his status as both senior lawman and unbroken human survivor.

The fact that the mountain was to be dragged with hair ropes down to Mejurrin to "box up" the gap between the twin peaks is also a potentially *murlal* (incestuous) act inasmuch as this would have been placing the body of a relative back in same moiety country, home to "close up" classificatory fathers, brothers, and sisters. The features of the land and socialized individuals are expected to remain differentiated and distinct rather than merged into a single entity. Referring back to the locating of the life source in the soft "gaps" between the collarbone, in the unclosed frontal suture of the infant's skull, and in the hollows of the rock caves, it is clear that the closing up and opening of social-physical gaps is a theme that is multivalently reworked in the Ngarinyin imagination. The widow's demand that her husband return to his grave, "get in the same hole," is just one of these overdetermined images of closure and completeness. In the proper exchange channels, a prestation would move between clans of opposite moieties rather than ones within the same moiety, as in this case. The appearance of the daylight, causing the hair belts to break, brings a sudden end to the illicit action occurring under the cover of darkness. *Brarr* (daylight) is said to "sweep up, clean up" after the night. These hair belts or ropes—*jundul*—often appear in contexts that emphasize their symbolic value as umbilical cords—*dinjil*—and have one incarnation in the *biyu,* death cords, that have to be walked like a tightrope into the realm of the dead, a feat that can be carried out successfully only by *barnman* or doctor-men, from whom the cord emanates from either the navel or the top of the head. These ropes are now called "radar" by Ngarinyin people. Normal humans will become tangled up in the death cord and fall to the ground. Ngarinyin people say that prenatal infants stand upright inside the womb and are kept upright by the umbilical cord, which prevents the child from falling out prematurely (also see Lommel 1969:33).[3] The hair belts' breaking in the Winjagin story is congruent with imagery of the umbilicus of the newborn child breaking after it falls through the rock-chasm into a realm of light symbolized in Brarr Wodenngarri, the daylight Wanjina.

This birth imagery, congruent with the insights of Van Gennep (1960), is overdetermined by the symbolic structures of the circumcision ceremonies, Walungarri, which equate the foreskin with the umbilicus and repeat the severance from the maternal body. Damalarr, the charcoal from which the python takes her name, is also the substance that is applied to the healing penile wounds of initiates after circumcision. There is a strong sense, then, in which the widow is herself made equivalent to the transformation of the initiates' genitals, which Native Cat introduces at the same time that he precipitates his own Oedipal death. In that part of the Winjagin story where the first rays of the morning sun make the hair belts snap, there lies an analogue of the crucial "last movement" of the ceremony for "making man," which occurs at the moment of the sun breaking the horizon, after the three nights of continuous dancing, when the taut, stretched-out foreskin is cut by the "butcher" (a colloquial term for the circumciser). His maternal links eclipsed, rising from the ceremonial ashes, the "new man" is re-born from his brother-in-law's thighs, after being hidden in the "ground" of his maternal relations. Like Wijingarri, he gets up from the ceremonial "grave" after three nights. His transformed social self is marked by the new importance of his brother-in-law in his life. His actual father has nothing to say in this now that he has been re-born from the brother of a future actual or potential wife. This action has, in some important psychical respects, made his future wife into his own new mother, since the initiate is now just like his father. The brother-in-law (called in this context the "nurse") as "mother" and his sister (the future wife) form, at this juncture, a single psychical entity. The de-hooded, charcoal-daubed member is simultaneously an embodiment of the "widowed" maternal body, now an internalized object, bound to the transformed subject. The doubling of the subject is a response to the intense fear of loss, both in death and in initiation.

It is seen to be the "proper" thing that the Wanjina-child remains in a separate hill, just as the widow-python remains distinct from Mejurrin, and from the place where her husband died. The tensions inherent in the unresolved desire for closure are the creative forces themselves, socialized in the indirect exchange system, the *wurnan.* The stories become overlaid and complicated exactly because of this desire and resistance working through and against each other. In one version of the story, the widow-python creates the cave, cleans it out, and the Daylight, *brarr,* comes and lays down inside this cave made from the widow's own body.

One fragment of the mountain Winjagin is called Jag Nyoningarri (literally "he split it off her"), which is also the name of one of the sons of the male traditional owner. His daughter takes her Unggurr name from the rock itself. This splitting off of brother and sister, actualized in the name Jag, which refers to a Wanjina, Wurnbijngu, "chopping out" a spear-thrower from the body of a corkwood tree and thereby nearly severing part of the mountain, reflects the radical avoidance relationship between brother and sister, so integral to the story of Winjagin. The forked structure of the spearthrower, *yanggal,* is shaped in the image of the "forked" relationships between avoidance relations, stemming back to an original unitary block. The social structuring of this originary pool of undifferentiated libido provides the transcending thrust (of kinship system as "social technology"), which projects the human subject, as a spearthrower projects the spear, toward an acceptable object of desire and into a wider world of social and object relations.[4] Elkin (1933:455) found that the Corkwood tree from which the spear-thrower is cut in Ngarinyin country belonged to the Wayangarri (skin) clan (confirmed by contemporary Ngarinyin people), and the stories about it relate the "skin" of the corkwood tree with the skin of the kangaroo. Wayangarri people call Garnjingarri people "mother." They own adjacent estates.

In these stories "the men of the time tried to make *yarnngal* out of the *waya,* skin, that is the bark, of this tree, but finding it was not strong enough, they used the wood instead, and found it successful" (Elkin 1933:55). This little story, which seems in the "just so" vein, is also replete with body imagery, with metaphors of human skin and trunk, with the "splitting" effect of the stone axe as it is swung into the core of the wood to break suitable pieces off the main body. The skin's (bark's) "uselessness" is also how the *mamala,* or foreskin, is referred to. This is offered as a rationale for circumcision (*Walungarri,* the term for initiation ceremony, is said to derive from the verb *walag,* "to strip off, to tear, as in to strip bark from a tree").

The process of the splitting of the major protagonists in the story is a working through of desire and social differentiation, the implementation of the *wurnan* sharing system to prevent closure at the same time as fully acknowledging the power of incest passions. In the final count,

a. the native cat is married to two sister pythons who each come to Winjagin
b. both are wrapped around a single stone but looking in different directions
c. one or both of whom are then grabbed by the *umbaru* (a local avoidance word), (sacred object/son-in-law) who becomes her second or "side-ways" husband
d. one sister then disappears into a spring at the base of the mountain
e. another or the same one creates a cave out of her body, which the Daylight Wanjina/child-image lays down inside
f. she simply stays wrapped around the rock
g. the sisters are also seen wrapped around the twin peaks to the south, which were once a single block

This dizzying flux of identities exists in concert with the powerful counterpoint of an insistence that the protagonists "lie down and remain" in one place, just as the Lazarus-like Wijingarri was also told to "go back and lay in the same hole."

Within Ngarinyin communities there is constant discussion of the virtues or otherwise of "stopping in one place." While this moral injunction needs to be firmly situated in the context of pastoralism and the pastoralists' need to maintain the fixed address and availability of Aboriginal workers and consumers, this is far from being the only strand to the tethering rope of permanency. Widows in particular are expected to remain in or near their own camps and look after their own needs until the mourning period is over. Because they have to satisfy their own needs, they are known as "hunting women." Such people will usually offer up as the reason for staying home that they have to "look after dogs," and the companionship that is shared with these camp dogs patently does offset the loneliness of this period of life.

The political and moral tensions between moving and stopping, containment and action, are overdetermined in the lives of Ngarinyin people, and the stories associated with Winjagin are but one point of cohesion between mythopoeic and historical experience and interpretation (see Rumsey 1996).

The trip to Winjagin brought the poetic resonances of the stories home in a spectacular fashion. As we approached the hill across the plateau, great ribbons of smoke could be seen wrapping themselves around Winjagin, following the contours of the sandstone "terracing" that winds around the mountain. It was the end of the dry season, and the old grass was burning, much to the delight of the older people, who fear long grass for snakes. The blackened, smoldering stubble left by the fires was pointed out as the burnt hair of the widow-python.[5] Later that evening a band of cloud circling the full moon was pointed out as the python wrapped around the mountain, reflected in the sky for us as a sign of acknowledgment of our presence.

From all the signs in the country, it was clear to everybody that Winjagin was "opening her *liyan* (gut feeling) to us." After all, they pointed out, couldn't I see that as we got up closer to this long unvisited place, the mountain moved toward us, evidenced in the fact that it grew bigger as we got up close rather than "stay little" as it was when we first sighted it across the plain?

The mountain was growing and shifting in front of our eyes, revealing an inherent instability derived from its grounding in the lived body, simultaneously human and python. If there are many Ngarinyin stories that talk about the transformation of soft organic substances into crystalline states, this mineralization is never complete or static. Diamonds, for example, remain the soft kidney fat and emotional seat of ancestral and living subjects. Quartz stones can enter and exit the permeable human body, becoming soft, then hard, then soft again as they move through different media. These are the "greasy stones" that characterize Ngarinyin country.

The performance of the Mejurrin song that I witnessed in 1997 illuminated the kinetic embodiment of place in a powerful way. The song-boards depicting the python-wrapped twin peaks, having been transported from the neighboring community on the back of a Toyota, were mounted on the shoulders of the dancer in much the same manner that the Wanjina are said to carry caves on their shoulders. As the dancer stamped across the ground, the twin peaks shook and shuddered, tilting first in one direction and then another. The body of the dancer is the medium through which the image of place becomes animated and infused into the "stomping ground." The clouds of dust arising from the dancer's feet obscured the actual point of contact between the dancer's body and the ground, lending the impression that the dancer is moving through a red haze, or even walking on clouds. Clusters of green leaves at the knee and elbow joints add to the flickering, kinetic image of the body. Mejurrin became present in a dance ground several hundred kilometers away from its actual physical incarnation.

This mythic performative complex suggests to me the necessity of a theoretical approach to the interaction of person and land based on an exploration of the qualities of human and other animal bodies and the imaginary structures that arise from and make awareness of the body possible. Ehrenzweig (1967) invented the term "peomagogic process" to describe the imaginative oscillations between scattering and containment, the rise and fall of inarticulate perceptions, unconscious fantasies, and enteroceptions that create the labile sense of self at any given moment and impart definition and depth to the world. This sense of the shifting coherences that the human imagination creates out of experience can be usefully combined with psychoanalytic insights to show how objects can be internalized as more or less integrated parts of the self, as well how parts of the self may split off from the core ego to become alienated and projected into other people or other objects at the same time that they are bound to the subject (Fairbairn 1944; Mitchell 1991). To date, Morton (1987, 1989) seems to have been best able to maximize the phenomenological insights and psychological intimations of Munn's work. My only criticism is that he sometimes accepts too readily Munn's distinctions between what is experienced as being "outside" and "inside" the self. A phenomenological method informed by psychoanalysis would thoroughly problematize this distinction between the "outside world which is 'proximal' as opposed to the inside world which is 'distal'—that is beyond the subject's field of sensory presentation" (1989:289). Of course, the inside of the body, and by projection the inside of the land, *does* present itself to consciousness as enteroceptive images, fantasies, and sensations seeking articulation. The creative/destructive tension between the visible and invisible worlds may be founded upon this hierarchically organized asymmetry of bodily experience, conflating behind and in front, inside and outside the body, above and below the surface of the country. It could be further argued that these corporeal asymmetries have significantly contributed to the asymmetrical exchange systems that organize Ngarinyin sociality around the same themes of unstable equilibrium, fragmentation, transmutation, and interdependency that, enveloped within feelings of perpetuation of the self, characterize the subject's relationships to country. One such contrast that is utilized in the social system is a function of the moiety division in which Jun.gun, the Owlet Nightjar, is said to live inside tree trunks and other secretive hollow places and is heard but not seen, whereas his counterpart, Wodoy, the Spotted Nightjar, lives in the "open places," making himself visible on bright nights.

Conclusion

So "why must place move?" The question was proposed, in a rhetorical manner, by Tony Swain in *A Place for Strangers* (1993). The two components of "Aboriginal ontology" that Swain derived from Nancy Munn's work on Walpiri cosmology, the intentionality and interdependency of the places created by primordial beings, seemed to offer grounds for a fruitful inquiry. But this ground fell away as Swain argued for hard dichotomies between the "ubietous," place-oriented ontologies of social worlds surviving only in the desert and kin-based ontologies elsewhere. Keen (1993) has already taken many of Swain's assumptions to task empirically.

Swain is not the only commentator to assert the "primacy of space over time" in Aboriginal ontologies. His claim, however, that "Aborigines denied both the body and kinship in order to express the fact that all rights and obligations were derived from people's existence as extensions of places" (1993:38), takes the position to an indefensible conclusion. Lattas (1996) attacked this notion by raising the objection that it is totally off the track to set up a schema of "ontological alternatives" in which Aborigines had to choose between place or body as primary principle. Lattas replied that neither place and body nor place and time can be set up as paired "opposites" (28).

Some of Swain's problems seem to be based on his misunderstandings of Nancy Munn's classic treatment of constitutive relationships with country (1970). But the suggestion of such misunderstandings is contained in Munn's early scheme, which obscures the extent to which the embodied imagination remains an active agent in creating relationships with country. Munn's description of the "double movement" of the transformative process speaks of "on the one hand a process of separation from the originating subject; on the other a binding of the object to the self in permanent, atemporal identification." This allows the country to act as "the fundamental object-system *external to the conscious subject* within which consciousness and identity are anchored" (1970:143, my emphasis). While Munn's structural scheme certainly provided valuable insights that must be acknowledged—and its influence in shaping subsequent anthropological thought has been profound—these structures now form the ground upon which a theoretical approach to identity and transmutation of the human subject can be considered in terms that include the essential plasticity and mobility of the imagination. Such an approach will problematize Munn's notion of an "object-system external to the conscious subject," of there being any such thing as a "non-sentient environment" and the idea of "permanent, atemporal identification" (1970:143).

Morphy followed Munn in suggesting a "triadic relationship between the individual, the ancestral past, and the world in which he or she lives" (1995:187). In this scheme, the ancestral past, objectified in the landscape, becomes reproduced by lived social interaction with that landscape. Morphy attempts to avoid assigning a determining role to what he identifies as "social or cultural structures." These structures, he suggested, are "semi-autonomous" but "inter-dependent" and reproduced by human action. Yet his conclusions offer a view of human relationships with the landscape still grounded in the determining structures that Munn's early work had enunciated. That is, "the ancestral beings, fixed in the land, become a timeless reference point outside the politics of daily life," "the ancestral journeying had . . . to be frozen over for ever at a particular point in the action," leading to a "subordination of time to space" (1995:188). For Morphy and Munn, "untrammeled creativity" (1995:189) is reserved for the Ancestral beings. Living human subjects "submit" their lived experience to be structured by the visible sediments of ancestral power frozen in the landscape. These structures, argued Morphy, are "outside the human world" (1995:189), just as Munn had posited the "creative locus 'outside' the individual" (1970:160). This theoretical position potentially inhibits further exploration of human relationships to country. Space and place have meaning and existence only in relation to the positioned, mobile, and intentional human body.[6] I have argued that rather than "taking on the determinate, unchanging structure of the object world" (Munn 1970:150), the living human subject has available a range of ideational material in the mobile landscape that fuses images of human, animal, plant, mineralized, and stellar bodies. The animal bodies, in particular, having all been human at one time and continuing to roam across the country, allow for exegetic distinctions between present and creative time to be drawn but without any absolute separations, since each human life is originally "found" in an animal body. The transformative series for human subjects is human body- animal body (including instantiations in country)—human body ad infinitum. The Ngarinyin worldview has allowed human subjects to "find" themselves and their relatives in a shifting but patterned landscape reflecting the lived-in human body.[7] Far from being "frozen over" or "outside time," human experience continues to draw lifeblood from, add clarifying detail to, and animate the mythic structures of country. Human emotional investment makes the country "grow big" and the stories of creation visible.

Notes

1. Kolig (1981), Munn (1970, 1973b), Morphy (1995), and Swain (1993) were all inclined to equate human creativity exclusively with innovation in their varying degrees of separation of ancestral subject from human object in Aboriginal cosmologies.

2. I note here Morton's comment that "male and female contributions to the dreaming are thus caught up in an eternal dialectic between 'high' and 'low.' Men 'lay down' the country, while women 'lift it up' " (1989:280).

3. I was interested to learn that the umbilical cord, *dinjul,* in bush births at least, shouldn't be cut off at the navel but rather have a piece of woven hair or sugar-glider fur tied tightly around it so that it gradually loses its blood supply and drops off after about a month. The intent seems to have been to prevent a radical severance of the child from its chrysalis/matrix, which could lead to disturbance in later life—"don't make 'im jump," as people say.

4. Morton (1997:157) has brought to light the fact that the native cat (the Spotted Quoll) really has a "double penis, an actual one and a long secondary appendage, which like the penis itself, becomes erect during mating." The spear-thrower, with its minor and major axes, could, in some respects, be said also to be a "double penis," as well as an originary matrix or cradle/receptacle from which the spear emerges.

5. This cutting and burning of the hair is a form of penitence and denial that is practiced by all those, male and female, in a classificatory relationship of being an "in-law" to the deceased. People said to me, "We *gotta* cry for that bloke," indicating their need to absolve themselves of any blame in the death. Only murderers are regarded as having long, thick hair. In 1938 a Ngarinyin man, in the course of relating to Pentony a dream in which he grabbed hold of another man's hair, it broke off, and he then burnt it, said that "when anything is burnt it is finished" (Pentony 1961). It is possible to bring into the interpretation, then, a sense of Damalarrngarri denying responsibility for her husband's death and embodying the permanency of death in her own burnt hair, finishing with him forever.

6. Franca Tamisari (1997) has reviewed and critiqued the prevailing position emerging from Munn's and Morphy's work by applying a phenomenological approach deriving from the later work of Merleau-Ponty, focusing on the central issues of mobility and visibility in Yolngu cosmology.

7. Buttimer (1976:284) used the works of Merleau-Ponty to explore the notion that "each person has a natural place which is considered to be the zero-point of his personal reference system. This natural place is set within a membered spatial surrounding, a series of places which fuse to form meaningful regions each with its appropriate structure and orientation to other regions. Each person is surrounded by concentric layers of lived space."

7

Strangelove's Dilemma

Or, What Kind of Secrecy Do the Ngarrindjeri Practice?

James F. Weiner

In Stanley Kubrick's famous movie *Dr. Strangelove*, that marvelous spoof on the gravid story *Fail Safe*, we find, as the rogue U.S. strategic bomber is on its way to release its nuclear load on the Soviet Union, that the U.S. Strategic Defense War Room finally learns of the existence of the Soviet Union's "secret weapon": the "Doomsday Device," which will destroy the entire world if a nuclear explosion occurs on Soviet territory. The Doomsday Device was designed as the ultimate deterrent in the Cold War of secret technology, deterrent and counterdeterrent. But Dr. Strangelove, sitting among the generals of the U.S. War Room, remarks that the Doomsday Device could do its work of deterrence only if the Other Side, that is, the U.S., knew of its existence. As it was, it failed to perform its function because the Soviets forgot to reveal its existence.

In 1995 in the state of South Australia, two groups of Aboriginal women of the Ngarrindjeri language group found themselves in a similar quandary. One group, who came to be known as the proponent women, claimed knowledge of a women's secret tradition of great antiquity associated with Hindmarsh Island, in the mouth of the Murray River, and its surrounding channels. Part of this hitherto unreported complex stipulated that Hindmarsh Island must remain separate from the mainland in order to maintain both the proper procreative functions of women's bodies and the reproductive capacity of the cosmos in general. The requirement of separation was appealed to as justification for opposing a planned bridge between Hindmarsh Island and the mainland town of Goolwa, a bridge that was intended to service the marina that had already been completed on the north end of the island. But shortly after the construction of the bridge was halted in mid-1994 by virtue of a successful application under the Commonwealth Aboriginal and Torres Strait Islander Heritage Protection Act (1984), another group of women, who would become known as the dissidents, made a number of dramatic public pronouncements disputing the existence of such a tradition in Ngarrindjeri culture. The dissident women did more than claim that they did not know of the particular secrets and its associated cosmology asseverated by the proponent women and Doreen Kartinyeri, their spokesman and primary custodian of the secret knowledge. The dissident women would have conceded much of the proponent women's case if that was what they were saying, for by definition, such a regime would include members who did not know the secrets. But the dissident women maintained that their culture did not have a regime of secrecy of any kind at all, and in fact did not even have separate men's and women's religious or ritual practices.[1] This was apparently a much more radical claim, indicative of a far more radical disagreement among the Ngarrindjeri themselves. The dissident women's characterization of their system was, however, consonant with the description of traditional Ngarrindjeri religious knowledge given by the (now deceased) anthropologists Ronald and Catherine Berndt in an extensive survey of precolonial Ngarrindjeri life (1993), and the testimony of a more recent ethnographer of the Ngarrindjeri, Philip Clarke, a cultural geographer. The Berndts reconstructed their portrait of traditional Ngarrindjeri culture from the accounts provided by three elderly Ngarrindjeri in the 1940s, one of whom was subsequently identified as the original source of the proponents women's "secret business," as it came to be called. But the Berndts chose to characterize Ngarrindjeri society as one in which both elaborate regimes of restricted knowledge per se and gender-based divisions in religious knowledge in particular (both of which were found in numerous other areas of Australia, in particular, the Central and Western Desert) were either absent or not extensively developed.

The proponent women and the dissident women therefore seemed to be disputing not the mere existence of particular secrets but, apparently, the fundamental epistemological foundation of their culture, religion, and social world. It was not phrased as a disagreement between orthodox and heterodox versions within the same religious system, as has been maintained by at least one legalist (Andrews 1996). This publicly reported dispute, plus statements by other Ngarrindjeri that the proponent women's claim had been fabricated for the express purpose of stopping the bridge, spurred the conservative Liberal Party–dominated state government of South Australia to hold a Royal Commission in 1995 to investigate, among other things, the claim of deliberate invention. After more than five months of hearing testimony, the Royal Commission concluded that the restricted women's knowledge had been fabricated in 1993 in order to block the construction of the bridge.

It appears as though the dissident women, like Dr. Strangelove's anguished U.S. generals, were distraught not so much because they didn't know the secrets but because they had not been told there was anything secret in the first place. If in fact Ngarrindjeri was a system that included restricted knowledge, as a result of the Hindmarsh Island bridge affair the proponent women had to confront the seeming paradox of losing or destroying knowledge by keeping it too well hidden, by holding on to it too tightly, by not releasing it. In this chapter, I present a hypothesis concerning the nature of Ngarrindjeri secrecy. This hypothesis stems from a consideration of the form that loss of knowledge may take in different traditions and the social uses to which the deliberate relinquishing of restricted knowledge may be put.

Knowledge as Metalanguage

I begin with the following question: What version of knowledge would we have to fashion to make of the conflicting claims of the proponent and dissident women plausible alternative views within the same system? In the best-known cases of regimes of restricted knowledge, such as those in northern Australia, the Sepik River region of Papua New Guinea (see Wassmann, chapter 2 above), and Africa, the forms and social mechanisms for revealing knowledge itself are highly elaborated and hedged with formality. The manner in which secrecy works socially is largely a function of these mechanisms. In the case of Hindmarsh Island, let us also begin with the mechanism through which the existence of the knowledge was made known.

The female consulting anthropologist was persuaded by a professor of law, Cheryl Saunders, acting on behalf of the federal minister for Aboriginal Affairs, to write an anthropological assessment of the proponent women's claim. She was given only two days to accomplish this, and so her report was essentially her edited account of what the primary custodian, Doreen Kartinyeri, related to her in a series of conversations. The report consisted of a main summary of twenty-five pages and three appendices. The first appendix was a two-page list of the Ngarrindjeri people associated with the claim. The second appendix, of twelve pages, was the anthropologist's rendition of Kartinyeri's account of the secret women's business. The third appendix, of four pages, was the anthropologist's analysis of its broader cosmological significance in terms of what she construed to be the Ngarrindjeri women's "cultural logic" (Fergie 1994). The final two appendices the anthropologist placed in envelopes and marked "Confidential: To Be Read by Women Only." The strategy of the Royal Commission, as well as the counsel representing the bridge developers and the dissident women, became largely an effort to deduce or force a revelation of the contents of the "secret envelopes," as they came to be called.

The parallels between this case and the middle Sepik River region of Papua New Guinea would then be striking. Wassmann, in chapter 2 above, has already cited Harrison's comment on the Manambu to the effect that new myths are constantly being created and tested in the public arena, and it is worthwhile to repeat that passage here:

> Men claim that mythology never changes, and that someone who tried to alter myths or promulgate false ones would invite affliction by the totemic ancestors. But, in fact, myth is manipulated continually. On average, a completely new name-dispute breaks out in Avatip once a year, provoked by some group challenging a myth of another group with a newly-fabricated rival myth of its own. Mythology is therefore being constantly produced. Whether or not it gains currency depends on its proponents' success in the debating-arena. (1990:141)

Let us next observe that the South Australian Aboriginal Heritage Protection Act of 1988 governed the procedure of inquiry in the Royal Commission to a marked extent. Specifically, section 35 of that Act states that "(1) except as authorized or required by this Act, a person must not, in contravention of Aboriginal tradition, divulge information relating to—(a) an Aboriginal site, object or remains; or (b) Aboriginal tradition." Periodically and regularly, the cross-examination and testimony took directions that stimulated the counsel for the consulting anthropologist to object that the Royal Commission was in danger of contravening section 35 of the State Act. In order to allow testimony to proceed, Commissioner Iris Stevens would clear the courtroom of all observers and allow the divulgence of testimony in "closed session."

But the imposition of this restriction within the Royal Commission was not only constructed wholly within it; it failed to affect the flow of information outside the Royal Commission inquiry and could even be said to have stimulated this flow. Thus, at several points in the Royal Commission, the consulting anthropologist and her counsel insisted that what the public had claimed to learn about the secrets were only uncontextualized fragments.[2] In so doing they were acting very much as the Manambu elder would in response to a challenge to his own secret knowledge. The fact is, these fragments kept leaking out and people kept building hypotheses around them and trying to piece together a portrait of Ngarrindjeri culture and knowledge and religion from it—and after all, is this no more nor less than what an anthropologist studying a regime of secrecy does? As Harrison (1990), Keen (1994), Morphy (1991), and others who have worked with elaborate regimes of secrecy in Papua New Guinea and elsewhere in Australia have noted, secret knowledge ultimately infiltrates the public domain, and in fact it is this inevitable and uncontrollable leakage that motivates renewed efforts to assert restriction.

The perception of the inevitability of leakage inclines us to some variety of what Bakhtin (see Morson and Emerson 1990) and Hanks (1996) call dialogism as a feature of discursive life. It allows us to approach the Royal Commission as itself an inevitable and integral channel of Ngarrindjeri cultural articulation. In contemporary Australia, where Aboriginal claims of all sorts are contested by state and commercial interests, these are central elicitory components of Aboriginal culture. As a result of this, we can see Ngarrindjeri and Euro-Australian speech acts not as colliding within some cultural or linguistic no-man's-land but as dialogically constituting a culture of confrontation and challenge within which Aboriginal and Euro-Australian rhetorical forms become thoroughly implicated in each other's discursive manifestations. This further leads us to consider what could be called *the conditions of performative acceptability* in any given speech encounter. Focusing on conditions of performative acceptability frees us from the necessity to accept the naturalness or boundedness of "a language" or "a culture" and the Whorfian "world view" to which it often leads in anthropological thinking about language. It places communicative efficacy at the center of anthropological investigation and views the emergence of distinct and coherent "cultures" and "languages" as a consequence rather than a precondition of it (Hanks 1996).

From this point of view, secrecy is not a quality of data of knowledge or language per se. It itself is a metalanguage: it provides a higher-order context within which the boundary between semantic element and grammatical frame becomes dissolved. It always works to convey the message "*what* is secret is not as important as *the fact that it is* secret." In other words, it erodes the boundary between interpretation and thing interpreted. This is why the anthropologist's account of Doreen Kartinyeri's secret business (the first secret appendix) also became secret (the second secret appendix), and which is why Commissioner Iris Stevens had to periodically clear the courtroom for closed sessions to proceed. By doing so, by performatively *interpreting* section 35 of the State Heritage Protection Act in her own way, the commissioner made her contribution to building the domain of restricted knowledge in Ngarrindjeri culture no less than the consulting anthropologist did.

No less than that of judges and royal commissioners, the creativity of the anthropologist also cannot be factored out of the equation, which is what makes Heritage Protection Acts that attempt to specify "aboriginal tradition" so impossible to carry out by anthropological standards (see Weiner 1999). It would be pointless to argue that the anthropologist does not contribute to ordering and making systematic the knowledge and social practices of his or her hosts. But both the anthropologist and the Royal Commission proceeded with an overly restricted view of what language and revelation consist of, and both preferred for exactly opposite reasons to see the avowal of nescience—not-knowing—as an adventitious intrusion of the political into the realm of the epistemological. The farcical elements of the Hindmarsh Island Royal Commission emerged because the inquiry proceeded upon the assumption that there was a version of Ngarrindjeri culture that existed independently of the anthropologists' and the commission's attempts to configure and interpret it, and hence repressed the dialogic properties of encounters of this sort where the nature and extent of culture and knowledge are contested.

Ordinarily, such knowledge is not some recondite and arcane piece of lore unconnected to people's everyday public lives, as was patently the case of the secret women's business in the Hindmarsh Island case, at least from the point of view of the dissident women. Knowledge is a key to some vital and salient behavioral complex within public life, as well as an analytic and conceptual perspective on it. That is why some anthropologists, such as Moore, Wagner, Strathern, myself, and others, refer to "social knowledge"—the way that perspective and competence are generated through social interaction as well as by means of some cognitive reconstitution or construction of them (though it was almost exclusively to the latter that the appeals to the proponent women's knowledge were made in the context of their application, and afterward [see Bell 1998]). This, by the way, is a perspective that could be obtained only in the context of prolonged daily cohabitation with a community, where the effects of secrets that ultimately find their way into the communal consciousness and there exert an effect on public discourse can be observed, recorded, and interrogated. However, no ethnographic documentation on this issue was or has been adduced before, during, or since the Royal Commission. It is significant that the two most recent ethnographers of the Ngarrindjeri themselves, Philip Clarke and Steven Hemming, who otherwise took opposing views on the validity of the proponent women's claim, had documented no evidence of the existence of this women's business before the claim by the proponent women was lodged.

This is not to say, however, that we don't now have a great deal of information about present-day Ngarrindjeri sociality contained within the transcript of the Royal Commission. When questioned about knowledge concerning female reproductivity, time and again Ngarrindjeri women attested to the fact that they were told nothing about the female "facts of life" by their mothers and other elder-generation relatives.[3] While not possessing the status of secret-sacred knowledge, these statements attest to a sociality in which conventional understandings of feminine reproduction are left tacit in a somewhat different way than our Western conventions are. It could be that an overt focus on the power of Aboriginal Law, as a local Ngarrindjeri and as a pan-Aboriginal cultural marker, and as an avenue toward political and economic advantage within a Western nation-state, deflects attention away from how a culture of restriction treats its own conventions with great circumspection.

Focusing on social knowledge displaces what we might think of as "culture" from the realm of the purely cognitive and subjective to the intersubjective, the communicative, and the relational. It makes knowledge as much a function of what people do and say, in particular with other people, as it is a function of what they can individually remember, asseverate, or believe in.

The contrast between "restricted" and "unrestricted" communication is thus only sharp and discrete at what we would call the "ideological" level. Considered in terms of the practical or praxical constraints on communicative adequacy in a community, it is more a continuum. Men and women everywhere "know" different things and thereby selectively communicate with each other, especially when such communication is governed by conventions of cross-gender appropriateness that are common in non-Western societies. Foi men of Papua New Guinea, for example, exhibited great reticence in discussing matters of childbirth and procreation, preferring to see such matters as women's special expertise. But it cannot be automatically read off from such divisions of communicative labor that men's and women's knowledge in such cases was unknown to the other gender, or that such contrasts supported or were supported by a *general* system of restrictions on communication, since a common lexicon and grammar have to ground any metasemantic distinctions between "men's" and "women's" language and speech styles. Similarly, each member of a community has "specialist" knowledge, broadly speaking. The existence of specialization does not entail that knowledge associated with the specialization is restricted in the marked sense that was at issue in the Hindmarsh Island bridge case.

The appeal to "inside" and "outside" aspects of language use implies, furthermore, that secrecy does not parcel out discrete domains within a tradition; there is a public component and a restricted component to every datum of knowledge, to every practice, to every institution. Of the Telefolmin of the West Sepik Province, Papua New Guinea, Marilyn Strathern observes:

> While the process of male growth is secret, the results are open and the stage of initiatory sequence visibly advertised in men's apparel.

> Each man thus presents on his exterior the effect of the secret interior process by which he had grown. What is true of individuals could also be said of communities. (1991:89)[4]

It was claimed by the anthropologist (see, for example, Transcript, p. 5929) that the Ngarrindjeri transmission of the secret women's knowledge was closely tied to the institution of *putari* (healer), which in the female role focused on midwifery skills and procedures. We don't know how many midwives or female *putari* there are in Ngarrindjeri society today. It may be that there are none, and even if some women claim to be *putari,* we have no information on the *current* social practice of midwifery, except in the experiences of nurses' aide training narrated by some female Ngarrindjeri witnesses in the Royal Commission.[5] The women's knowledge might be, probably is, by Ngarrindjeri standards arcane, and in the case of those who have embraced Christianity, might even be dismissed, repudiated, or denied. In this case, the consulting anthropologist's dilemma is real, for both the state and the federal acts prevent us from situating the belief, *and its public denial,* as a function of current Ngarrindjeri behavior, just as is the case with confrontations over revelation between the Baktaman and the Bimin, the Gunian and the Yulbaridja, and the Yolngu and the Europeans—all of which I will discuss in the next section. If it is not sedimented in behavior, it is beyond the reach of the empirical. When I maintain that such knowledge must be "sedimented in behavior," I do not insist that there be a positive correlation between ritual-mythic accounts of the world and social life. The relationship between such domains (as adumbrated by the anthropologist, of course, for one's informants may not recognize such distinctions [see Mathews 1996]) could be one of mutual contradiction, Freudian repression or repudiation, dialectical encompassment, or interpretive or transformative restatement, none of which easily meets the Durkheimian requirements of religious regulation, patterning, and ordering of the societal. But whatever that relationship, it is meaningful, again, by dint of the anthropologist's own efforts to render its terms into his or her own language.

To repeat: One cannot, I feel, argue the issue of whether the alleged secret women's knowledge was consistent with what is known about Ngarrindjeri culture without simultaneously determining the status, both behavioral and ontological, of the particular *regime of secrecy* that it is alleged or inferred the Ngarrindjeri possess. Obviously, there are different regimes of secrecy. In the Sepik (Papua New Guinea), in Arnhem Land (Australia), and in the Central Desert (Australia), we find the phenomenon of restriction of knowledge linked with specific theories about the nature of language and other expressive vehicles that make restriction inevitable. Specifically, in many societies with well-established regimes of restriction, language itself has an inside and an outside version, a concealed and a public gloss. As intimated by Tonkinson (1997), the distinction between "inside" and "outside" in Arnhem Land is first and foremost a grammatically salient category of the semantic system, and hence would be a central dimension of every instance of uttered speech. People, purely by virtue of speaking, would become aware of the layering of meaning that the structure of their language makes possible. There are multiple names and referents for every object, and the knowledge of these multiple referents is variably distributed. The variability of this distribution is what constitutes the restriction. The Kpelle of Liberia, who participate in the widespread Poro secret society, have a word *meni,* which the ethnographer Beryl Bellman translated as their version of Schutz's "multiple versions of social reality": "Each potential speaker makes the decision of whether to talk or not largely by identifying the particular auspices of, or meaning context for, the social situation. In Kpelle, these auspices are called *meni*" (1984:43–44).

Meni is the social frame, the interactional context that makes a certain assumption of discursive authority appropriate and effective for the Kpelle. How would one go about discovering whether such metalinguistic or metadiscursive features, so important for making restriction do social work, were ever at any time components of the Ngarrindjeri language, or their discursive world more broadly? And since Ngarrindjeri is not the language of use among Lower Murray people today, in what form of their communal language usage do such features manifest themselves? Any anthropologist seeking further information on the nature of contemporary Ngarrindjeri language usage must, it seems, arm him/herself with these and other similar questions.

In the Sepik, what is hidden through a system of secret names is the connections between totemic places that gives the account of ancestral creator beings coherence and meaning (see Wassmann, chapter 2 above). But the cosmology itself, as an account of creation, is concealed from most people. What, then, do people know, or have to know, to allow them to "function" in the religious life of their community? If a regime can be characterized as one that avoids ostensively articulating its conventions, then getting by in life becomes more a matter of strategic improvisation than of conforming to rules.[6]

> In later life each form of religious acquisition, whether the introduction to a new song, a sacred object, or some other form, involved aspects of initiation. In this respect, a man's learning process was never quite completed during his lifetime. Any man, even the most learned, when confronted with an unfamiliar ritual, myth, or sacred object once again becomes an initiand whose ignorance requires formal education. Even today, fully initiated men in the Fitzroy area, when faced with a new important religious item, will begin a ritual wailing to express their grief at having missed out for so long on something so eminently important. (Kolig 1981:66)

The discrepancies in knowledge and authority created by a regime of restriction thus are always relative. A culture does not consist of a finite number of premises that can be exhaustively cataloged or known and that are subsequently parceled out to create politico-epistemic division. Anthropologists themselves fabricate these premises as part of a formalized account of a behavioral nexus that they ever encounter only in its contingent form as social event.

The Problem of Loss of Knowledge

I want to now speak about the phenomenon of "loss of knowledge" as it has been reported from certain areas of Australia and Papua New Guinea. In *Partial Connections,* Marilyn Strathern discusses Barth's analysis of systems of restricted knowledge among the Mountain Ok groups of western Papua New Guinea. Barth made famous the image of the Baktaman ritual specialist struggling against the perpetual threat of knowledge loss in its transmission from elder men to those of junior generations.

> A general command of Baktaman culture was in no sense thought to entail the foundations for knowing cult forms and procedures. Indeed, the Faiwol seem to live with the constant fear of loss of the vital knowledge. With the necessity, as they see it, of deception of the uninitiated, and the sacralizing power of secrecy . . . the general idea among them is that transmission from elder to junior is in perpetual danger of being lost. . . . In cases of recognized failure of transmission, however, the traditions of neighboring groups are,

> under fortunate circumstances, available to replace the parts of one's own tradition that were lost. (Barth 1987:26–27)

Strathern goes on to argue that Barth has insufficiently distinguished between loss of information and loss of knowledge:

> Barth makes it clear that experts are concerned with providing the vehicles for thought, for making hidden meanings appear, constantly generating for themselves the very traditions that must change in the course of regeneration. Yet this must surely cancel any lingering anthropological notion that "tradition" only survives if it is kept intact as a positive tracery of connections between events, images, meanings. We have to, as he stresses, get our ontology right. On this evidence, that exercise must surely include loss of knowledge as part of the data, not as loss of the data.
>
> What is lost are imagined as once existing vehicles or media for communication. But I have suggested the *knowledge* that they are lost is not, so to speak, lost knowledge, it is knowledge about absence, about forgetting and about an unrecoverable background. That sense of loss stimulates the Baktaman initiators, it would seem, to make present images work—not to filling in the gaps, for that cannot be done, but making what is present do all the differentiating work it has to do, and thus creating information for themselves. (Strathern 1991:97–98)

Strathern argues for a different positioning of what is "present" to anthropological analysis. For Melanesians, she maintains, connectivity and communication in social life are not problematic. In places like Papua New Guinea and Australia, connectivity, and the establishment of some mode of conventional communication exchange, overreaches and overextends itself, not just between persons and domains within a language but between what we take to be discrete languages and cultural communities themselves. But since it is harder to conceive of what the loss of social connection might mean epistemologically than the loss of "factual knowledge," Strathern thereby renders problematic the notion of culture as a catalog of thought that comes before and defines social action. *The loss of knowledge, then, is first and foremost an indication of the nature, quality, and extent of social connectivity.*

Strathern and Barth, and all the rest of us who have commented on the Baktaman and the Mountain Ok since Barth's pioneering studies (Barth 1975, 1987), were also intrigued by a system in which the perception of entropy of information was not an effect of contact with an alien, dominant, and intrusive tradition but rather of an endogenous conception of convention, information, and efficacy of knowledge. Here is a tradition whose own notion of "outside" looked "inside" to us anthropologists.

The recent public politics of Aboriginal cultural revitalization has focused heavily on the image of steady and irreversible loss of culture as a result of intrusive policies of assimilation and cultural erasure by white Australians in the past 150 years. I want to suggest, however, along the lines of the Mountain Ok example, that in societies that are organized around regimes of gradated and restricted knowledge, the necessity to retain, replace, or reconfigure knowledge in the face of the experience of its loss is an *internal* mechanism of knowledge revelation and creation themselves. As Myers says for the Pintupi: "The particular notions captured in the Pintupi metaphors of 'holding' (nursing) and 'losing' (relinquishing, as with death) represent permanence and continuity of society's ground rules in terms of biological reproduction" (1986:243). Morphy, in a somewhat different vein, says of the Yolngu, "It is one of the ironies of a system of restricted knowledge, at least of the Yolngu type, that knowledge both gains and loses power through its release" (1991:98). Loss and consequent attenuation of knowledge motivates renewed attempts at both restricting knowledge and creating new knowledge to replace what is lost or devalued through transmission and revelation.

The conditions for this retention of form in the face of "loss of data" are also present in Aboriginal traditions. Kolig thus suggests:

> A myth contains many reference points to other myths. The elaborate narrative of an Aboriginal myth is an exegesis of the sacred songs that epitomize the mythic plot in a scant few key words (see, e.g., R. M. Berndt 1951:17, 88). Exegesis of the often meager hints given by the key words can naturally be manifold. There is ample leeway for the varying interpretations. Moreover, the sequence of the verses is unstable and can be, and in fact often is, changed around. . . . The flexibility of the myths and the interlocking of mythical tracks make it relatively easy to establish connections on a geographic and symbolic basis. (1981:42)

Here we have a situation in which form and information are not extricable from each other, and in this case we would have to highlight the special features of myth in preserving this indissolubility of context and content. Because the form of myth is also its content (see Wagner 1978; Weiner 1995c; Lévi-Strauss 1963), the Aboriginal creation myth as we have come to know it, as a story of a journey across the land by creator beings of various sorts, contains both information and its form (in this case, the place names, their external nonlinguistic spatial anchorings, and the content of the story, which gives them cultural-religious significance)—hence, both are lost and gained together, unlike the Baktaman, who lost information without losing form, or the Foi, who lost form without losing information.[7]

What we need to highlight here is something that I've called elsewhere the form of interpretational praxis (Weiner 1995c, 1995d). We usually look to our informants' exegesis of a myth as providing a "plain language" account of its "significance." But it could be the other way around: it could be that myth is the form that local exegesis takes of otherwise inscrutable or concealed "everyday language," as the Kimberley example given by Kolig indicates:

> The *Djularga* line is . . . divided into two main parts, in keeping with the two separate sections of the mythical track. The northern part of the track . . . is associated with the Gunian, . . . and other groups of the Fitzroy area. From the Fitzroy perspective, the Gunian are the main repositories of the northern manifestation of the *Djularga* tradition. . . . At the "territorial" border between the Gunian and their southern neighbors, the Wolmadjeri and Yulbaridja . . . [a]ccording to the prevalent Gunian version, the mythical leader refused to hand over the esoteric secrets to the new leader who was supposed to bring them to the Wolmadjeri and Yulbaridja.
>
> The Yulbaridja version knows of no such vital denial of esoteric secrets. . . . The location of the track and the mythical plot give the Yulbaridja ample opportunity to link themselves with this tradition, and today most of them claim membership in the *Djularga* lodge.
>
> . . . In the case of the Yulbaridja, the establishing of this link between their tradition and a northern one was probably intended to provide religious justification for their presence in the new habitat . . . The mythological denial of vital secrets in the Gunian version of the myth represents their symbolic rejection of the Yulbaridja land claim. It is also a rejection of the present religious dominance of the Desert Aborigines. The Gunian interpretation attributes inferior status to the Desert traditions by implying that vital secrets had been withheld from them—and that only the Gunian remain the true repositories of the *Djularga* tradition today. (1981: 48–49)

To paraphrase Lévi-Strauss once more, it is not the political that is determined in the mythopoietic; it is the mythological that is determined within these very concretivities of social and political life. On the other hand, religious systems in Australia were by and large integrally tied to intimate knowledge of terrain, territory, and topography (see Rose, chapter 5 above), and when certain Aboriginal groups were dispossessed of their land, a prime component of the objective and material basis of this system of restriction was removed. In such cases, several alternative strategies for the reinscription of these articulatory mechanisms can be noted among contemporary Aboriginal groups. But some of these mechanisms for reinscription also predated European contact: "Religious elements have always been deliberately offered and sought after, exchanged and traded. The religious potency of objects and intellectual contents was traditionally believed to increase proportionally across distances" (Kolig 1981:111).[8]

The problem that arises is the nature of "outsideness." If we can imagine Aboriginal groups living at a great distance from each other nevertheless linked through such religious exchange networks, how external to the system were Europeans, with their new myths and rituals? The response of the Yolngu on Elcho Island in 1957 indicates that in Sahlinsian terms, a wholly Yolngu appropriation of Christian power and religious knowledge was attempted in the so-called Adjustment Movement. As Berndt noted:

> It is interesting that "formal" leadership devolves primarily on *jiridja* moiety men, rather than *dua,* since traditionally the *jiridja* moiety is associated with "introduced" and alien features, while the *dua* is said to be more conservative. . . . In local terms this represents a conceptual division of responsibility, as between "change introduced from outside" (the concern of the *jiridja* moiety) and "concentration in indigenous themes" (the concern of the *dua* moiety); this has provided a certain degree of resistance to alien pressures. (1962:36)

Now, given that we have identified a mechanism *internal* to societies of both New Guinea and Australia for the deliberate articulation of incommensurate frameworks, what kind of payoff in terms of social effect or meaning is obtained in such systems? Let us return momentarily to the Baktaman.

How Much Dispute Is Too Much for One System?

In *Cosmologies in the Making* (1987), Barth set out to describe the local variations within a regional cult and ritual complex among the so-called Mountain Ok communities of the Fly-Sepik headwaters region of western Papua New Guinea. Let us take two examples of the kind of ritual variation that Barth confronts. In the first, the Baktaman smear the initiates in Mafomnang initiation with the fat from domesticated pigs, while the nearby Bimin-Kuskusmin smear the faces of their Mafomnang initiates with the fat from wild pigs. In the second example, the red facial paint of the Telefolmin is secretly associated with menstrual blood while the Bimin-Kuskusmin represent menstrual blood by the color black, rather than red. The Baktaman themselves would view with horror the infusion of such a polluting substance into such an initiation; it "would be completely destructive to the integrity and good-sacred properties of cult equipment and activities" (4). Barth concludes:

> It is no doubt necessary to be somewhat attuned to these cults and symbols to realize the full impact of contrast and shock that such differences generate. Clearly . . . the symbolic objects and acts that I have picked out here are of a kind, though opposite; but they also enter deeply into an elaborate set of connected meanings and ritual statements as to dramatically explode and destroy this common base. If one were to imagine a Christian from one English village who entered the church of a community some miles away and found an image of the devil on the crucifix, and the altar wine being used for baptism, this seems the closest analogy I can construct. (Barth 1987:5)

We are being asked to consider that different ritual practices within an otherwise culturally, socially, and ecologically uniform area might be so divergent as to appear almost demonic by our standards. It is clear, however, that such variations in ritual practice may be a crucial focus of local cultural differentiation in this area and that such differentiation has its own sociopolitical functions in this region of Papua New Guinea. I mention this only to show that anthropologists under different circumstances can accept this measure of divergence without calling into question the "coherence" of a regional cultural system and that we might want to reduce the scope of the dissident and proponent Ngarrindjeri women's disagreement in the same manner.

In societies that are small in population and whose social divisions are based on variations in access to religious and cosmological propositions, there is by definition the likelihood of great disparity in individual cosmological knowledge. Under such conditions, "the analytic danger is that the insights obtained from someone with specialized knowledge may have little bearing on the way in which, say, ritual symbols are apprehended by the population at large" (Tuzin 1992:254).

We can now ask, What does a form of social life, which we describe as a structure or a system, reproduce? In Strathern's view, it does not reproduce or transmit or pass on information per se, as Barth seems to feel. Rather, it reproduces a certain technique of making information visible, that is, a social technique of symbolic reproduction itself. The difference between the Foi and the Baktaman can be said to be very great from our viewpoint, as great as that between the Baktaman and the Bimin-Kuskusmin. Here, subjective interpretation seems to run counter to the project of comparison, unless we can make the elicitation of conventional forms of subjectivity itself the datum of comparison—this is what Strathern does in her book *Partial Connections.* To understand Aboriginal and Papua New Guinean articulations of identity such as are at issue here, it might be necessary to admit that the actual bits of information that the processes of identity draw upon are less important than the structure of the regime of articulation itself. As Strathern puts it, "Everything is in place: sociality, the values, relationships. But what must be constantly made and remade, invented afresh, are the forms in which such things are to appear" (1991:98).

But as I have argued previously (Weiner 1995b), we only abstract *form* from the very same concrete acts of social relationality from which we adduce the flow of information that such form manages. How then do we distinguish between loss of form and loss of information, if in each case what is lost is a certain technique of relationality itself? In the case of Hindmarsh Island, one answer seems to be that the invocation of a hidden conventionality ultimately served to publicly differentiate factions within the Ngarrindjeri community, each of whom were articulating a different relation to an image of traditionality and indigeneity. This information was not adduced under the terms of the Hindmarsh Island Bridge Royal Commission, because neither set of protagonists could provide a satisfactory account of the social constitution of knowledge in the contemporary Ngarrindjeri community.

This leads us back to the Adjustment Movement. Berndt quotes the shock of his Yolngu informants in the 1950s when confronted with the evidence that the white men had been publicly showing their most secret objects and ceremonies:

> "They took pictures of our sacred ceremonies and *rangga,* and we got excited. Why do they do this? We understood this when Warner, Thomson and the Berndts were here. But why do they come again and again to study us? They take photographs of sacred things and show them to all the people throughout Australia and other places. . . . We got a shock. We're not supposed to show these *mareiin,* these *rangga* to just anybody. . . . All this made us think . . . then we saw a film at Elcho church. It was from the American-Australia Expedition, and it showed the sacred ceremonies and emblems. And everybody saw it. . . . We've got no power to hide (these *rangga*): they are taking away our possessions." (1962:40)

It is this "unarticulated background" of relatedness as against linguistic, mythical, and religious differentiation, that was revealed in the manner of a figure-ground reversal in the Adjustment Movement Memorial. But the public revelation of the Ngarrindjeri women's restricted knowledge had exactly the opposite effect: it revealed a lack of background consensus concerning Aboriginal femaleness and religiosity. The proponent women were thus in a situation more like that of the Ok. We can consider that the Ok, in contrast to the Yolngu, *lose* the unarticulated background deliberately through restricting knowledge transmission (recall the "horror" of Baktaman when confronted with the form of Bimin Mafomnang initiation; the Yolngu, on the other hand, *retained* it by revealing the form that they hitherto could not articulate).

The Baktaman, Kimberley, and Yolngu examples lead us to speculate that practices concerning restriction are part and parcel of traditions that recognize the potency of the distant, the exogenous, and the innovative and that have institutional internal mechanisms for appropriating, controlling, and apportioning objects, discourses, and knowledges that are seen to have an external source. I think this hypothesis has something to contribute to the Ngarrindjeri case. I suggest that despite the seemingly intractable epistemic discrepancy given voice in the Royal Commission, the dispute between the proponent women and the dissident women sounds very much like the disagreement between the Gunian and the Yulbaridja concerning whether the secrets of the Djularga cult were or were not passed on to the Yulbaridja. Further, I would like to make a case for seeing the confrontation between the South Australian state and the Ngarrindjeri as not radically divorced from the internal contestations between proponent and dissident women: both conflicts were shaped together within and outside the Royal Commission and can be said to have been contained within the same kind of events of language contextualization—what Hanks calls "metalanguage"—that we normally include as a label for "a culture."

The preceding argument leads to an important general principle, as Hanks has phrased it:

> No phrasing, no genre, and no amount of caution in speaking can insulate an utterance from the technologies of metalanguage. Socially, it is the ubiquity of talk, the vicissitudes of human judgement, and the play among different fields of reception that open the utterance to later construals or misconstruals. As Bahktin observed, certain forms of authoritative or dominant speech are designed to control these factors by defining their own interpretation so finally as to freeze it. But language alone can never achieve this. . . . Similarly, social groups develop institutions such as censorship, copyright laws, ethical codes, and the entire apparatus of propriety to control speech but the grip is tenuous at best. (Hanks 1996:274)

The courtrooms of Australia are now just as important venues of cultural revelation as the ritual dance grounds; they are one more contemporary arena in which groups vie to force others to reveal their restricted knowledge for socially appropriate purposes. We should view Australian lawyers and politicians as being at least partly responsible for the shape of cultural difference, even at the same time that they try to disconfirm and delegitimate it for rhetorical purposes. It might be objected that I am merely dignifying in the language of relationality a more insidious latter-day colonization of Aboriginal intention and creativity. But perhaps all I am suggesting is that Euro-Australian solicitors and judges are now akin to the Iatmul and Manambu elders of the Sepik River of Papua New Guinea, who confirm the limits of their knowledge by casting doubts on the extent of their rivals' knowledge.[9]

After World War II, a label emerged for the "culture" that included two very similar yet ideologically opposed super-states locked in competitive military-industrial struggle. This rubric was the "Cold War," used to describe a communicative arena wherein deception, espionage, and secrecy nevertheless intimately bound adversaries and created out of that willful intention to miscommunicate and mislead a conventional form of allusive and elusive communication itself. The Royal Commission, despite its findings of fabrication, had the effect of inserting secret women's business on Hindmarsh Island squarely within the arena of Lower Murray social knowledge, where it is now there to stay. Although the proponent women quite publicly announced that they had burned the secret appendices late in 1996, this cannot lead to a temporal reversal of people's consciousness and intention. Once you have cooked up a symbolic treat and forced people to consume culture, you have to reap the nutritive consequences of such nurturing, as Marilyn Strathern has said. A relationship of conflict and contestation can socially and culturally bind participants just as closely and indissolubly as one of cooperation and mutual esteem. Doreen Kartinyeri and the Ngarrindjeri proponents, men and women alike, continue to depend upon the formal and legal challenges and resistances of the conservative federal and South Australian state governments for the success of their own culturally and socially regenerative and innovative efforts.

Notes

1. Transcript of the Hindmarsh Island Bridge Royal Commission, pp. 958, 3362. In the words of one of the dissident women, Mrs. Bertha Gollan:

> Q [Ms. Pyke, counsel for the consulting anthropologist]: Do you have any knowledge, in Ngarrindjeri tradition, of who is entitled to receive particular sorts of information. Whether some people are entitled to receive some information and other people not. Are you aware of anything like that.
>
> A [Mrs. Gollan]: That has never been. That was never, ever pointed out to anyone over at Point McLeay. That "You should know and not you."

See also pp. 4140–4141, 4467. The complete public portion of the transcript of the Hindmarsh Island Bridge Royal Commission can be found at the following Web site: http://library.adelaide.edu.au/gen/H_Islnd/.

2. See Transcript, pp. 5838–5839:

> Q [Mr. Abbott]: Have you any reason to believe that Doreen wouldn't remember what she had told you to put in that report.
>
> A [Anthropologist]: I don't think she remembers it certainly in the way in which she gave it to me, that's certain, but, I mean, there are a variety of ways in which you could think about this, which is that what you are actually seeing is just, you know, a process of somebody, in effect, giving another—I mean—yes, giving another version of stuff. I

mean, I don't—I know what you are saying, there is not a lot of accord between reports of what Doreen says are there, and what my recollection of—

Q: What you say—

A: What my recollection is, what is there is there. I mean, part of what she's said in some press statements of fragments of what are there with elaborations that are certainly not there, I don't know, or—

3. See, for example, Transcript, pp. 618–619, the testimony of Mrs. Bertha Gollan, one of the dissident women:

> Q [Counsel Assisting]: In all of your years on Point McLeay, did you ever hear any talk of any women's business.
>
> A [Mrs. Gollan]: No, never.
>
> Q: Was it ever suggested to you that there was ever any secret knowledge that was being passed on to you.
>
> A: No. When as children growing up, especially the young girls, we were never told how babies were born and the changing of us in our bodies—which is, well—now, these days, every mother tells a girl. We were never told that. We had to experience this on our own. So, if there would have been any sacred business, women's business, I know we would have been told. So, if the old ladies and my mother, if they didn't tell us the changing of our bodies and how our children were born, why weren't we told about the sacred business—which we were never.
>
> Q: Were you told anything about where babies came from.
>
> A: No. We had to find out for ourselves. We were told that the babies were found out under the big fig tree outside the hospital.

4. This makes Morphy's point once more: what is visible and public is a recognizable version of what is secret and hidden.

5. See Transcript, p. 950. In the cross-examination of the dissident woman Mrs. Bertha Gollan by the consulting anthropologist's counsel, Ms. Pyke:

> Q [Ms. Pyke]: And the basis for your belief that it is lies is because you have never been told that.
>
> A [Mrs. Gollan]: Because I haven't been told it and I know for certain that these other girls weren't told, because they were all gone. Who would tell a ten year old girl?
>
> Q: Do you not accept that it might be that some people were told things that you weren't.
>
> A: I do not accept it.
>
> Q: Are we to take the position then that, unless you know about it and it has been told to you, about any aspect of Ngarrindjeri history or culture, it doesn't exist.
>
> OBJECTION Ms Shaw [assisting Mr. Smith, Counsel Assisting the Royal Commissioner] objects.
>
> MS SHAW: We are dealing with secret women's business.

> COMSR: I don't know that that is what the witness has said. She said that, because of the fact that she was present at all these confinements dealing with child birth and that she discussed it with the various women, that she thinks that surely during that process she would have heard something. So, I don't think that is quite the same as saying that, unless she knows about something, that it doesn't exist.
>
> MS PYKE: All right.
>
> (pp. 953–954)

6. This, however, is not a straightforward categorical distinction, since as both Wittgenstein and Bourdieu have shown, the tactic of "conforming to the rules" itself requires a practical command of the strategy of rule-following.

7. See Weiner 1988:151 on the relationship between "sacred" and "secular" myths in the Foi past.

8. Apropos of New Guinea/Australian comparison, Kolig goes on to say in the next sentences: "Things common or banal at their place of origin might well become cherished treasures elsewhere. Take for instance fragments of pearl shell. They're hardly valued in coastal areas, but their worth increases steeply in the hinterlands" (151).

9. The Talmud speaks of Rabbi *Aher* (Rabbi "Other") "who is in opposition to most assent formulations" (Morris, "Community Beyond Tradition," in Heelas, Lash, and Morris 1996:240).

8

The Underground Life of Capitalism

Space, Persons, and Money in Bali (West New Britain)

Andrew Lattas

A great deal of contemporary academic work on cargo cults has sought to deny their reality and has preferred instead to speak about colonial inventions that are ideological artifacts of a certain primitivism that permeated the thoughts of administrators, missionaries, and other colonists (Hermann 1992; Lindstrom 1993; McDowell 1985). This new academic position prides itself on its ethics and studiously avoids the term "cargo cult," which is dismissed as the disparaging, mystifying language of colonial ethnocentricism. Even very good books, like Martha Kaplan's (1995) historical work on millenarian movements in Fiji, seem to be embarrassed by villagers' desire for money and cargo, which is said to be secondary to what is assumed to be villagers' more primary concern with politics and morality. Such ethical apologies for the natives' materialism imply their own ethnocentric ontologies. They imply a materialist-spiritualist opposition—where the desire for material goods and wealth is seen to corrode the legitimacy and integrity of politico-ethical concerns. In my work on cargo cults (Lattas 1992a, 1992b, 1992c, 1998), I have avoided this Christian-inspired, God-versus-Caesar dichotomy except insofar as nowadays it is used by informants influenced by charismatic forms of Christianity. Instead, I agree with the position of some of the classic academic texts on cargo cults by Burridge (1960), Lawrence (1964), and Worsley (1970), which document and analyze how millenarian followers made "cargo" into a sign of moral well-being—that is, into a means of ethically interrogating traditional culture and current social relationships. My own work has sought to reconstitute the insights of these classic texts by merging them with the insights of a Marxist-phenomenological analysis that treats commodities and money as new ways of objectifying and constituting sociality and subjectivities (cf. Castoriadis 1987; Taussig 1980, 1987).

My experience of cargo cult followers throughout New Britain is that on some occasions they will embrace the term "cargo cult" with pride as a description of the alternative road to modernity that will come through the dead, the underground, and cult practices. Yet at other times, followers will deny the applicability of the term to themselves, explaining that cargo cult followers are those who wait naively for something to come up all by itself, which is not what they do. Instead they work hard at trying to "straighten" relations among themselves and with the dead. Such ambivalences express the contradictions that villagers experience as they become caught up in the hegemonic gaze and evaluations of whites, government, missions—gazes and evaluations that they simultaneously internalize and wrestle with. Though theoretically underdeveloped, some of the best ethnographic documentation of those alienating experiences can be found in the classic work of Burridge, Lawrence, and Worsley, who treated seriously the moral problematization of identity that the white man's wealth brought. Modern academic ethical apologies and denials of the importance of "cargo" will not facilitate an analysis of the forms of ethical and racial problematization that the white man's wealth brings and that cargo cults themselves often reproduce while also seeking to alleviate (Lattas 1998).

I believe that a thorough analysis of the political and ethical meanings of "cargo" must begin from a cultural analysis like Michele Stephen's (1979, 1982), which explores how indigenous ways of producing change through contacts with the dead have been elaborated to encompass the world of white power and wealth. Stephen's work focuses on the ontological structures, the space-time frameworks, within which modernity becomes refigured. One of those structures concerns the way Melanesians use the worlds of the dead and spirits as mirror worlds (Bercovitch 1989; Feld 1996). Throughout New Britain, that mirror relationship is focused on the underground (Lattas 1998; Panoff 1968). This is the case for cults that I have studied in the bush Kaliai area and more recently in the Pomio area of East New

Britain and Bali Island of West New Britain. Cargo cults reinvent the mirroring practices of tradition that are now merged with the mirroring practices of the West so as to create new ways of forming the constitutive gaze of self-awareness and more particularly of a moral conscience.

The Dakoa Cult

I want now to document and expand some of these ideas by looking at a cargo cult on Bali Island, which was started in 1964 by Cherry Dakoa Takaili, a charismatic man often known as Dakoa or CDT. Sometimes Bali Island is listed incorrectly in government documents as Unea, though its correct local name is Unyapa. Bali is a small island whose population in 1970 was recorded as being 4,120. It is currently part of the province of West New Britain and lies about sixteen hours by boat from the provincial capital of Kimbe. It was first administered by the Germans from Madang at the beginning of the twentieth century before coming under the control of Talasea. The Germans established a coconut plantation that was later run by a series of Australian owners and managers. In 1932, German missionaries established the Catholic church, and Catholicism is still the largest denomination on Bali Island. Next in size is the cargo cult run by Dakoa, which calls itself Cult Mission, and then the Seventh Day Adventist church. Other, smaller denominations include the Baha'i faith, the Assembly of God, and Jehovah's Witnesses. All Bali villagers speak a common Austronesian language, which has been classified by Chowning and Goodenough as part of the Kimbe family language group. The traditional major crops were taro, bananas, and yams, though today sweet potatoes and corn have largely replaced taro. Villagers have also become heavily reliant on rice and tinned meats that they purchase through growing and processing copra and cocoa.

In 1967 an agricultural report stated: "Indigenes on Bali Island produced up to $20,000 of copra each year." This copra was produced by individuals but also by the cargo cult that was started in 1964 when Bali villagers donated coconut trees and labor so as to create a company called Perukuma Company, which they expected to have the same sizable income as that enjoyed by large European companies. This cargo cult company was the brainchild of Dakoa Takaili, a charismatic man who still leads the movement. Dakoa's cult is very different from other cargo cults that I have studied—like those of the bush Kaliai on the mainland of West New Britain—in which villagers have actively resisted planting cash crops. Bali Island is covered in coconut and cocoa groves, and Dakoa's followers are heavily involved in cash crops both as individuals and as cargo cult company participants. Perukuma Company produces mainly copra and some cocoa. In the late 1980s, as compensation for certain unusual violent punishments inflicted unlawfully upon cult members by police and council government officials, Perukuma Company was given five thousand kina in money by provincial government officials, which it used to build a cocoa fermentary. Today Dakoa purchases raw cocoa from Bali villagers, processes it, and sells it. He also operates like an unofficial banker on Bali island, for he converts into cash the numerous checks that are brought to him by teachers, government officials, and local villagers.

Unlike bush Kaliai villagers who still view cash crops and development as fraudulent, immoral activities, Bali islanders have embraced the world of commodity production and have reworked it into their own domains of truth and morality. Like bush Kaliai villagers, Bali villagers do have ambivalences about the cash economy and about accepting it on its own terms. Indeed, Dakoa's followers speak about the commercial work of Perukuma Company as a *karamap* (cover) for the true work that is being done for them in the underground. Followers also talk about their collective work for Perukuma Company and the redistribution of its profits among themselves as acts of kindness and love that will entice the underground to come and live with them. Incorporated into the hegemony of the cash economy, Bali cult followers are working their own idiosyncratic meanings about the transformative moral power of money, development, and companies. Whereas other Papua New Guinea villagers will sometimes speak of money as the root of all evil, as something belonging to Satan, on Bali Island a certain moral order has been projected onto the domain of money. It is not that cult followers see money as inherently good; rather, they equate the moral order and solidarity of their community with them working collectively for their company, which in turn is seen as working secretly with the underground dead for their benefit.

Dakoa's company portrays itself as a moral community that stands opposed to the violence, cannibalism, sorcery, and warfare of people's past. The unifying corporate activities of Perukuma Company are seen as creating and reaffirming codes of morality and solidarity among Bali islanders. The cult's company offers villagers the promise of becoming new sorts of subjects with new sorts of "stomachs" (emotions) that look favorably toward others. The production of copra and cocoa for cash sale acquires a moral dimension in that it indicates people's willingness to work together, to share and love each other. On Fridays, when Dakoa preaches to his congregation, he will tell them not to put too much time into subsistence gardening. He will suggest that they avoid crops, like taro, that require a great deal of care and effort; instead he will suggest that followers plant less time-consuming crops, like bananas, yams, and corn. Dakoa will justify this focus on cash crops by telling followers that "money is love." Money is said to be love because it cares for you; it helps you by buying soap, clothing, saucepans, rice, tinned fish, and tinned meat. Here the new pleasures brought by commodities are seen as a way of caring for the self. There is a satisfaction, a contentment, and a sense of order brought to subjects by commodities, and this is embraced as part of the project of realizing a new loving community that has all its desires cared for and fulfilled.

The cult sanctifies working for money; it embraces the commercial work of copra and cocoa production and gives these cash crop activities an ordering, moral significance. Dakoa will speak about money as "straightening" a village because it allows a village to buy important Western goods—like a car and a ship—that make possible a more comfortable, modern existence. Money is also said to "straighten" individuals because it buys soap and new clothes through which they can become "clean." The need to work copra for money both as individuals and collectively for Perukuma Company is also why Dakoa will caution followers about taking on the "big traditional custom work" of their grandparents. He will warn followers how certain underground white men who are their deceased relatives will look unfavorably upon them should they appear raggedy, unclean, and disordered, as not having made an effort to redeem their existence.

> I [Dakoa] don't like this big work of our ancestors. We must just come and do all the work belonging to money alone. It is when men have money that they have plenty of food. If we looked inside [your house], there wouldn't be any food, for you don't have money. . . . However if we work strong with money, then money will come to our company. This company of ours will then be able

> to work. Our company will then distribute the profit to come back to us. We will receive it from our company and put it in our houses and our houses will be smart. They will be clean and have plenty of food. The food from gardens, it is small. We plant it, but we need money to be fully satisfied. I talk to them [followers] about this. . . . You can't work too much on your own house and garden. . . . All the [underground] bosses will come to live with us and we can then change. However, there is still some thinking that comes and continues to bugger us up. Now, when the [underground] *masta* (white men) come and see it, it won't be any good. They will say, "Oh, Papua New Guineans, they can't gain the new existence for they are still ruining their way of life. They must wait longer. They are still not good and they themselves have spoilt it."

Money here mediates a certain break with tradition and is part of a consumer culture, but one that is directed at capturing the dead. The world of work is not to be focused exclusively on one's own house and garden, but ought to be a collective, cooperative world that will be judged by the dead. Bali villagers' understanding that they will acquire a new morality along with an improved lifestyle from cash crops and Western development probably has its ideological origins in the speeches and comments of colonial kiaps (government patrol officers) and missionaries (see Guiart 1951). This ideology can still be heard today in the speeches and conversations of Melanesian kiaps, agricultural officers, councilors, magistrates, and politicians, who continue to assign a moral, uplifting function to economic activities like cash crops, trade stores, taxes, school fees, and community labor for the church, school, and council. Perukuma Company has appropriated this official discourse concerning the civilizing effects of development and has merged it with the traditional transformative power of the underground. Dakoa's cult has projected this official discourse into concealed, subterranean voices where its echoes acquired new resonances and new forms of realization. In recontextualizing this official discourse, which ties together moral and economic change, Dakoa's cult has also sought to redirect its processes of change. The officially promised transformative power of money, companies, and cash crops has been displaced into underground terrains of meaning where development came to be developed differently. Here Western models of transformation were merged with traditional schemes for figuring processes of change and metamorphosis—for creating processes of creation. The civilizing transformative processes of pacification, Christianization, and development were localized as they came to be remediated by underground beings who in turn were whitened and Westernized through this newly found association.

The Coming of Council Government

In the mid-1960s, soon after Dakoa began his company, the administration tried to introduce council government. Dakoa opposed this idea, viewing councils as a white man's trick. Dakoa was and is still of the opinion that councils do not have very much meaning. He believes their meaning is not deep, for they do not tap into the true, secret powers controlled by whites that come from inside the ground. Initially, all of the thirteen official villages on Bali joined Dakoa's work, but soon four villages left to join the new system of council government. This led to some bitter conflicts between cult and council followers, conflicts that have left many painful memories. Those conflicts ended only recently, in the early 1990s, when council followers stopped demanding that police arrest and jail Perukuma Company followers for their *bikhet* (pigheadedness), for their stubborn refusal to recognize the authority of council government by attending its meetings and roll calls [*belo*]. In the 1960s and 1970s, the colonial administration was advocating council government. Under the guise of providing local communities with some form of autonomy and self-government, it wanted them to take up some of the pedagogic and practical work of government. Indeed, throughout New Britain, this official attempt to localize Western structures of governmentality was opposed by cargo cult leaders, who often had their own techniques of localization that simultaneously empowered local geographies, customs, and kinship ties. Throughout New Britain, cargo cult leaders denounced councils for creating meaningless extra work, creating prostitution, and undermining the moral order of villages (Lattas 1998:18–19, 67–68). When I asked Dakoa about patrol reports claiming that he had opposed self-government and independence, he told me that this was not so, that he did want these things but that true self-government and independence would come from the ground. It was a different form of localization that Dakoa wanted, namely, forms of autonomy and governmentality that sprang from local ancestors, myths, graves, and clan sites rather than from councils.

Internalizing the Dead

From its beginning in 1964, Perukuma Company was organized not just around commerce but also around moral beliefs concerning the underground, from whom followers received a strict code of ethical conduct involving the four moral principles "love, honor, belief and *harim* [obeying] talk." In terms of how it historicizes itself, Dakoa's movement claims to have received its major influx of ideas in 1973 when the dead came up as American spirits who entered followers' bodies. These underground spirits were led by their boss, by the president of America, a spirit called John F. Kennedy who entered the body of a young man while he was listening to the radio. Dakoa's followers speak of these American spirits as *tevil bilong mipela*—the souls belonging to us. They are also referred to by the Tok Pisin word for maternal relative—*kandere*—which throughout Melanesia is also used as a familiar form of address for strangers. Given that the clan system on Bali Island is patrilineal, one's distant relatives through women belong to another clan, and they provide a convenient way of thinking about both the distance of other countries like America and that distancing of kin brought by death. Indeed, different clans will have their underground wealth brought by different *kandere,* a Pisin word that followers self-consciously pronounce and merge with the English word "country." Here different forms of distance are made to overlap so that the familiar strangers of one's wife's and mother's clans are like the familiar strangers of deceased villagers who have turned white. Cult terms like *kandere* serve to familiarize not only the dead but also whites. The cleavages in the kinship system are used both to understand and to overcome racial cleavages, with this involving a twofold process that racializes kin and familiarizes race. In 1973, this dual process took the form of American spirits who surfaced and entered the bodies of followers. These white ghosts visited living relatives, who offered them food and shelter.

Dakoa's followers believe their cult work pulled these underground relatives into the surface world, where they could be again befriended by the living. These white spirits were quoted as saying: "This work of Dakoa's has pulled us up and we are now one [united]. We will work together. We have come to help you people." For followers, the arrival of American spirits signified their cult's development of a better relationship with the underground, who were said to have been previously dismissed by the surface world as *samting nating* (of little or no account). The Americans came and stayed for about a year, and Dakoa told me: "They came to straighten the work. In the beginning, when I started the work, there weren't many people, but as time went on and the work became strong then they increased." Men and women, boys and girls, young and old, all became possessed, during which they would speak not in local language but mostly in Tok Pisin. This new national language of progress, which had been originally learned and disseminated through Western plantations, schools, and towns, came to encode and articulate a certain whitening of the Melanesian self, whose compromised identity was further embodied in this spectacle of a black body possessed by a white American spirit. A few villagers went further in their claims to have successfully internalized modernity and the power of the dead, for these villagers tried to speak English and Latin, which was taken as further proof that the underground spirits were genuinely white and had access to Western knowledge. These possessions were an alternative way of realizing the movement into the modernity brought by the white man's world without losing the power and involvement of one's own past and dead in the present and the future. For followers, further proof that the newly arrived American spirits were concerned with the welfare of living descendants was provided by followers discovering at graves and *wowumu* sites cargo that had come up from inside the ground.[1] According to Dakoa, "Now, in terms of cargo, everywhere we saw the ground supplying it." When the American spirits left, they told people they were going back into the ground, where they would watch the living. If followers worked the cult strongly, then they would return; only this time they would stay and help villagers to build a new material existence that would include Western-style houses. Followers are still waiting for the return of these American spirits. Many expect them to return in the year 2000.

Dakoa believes that the government secretly allowed these American spirits to come to Bali. Dakoa is here referring to a secret government made up of sympathetic underground white men who conceal their true identity and allegiances from a more hostile government with which the living ordinarily have to deal. Dakoa often speaks of a secret government run by those "inside," by *kandere,* by this more benevolent race of *masta*. This alternative underground state that occasionally surfaces to intervene in the surface world is a state of wish fulfillment whose utopian possibilities and persona subvert the coerciveness of existing state structures. Through an alliance with this benevolent race of underground *masta,* Dakoa's followers subvert the moral authority of whiteness that underpins the demands of a black Melanesian state that is criticized widely for its corruption, inefficiencies, and coerciveness. Not only did Dakoa's work allow American spirits to come to Bali, but Dakoa claims that it has also allowed ordinary Melanesians to travel more frequently to the lands of *ol masta*—like Australia and America.

Reinternalizing the Dead

Dakoa's cult describes itself as a church, and indeed, followers meet each Friday for services—because Jesus was killed on Friday. Jesus is said to be a picture for the suffering of cult followers, whose pain will be repaid by the underground. Some followers speak of a black Christ's body lying in the ground, where its blood forms a bank. These Christian images were also employed in 1974 when followers tried in a different way to reinternalize the dead; followers spoke of this as becoming close and "one" with the dead. In 1974 followers sought to create Bali's own version of the holy communion by visiting the graves of relatives, where they secretly dug up the bones of the dead. Some bones still had flesh on them, and followers told me how they ate the "meat" and drank the "water" or "soup" that dripped from these bones. Dakoa claims they did this so as to gain "power" from the dead, so as to "*kisim*" (receive, take on) the power belonging to the ground: "With this here, they [cult followers] said that they would all drink the water [body fluids] and this would be their power." At the village of Penata, followers waited ten days before digging up a body; they wanted to find meat and fluid, but they did not want the corpse to smell too much through being too badly decomposed. The fluid that dripped from the flesh and bones was described as being like coconut oil. Some followers rubbed it into their eyes so that they could see all that was hidden in the earth. They also drank it so as to no longer be afraid of the dead when they visited cemeteries at night. These actions led to a confrontation with government officials and to the jailing of Dakoa's followers, who were taken to Kimbe along with an arm from a corpse. At Kimbe, followers argued successfully that their actions were traditional custom, which was an exaggeration on their part. Though there had been traditional practices of cannibalism on Bali, they were part of regimes for punishing either transgressors or the captured members of rival warring clans. Today Dakoa claims that this exhumed arm has had its picture placed on cases of cargo and that this is done by the underground, which secretly supplies this cargo as a way of celebrating the importance of Dakoa's work. Here the symbol "handle with care" that is used in international trade is reinterpreted by Dakoa as a secret symbol of his cult's own handiwork.

Many followers saw the digging up and eating of the dead as copying the work of Catholic priests, whom they accuse of seeking to monopolize the graves, bones, corpses, and power of the dead. Dakoa expressed anger to me about whites' seeking to control the burial of corpses on Bali Island. He saw his followers' digging up of the dead as an attempt to regain access to a lost ancestral power that whites had usurped. Dakoa is still suspicious of the Catholic mission, and he told me: "The mission wants us to bury people in its area, but we must bury them in the area belonging to us. We now plant them here." Like many other villagers throughout New Britain, Dakoa believes that the Catholic mission and its priests secretly receive cargo and money from the dead bodies that they bury. It is widely believed that after three days a ghost will appear at a new grave, carrying money that priests often secretly go to collect.

Some of the bones of relatives that Dakoa's followers dug up were taken and stored in domestic dwellings. Many saw themselves as copying the traditional customs of their grandparents, who would bury a relative, wait for the corpse to decompose, and then dig and remove its jaw. Along with some food, this jaw would be kept in a basket inside a house, where the soul of the food would be eaten by the ghost of this deceased relative. Later, if the owner of the house wanted some kind of help, he would tap on this jawbone and ask its ghost for help. This otherworldly form of help is what cult followers sought when they dug up the bodies of dead relatives, only now they wanted to internalize and use the dead to find the white man's lifestyle.

The Four Corners of the Earth

Alongside the production and selling of copra and cocoa, Dakoa's company looks to the earth for new forms of governmentality and new corporate bodies that will incorporate and position villagers differently by reclaiming anew the underground, ancestral past so as to provide a new beginning and a new future. Dakoa's cult has developed a new spatialization of thought and sociality using the underground to resituate the living. Part of the cult's creation of new imaginary geographies for repositioning people and their perspectives involved internalizing the perspective of the underground through the development of a new virtual geography. This is where the abstract space known as "four corners" is read into diverse local practices, beliefs, and sites. This new imaginary geography is sometimes said to be modeled on the compass, and it provides followers with a new domain of meaning—an underground meaning that forms a secret underpinning space that can be read into the diverse aspects of existence. This common abstract space allows a new form of situatedness, a new way of dwelling in the world. It relocates the diverse aspects of everyday life within the realm of a new cartography that amounts to placing existence under a new set of shared circumstances or conditions. Thus, for example, cult followers have a strong understanding of Perukuma Company as part of what is called the "four corners of the ground." This set of four corners consists of: government, company, church, and *lo bilong tumbuna* (the law of the ancestors). Another set of four corners includes the cult's ethical code of "love, honor, belief, and obeying [*harim*] talk." It forms an alternative moral law for living human existence, superior to that offered by the Bible, whites, and their churches, as well as that offered by the customs of one's grandfathers, who are often criticized for their warfare, sorcery, and cannibalism.

At the cult's headquarters, at Nigilani where Dakoa lives, there is a concrete sculpture of a star that has four points, and at its center there are four circles stacked on top of each other so as to form four steps. Dakoa's explanation of this sculpture was this: "It has four corners, it is the four corners of the ground. It is the four corners of the company, the four corners of God." On another occasion, Dakoa told me:

> There are two lines: East-West, North-South.
>
> Those who don't have a lot of knowledge say "God" for these four corners, but with us we say that we follow the compass. We picture it like this: God is North, North is on top, West is America, East is the strength of the ground, now with the South it is us, us black skins. This is the compass.

Here God stands as the opposite double of Melanesians, while America in the West stands as the opposite double to the *wowumu,* who are the "strength of the ground." Dakoa's compass came out of studies that he calls his Five Year Plan, and in the above quote he speaks of it as a substitute for God. This should not surprise us, for like God, it is an underlying, all-encompassing reference point or framework. One of the preachers in Dakoa's cult is a shaman called Tsigomori who was dismissed from the police force for his cargo cult participation. He told me how in dreams he had seen Dakoa's body twisted so as to form a compass, with Dakoa's two legs marking out one axis and his two arms marking out another, intersecting axis. Indeed, one of the cult's beliefs is that the four corners will yield a new God-king for Papua New Guinea, and most followers see Dakoa as that person.

It is not only Dakoa who dreams and hallucinates meetings and conversations with white spirits, for such visitations are frequent and the spirits who visit Dakoa, like his late first wife, will also visit cult mediums known as *profet* (prophet) and other followers. These spirits will often supply new information that will emphasize, elaborate, and develop anew cult doctrines like "four corners." It is significant that Dakoa's cult seized upon an item of Western technology (the compass) to provide the organizing metaphor through which to orient his followers' understandings and relationships, for a compass not only maps out space but also moves people through space. It moves them from where they are in the visible present to new future regions that are currently unseen. A compass also allows people to find their bearings when they are lost, or when there are no immediate, obvious marks through which to navigate or chart a course. This direction-finding device becomes a metaphor for all sorts of other ways of discovering and moving toward unseen regions; like moving toward or into the white man's world or into an underground world of meaning. Dakoa's company seized upon the compass as a way of charting a certain spatialization of relationships using a European model of space, and this was part of the process of internalizing a Western outlook or perspective. It is also true to say that Dakoa was reinventing this sense of what was a European perspective. He saw the masters on the surface of the earth as tricking Melanesians about the true road to the white man's world, which he instead sought to discover through unearthing the perspective of underground whites.

The four corners forms a new blueprint or ground plan, that is, a new organizing scheme that seeks to become what Bourdieu might call a new habitus. Within its new organizing framework, different differences can be resystematized, and to use a phrase of Lévi-Strauss, rendered similar in their differences. Dakoa's movement has many other sets of four corners. One old man, Topres, described how followers built a *bikpela* (large) set of four corners that consisted of four large houses at the cemeteries of four cult villages. Later, Topres was visited by his deceased father, who informed him about another *liklik* (smaller) set of four corners that belonged to each individual; it consisted of their head, ears, eyes, and mouth. Topres quoted his father's ghost as saying:

> This [the four houses] is the big four corners, and it belongs to us all. However, there is this smaller four corners, and it belongs to you as individuals [*wanwan*]. With you, if you follow it, then when something [from the underground] comes up here, you will think about it, and it will be easy for you. Now, if they [underground] put something out into the open, then you will see it, and you can go and take it. It will hide from others. You will hear them [underground] talking, and the two of you will be able to talk together. They can give you something that hides. It is not enough for someone else to see this.

The four corners that belong to each individual are made up of those thoughts, visions, sounds, and talk that go and come back from the underground. The sensual and intellectual apparatus of each individual is respatialized; all of those different ways of apprehending the world that are focused on the head come to be repositioned. The head is reterritorialized into a four-cornered space, and this introduces a clandestine geometry into people's being, with their perceptions and forms of knowledge participating in the hidden underground order of existence. Such beliefs produce a new body image for followers, incorporating the four-cornered scheme into people's bodies as an underground, secret corporeal scheme that allows the underground's knowledge, vision, hearing, and talk to inhabit their being. It is this small four corners within each individual that familiarizes the dead. Topres was told by his father:

> We as individuals have a four corner. However, not everyone knows. I am telling you this so that it will be easy for you, for something [underground cargo] to come up or for [your deceased] fathers to come up or for the strength of the ground [*wowumu*] to come up. It

> [an underground presence] will come up from hiding. It will come up in thinking or it will come up to your eyes or it will come outside into your ears or it will come as talk.

The four corners that belong to the head belong to an individual's knowledge, and it is a certain principle of concealment that has to be maintained in terms of what is received from the ground. According to Topres' father: "This [the small four corners of the head] is taboo [a secret]. I'm going to show you but you must hide it. It will then be easier for you to run into your [deceased] mother and father and into the strength of the ground."

Topres went on to explain to me that one reason Dakoa's work had yet to be completed was because followers had not finished restoring the concrete sculpture at Dakoa's headquarters so that the cult's flagpole could be hoisted onto it. The reshaping and repainting of this four-cornered star would establish a "clean" house where a Melanesian God-king could come to reside. Topres said:

> "With this cement, there is still a lot of work to be done. The timber [mast] for the flag is there and ready, but look at the cement. Its work is not yet finished. We must break its hands [those of the star], and we must work them to be shorter. This has been done, and it looks good, but the women have not yet washed it, and we haven't yet painted it." I spoke to the boss [Dakoa] like that. I also said, "If you told us to hurry up, then the women would quickly wash the cement. The cement would then be painted quickly. It's then that the king and God could together come up quickly." We know about the road. We have seen it, but there are some steps that we haven't reached yet.
>
> Look, you [addressing Lattas] have come here, and we are now capable of standing up the law. However, with the king, is his flag to stand up on the ground or will it be with all this rubbish [speaking disparagingly about the unfinished sculpture]. With the king, we have to clean his house, and then he can come and sit down. He could then sit down happily. He would sit down happily if we worked his house, if we cleaned his area . . . where the flag goes, at the four corners that are the cement. Now, this four corners has meaning, and its meaning is what we run on. Now, with the four corners that is made of cement, its work hasn't yet been completed. If the law stands up on it [the concrete star], then all of the [underground] army, all of the spirits, and all of the strength of the ground could come. The flag will then be out in the open. It will be flying, and it will pull them all to come here, along with all the cargo belonging to us.

It is on the compass that a new law is to be hoisted. It forms the house that will be inhabited by a Melanesian king and god. The compass is like a divine plan, an encompassing totaling scheme within which the governmental structures of king and god—of money and love—can reside. The compass creates a new ordered terrain for flying a flag that symbolizes the hoisting up of a new law of existence, which will be fully completed when it draws the underground to the living. As a spatial scheme, the compass creates a new abstract space of meaning in which all sorts of differences can be remapped and brought together within the promise of new geometrical symmetry that also promises to bring together the underground and surface worlds, Europeans and Melanesians, dead and living.

Names and Power

One of the points that Dakoa makes is that whites exist with three corners; this is reflected in their church and its worship of the Holy Trinity: God-the-father, God-the-son, and God-the-spirit. According to Dakoa, this leaves out a fourth corner, the ancestors *(tumbuna)*. Likewise, when in church services whites make the sign of the cross, they mention "God-the-father, God-the-son, and God-the-spirit," but they fail to mention a fourth corner, which Dakoa believes is an underground spirit belonging to him called CTD. Dakoa speaks of *mipela blakskin* (us black-skins) as composed of four corners consisting of three spirits in the underground and a body or "shirt" in the surface world. Dakoa has reinvented the ground as field of separation and identification for his followers. Rather than situating Melanesians in the white man's triangle, Dakoa has created a new space of thought and identity where he displaces the spiritual trinity into an underground world that belongs to Bali and its past. At the same time as he creates a new spiritual trinity, Dakoa also keeps a "shirt," a fourth corner, in the surface world so as to create the distance that makes possible a personal dialogue with the past. This four corners also allows him to both preserve and reconstitute a certain traditional dialectic between the seen and the unseen aspects of existence. The three underground spirits of Melanesians are sometimes referred to as three namesakes *(wannem)* who are also three *masta*—three Americans. The subterranean souls of the living are certain idealized whites, with followers referring to Americans as *tevil bilong mipela* (our souls). If a person works hard for the cult, then their underground namesakes will also work hard making cargo for that person. Conversely, if a follower is lazy, so will their underground *wannem* be lazy.

In the case of Dakoa, his three underground spirits are referred to as three capital Ds. One of these Ds is the D in GOD, who is also equated with Luangeh, the half-snake and half-human ancestor who ran away from Bali. A second D is equated with a spirit known as LTD, who secretly "bosses" the Papua New Guinea Banking Corporation along with all the other large companies belonging to whites. This spirit is also known as D-supply. The third D is a *wowumu* known as CTD. Through these three capital Ds, Dakoa multiplies his presence and power. He globalizes himself into an encompassing totaling persona. These three underground spirits circulate Dakoa's name so as to refamiliarize the underground and the surface world in a way that will overcome the cleavages separating the dead from the living and Melanesians from whites.

Dakoa gets his advice and help not from his deceased father and mother but from white namesakes who operate as his hidden reserved self and power. Dakoa speaks of his three underground identities as "the strong men of work." When I asked him if he had named these three underground spirits, he replied: "No, it is theirs. If it was a name that we put it would finish but this is a strong law from a long time ago. It [one of these namesakes, a *wowumu*] is a stone."

Apart from capital Ds, Dakoa's spirits also have other names, of which D is a part. These other names consist of capital letters that in turn are abbreviations or acronyms for other words or names. Thus in the case of a D-spirit known as CDT, the letter C stands for Cherry, which is the Christian name that Dakoa received in the early 1960s, when he joined, briefly, the Seventh Day Adventist Mission. The other capitals are D for Dakoa and T for Takaili, which is Dakoa's surname, his father's name. Dakoa understands the name CDT as being further abbreviated in advertisements and signs for Compact Discs, for CDs, that he sees in posters around town and in newspapers. For him, these advertisements are secretly celebrating him and his work; but he is also puzzled about why they keep leaving off the T, for his father's name. One of Dakoa's other underground spirits is LTD, whose name is an acronym made up of L for Luangeh, T for Takaili, and D for Dakoa. LTD is said to be the secret boss of all the companies in the surface world, and this is why his name is found as an abbreviation at the end of the names of large corporations. Dakoa explained to me that this capital D known as LTD had the job of ensuring that large companies remained financially successful and did not go bankrupt. In secretly containing Dakoa's initials, the corporate abbreviation "Ltd." is a secret form of homage to Dakoa and his power. Indeed, it is because large corporations are secretly attached to Dakoa's name and cult work that they are successful. Those corporations "capitalize" on his capitals.

Capitalism, Companies, and Corporations

Dakoa claims that when he was first forming his company he went and asked the government for permission and the government agreed and helped him by officially registering Perukuma Company. The Australian colonial official who did the necessary paperwork is seen to be the underground capital D known as LTD. I was told that when this spirit came into the surface world, he changed *(goligoli)* into a *masta* so he could help Dakoa to create a company like the ones that whites used to make their money "come up." Perukuma Company is directed to the dead and the "strength of the ground"; it is a form of ritual labor that will bind the underground to the living. As Dakoa put it, "We started up a company and the company has cleared all the roads. They are all completely clear. . . . Our work also joined onto some of the talk belonging to our ancestors when they worked custom to the ground. Now we also do this, like our ancestors did." The company that followers are working on top is also being worked in the underground by American spirits, only there it is not cash crops but cargo that is being worked. In the underground, the true value of company labor is being realized anew; there the underground makes up for the discrepancy in price that followers encounter when they see that the monetary returns on their copra and cocoa often bear little relationship to the work they put into their cash crops. Dakoa has also thought a great deal about the difference between the local price received in Papua New Guinea and the world price for Bali's cash crops. This difference between local and global prices is assimilated by him to the different remunerations offered by the surface world and the underground. The world price fascinates Dakoa because it is the price that comes from other countries, from *kandere,* that is from the spirits of the dead. Dakoa explained that in Papua New Guinea copra, oil palm, coffee, and timber would be bought by masters for a small price, but later it would be sold overseas to *kandere* for a much higher price. According to Dakoa, the profit from this difference is being collected by underground masters who will later bring it to the surface world as *kaikai* (food), which is also a cult euphemism for cargo.

Dakoa is waiting for the secret profits of Melanesian labor to be returned by the underground. He told me: "They haven't given it back to us yet. Later, they will give back a huge pay to us." Underground masters were also quoted as informing followers that later they would be given a special number to put on bags of their copra, which would now be delivered directly to the underground, where it would be bought at the overseas price belonging to *kandere.*

In their work for Perukuma Company, Dakoa's followers see themselves as secretly accumulating money with underground white men "so that we have enough money inside." Dakoa claims that for all the years his followers had worked, so had the underground also worked with them. His followers' unpaid labor was described as them building up an unpaid debt with the underground:

> Some *masta* [underground white men] have also worked money inside of these years [that cult followers have been working]. . . . All these years, they [underground whites] have been gathering money and we have not yet received any pay. We have been working the company; we have also been working with the ground. We go and work every night and we work reports [about meetings for the dead].

Until relatively recently, when its offices, safes, and books were destroyed by council followers, Dakoa's cult kept very detailed records of what work followers did: how many of them shelled coconuts, smoked the coconut flesh, stacked the copra into bags, cut grass, or worked in the new cocoa fermentary. This unpaid labor was written down in books by a company *kuskus* (secretary), who also recorded the unpaid labor of those doing *wok-nait* (night work). The latter refers to a special line of men and women whose job it is to travel around at night visiting graves and *wowumu* sites where they seek contact with the underground. When I asked Dakoa why they kept such detailed records, he explained that those in the underground were doing the same. When followers record an entry in their book, so does the underground also record that same entry in their own separate book. We have here a world of double bookkeeping, of doubled entries, which Dakoa explained to me as the need for the surface world and the underground to be aware of each other and to mirror each other's labors and processes of aggregation:

> Supposing we gather together for something belonging to the company, like to work a feast over something, then the *kuskus* [clerk, company secretary] must come and collect the number belonging to us [the number of followers gathered together]. . . . Now supposing you are the *kuskus* who is outside, well there is another *kuskus* who is inside, who *poromanim* [accompanies, is paired with, doubles] you, so that you come up as two. Now, everyone thinks there is just one, but there are two.

In the above quote, we see a certain fetishization of bookkeeping and counting in which cult feasts and meetings have their numbers recorded in duplicate so that the power of Western forms of knowledge can be assimilated and derived from the power of an underground world that is given its own alternative set of accounts. This underground secretary does more than rerecord the labors of his surface double, for he also supplements the pay or reward that will be received by the living in a future world. Some of that reward is received today in the form of cargo found at graves and *wowumu* sites as part of D-supply.

At meetings held in different villages on Friday, the total number of followers who attend is recorded by cult leaders and passed on to Dakoa and his secretary. The cult's secretary also records the taxes paid by followers to Dakoa. There are separate taxes for cult leaders, "work night" personnel, and women. These taxes allow followers to work successfully with the dead, and they ensure that people's underground cargo remains secure. The taxes were described to me by one cargo cult prophet, Devoku, as a process of "registering" with the underground. The writing down of taxes transmits the information to the underground, where it acquires added significance. I would argue that one reason bookkeeping was perceived as a form of creative power was because all processes of counting create new larger totalities. Processes of tallying and aggregation create new holistic meanings, and these become a way of figuring other social and cultural processes of unification—like followers coming together in acts of love that will then allow them to abolish their own differences in the surface world and also with the underground so that they can all move toward becoming one. It is through bigger and bigger totaling numbers that oneness will be achieved in the surface world, with this being a precondition for unity with the underground.

The cult's account-keeping practices do more than just tally up facts and figures, for they also extend and augment numerical processes of totalization by giving them another subterranean presence. The underground duplicates the marks of the living, reinscribing them in an alternative material world; such activity is part of the underground's longstanding function as a mirror world that reproduces, retraces, and completes the labors of the living. When I asked Dakoa to explain this double recordkeeping, he did so by saying that those in the underground and in the surface world needed to become "one," and in doing so they would become God. Dakoa spoke of followers honoring those in the underground, who in turn would honor them back, and these forms of mutual acknowledgment would overcome the separation of "inside people" from "outside people" so they could all become "one" and thus God.

The underground mirrors back the respectful concern shown by the surface world toward its reality, and it is through this mirror relationship of mutual regard that the surface world can become something more than itself, that it can trace itself out anew as a larger, more encompassing unity. The mirror space of the underground allows new connections and identifications to be established across diverse relations characterized by distance. In other words, this mirror relationship regrounds and merges various relationships of difference (white versus black, dead versus living, past versus present, surface versus underground, inside versus outside) that followers struggle to overcome through mimetic activities that make these various differences participate in a new kind of symmetry.

Like other ways of tracing the world, books are a way of marking and capturing the presence of a reality even though its moment might have passed. It is no accident that books were taken up as a way of capturing the alternative reality of the dead, the past, and whites, for books do create and preserve an alternative world of meaning. In offering another material existence for meanings, intentions, and desires, books generate a sense of capturing the alternativeness and otherness of those other material worlds of inscription inhabited by the dead, the past, whites, and the future. Books offer the promise of stabilizing meanings, of being able to accumulate and totalize meanings into new, larger domains of significance. The fascination of Europeans with tiny details, with recording and accumulating minor facts of sociality (such as when people were born or died, how many people live in a village, and how many coconuts they have), was seized upon by Dakoa's cult as offering new, alternative ways of knowing and objectifying one's community that seemed to approach the alternative knowing gaze of the underground. Perukuma Company's books contain detailed records of the dates when individuals were born or died. They also record the total number of births and deaths in cult villages. These books were said to be like the annual census lineups carried out by colonial administrators. It is a source of pride to cult followers that Perukuma Company keeps collecting these census records even though they are no longer collected by an inefficient Melanesian administration. These books refetishize the white man's knowledge while also displacing and remirroring that white knowing gaze into forms of objectification residing in the underground. It is the constitutive ordering power of a mirror relationship that is displaced into the creative powers and look of the underground, where the power of a mirror to create subjects is merged with the creative effects of a European pedagogic gaze and with the more familiar creative role of the traditional gaze of the dead.

It is a certain way of being known by the ordering gaze of the white other, which is appropriated and familiarized into an empowering subterranean gaze that will help to reorder and make people other than themselves. It is a new way of displacing, reobjectifying, and governing the self, which is realized in the otherness of Western bookkeeping knowledge and which now becomes assimilated in the remaking creative power of an underground gaze that also traditionally offered its own techniques of displacement, objectification, and governmentality. There is a marrying together of external perspectives for seeing the self and one's community.

I mentioned earlier that the cult recorded not just work on cash crops but also the night work of traveling around to graves and *wowumu* sites. Company books record followers' nocturnal experiences at these sites—if, for example, they heard a noise or someone speak, or felt someone move past them, or smelled an old person go by, or maybe even saw something like a bank or a person from the underground. The cult has redefined the meaning of work by merging followers' unpaid labor on cash crops with the unpaid labor of "night work." Indeed, all cult activities were said to be secretly paid for in the underground. Attendance at cult meetings had pay, and so did the punishments suffered by cult followers—their beatings and imprisonment. Cult taxes and cash crop labor for Perukuma Company was described by Dakoa as allowing the living to honor those inside, who in turn received [*kisim*] the "heavies" (suffering and woes) of followers as a debt to be repaid.

We see here the emergence of a new moral arithmetic associated with death, where the dead come to have their traditional forms of moral governance merged with the new value structures and forms of objectification provided by commodities, money, and bookkeeping. I interpret Dakoa's cult as partly drawing upon the structures of moral accountability that Christianity developed with respect to the imaginary geographies of Heaven and Hell. The cult has displaced those moral structures into the merged worlds of money and the underground so as to create another way of measuring and materializing that ability to work collectively which will draw the underground to the living. Here those new ways of being evaluated and objectified that are provided by money, whites, and Heaven and Hell are displaced into the externality of an underground world that contains its own familiarized masters who are aware of their true debts to the living. Expressed in cult notions of future pay for diverse forms of work is a certain totaling mathematization of the world and value that is part of the monetary logic of capitalism. It was Marx who analyzed capitalism as merging together and as rendering commensurate different use values within an encompassing common mathematization of value that he called exchange value. This takes place through money, which renders all goods and services measurable and proportionate within a common numerical structure of value. I see Dakoa's cult as creating a religion out of capitalism, both out of its fetishization of commodities and out of its encompassing mathematics, which Dakoa has transformed into a hidden moral arithmetic. Dakoa takes the symbolizing and totalizing possibilities of numbers and money and makes them part of a hidden underground moral economy that in its secrecy and powers of disclosure acquires an aura of truth and sacredness.

According to Dakoa, the money accumulating in the underground for the "heavies" of followers will be repaid when the "New Heaven" arrives. Along with being an example of the pervasiveness of the West's monetary economy, such beliefs are also a way of displacing the money economy into a new symbolic realm that partly suspends its operations while also acknowledging and conferring upon it a hyper significance. The world of money has its totaling governance acknowledged but also remade by having its influence permeate and come back from an underground world of primordial ancestors and deceased relatives where it comes back as a gift or a compensation payment. The logic of capitalism, where money mathematizes diverse forms of labor and products, is embraced as an empowering act that is grounded in the magic of numbers to measure and aggregate diverse human commitments and efforts. Yet in Dakoa's cult, money is not really fully part of the rationalization of everyday life, even though all activity is given a monetary quality. Rather, money is recognized for the mythological totaling dimension of value giving and creating that it obtains (see Mimica 1988). To the extent that money is merged with traditional mythic accounts focused on the power of the underground, it is because money, like the earth, is an all-encompassing domain of meaning and value creation that assumes mythic determinative proportions over people's lives. It is through working with these two all-encompassing causal domains—money and earth—that Perukuma Company will create a Melanesian king, which for most followers is Dakoa himself.

Tender and the Money Supply

The cult's fetishism of number is also expressed in its organization around the principle of four corners. From underground masters, Dakoa has received knowledge of how Bali Island is made up of four corners that hold four significant sites of cargo. Three of these are mountains that are said to be the three humped scrolls of the serpent God Luangeh. The fourth corner is a coastal cliff face known traditionally as Tender, which is to be found near the village of Penata. Followers believe that the three mountains are the secret origins of the wealth of three major corporations operating in Papua New Guinea. One mountain—Kumbu—is reported to be the secret underground origins of the Burns Philp Company. At this mountain was born Dakoa's grandfather, who later became the spirit LTD. At Kumbu, there is also a stone named Bimbimi, which Dakoa claims is where masters really go to make the "savings" that B-P, Burns Philp, often advertises:

> It belongs to the inside, this talk [knowledge] does. It [Burns Philp] belongs to the inside; it isn't just an empty company [*kampani nating*]. It comes from the ground. All of the masters go and "save" through it. . . . Now, with D, this D who belongs to working the companies, he belongs there, to this area, but this is a long story. . . . He died and he went and acquired this company. He then went and put it in the area at Rabaul and they call it B-P [Burns Philp]. It is Bimbimi. That is its name, of this road, of this company that belongs to all *masta*.

There is a certain doubling of names and identity going on here wherein we have the local name belonging to the ground and the public names that circulate in the corporate world of *ol masta*. According to Dakoa, his grandfather—LTD—put the public name of B-P [Burns Philp] onto the stone Bimbimi so as to hide its power: "He took this name and put it and he straightened everything like that so that other people could not recognize it [*luksave*]." Dakoa went on to tell me how in Rabaul there is a large company called the New Guinea Company, which on Bali is a stone called Ambueteketeh. A third large company that secretly belongs to Bali is the chain of supermarket stores known as Steamships, which is really a local mountain called Chiori, but "when you go on top, they all call it Steamships." These three companies have dual identities, for their public identity in the surface world conceals another made of stone that is their underground Bali identity. The inside and outside meaning of these companies, their surface world and underground presence, is also their participation in the creation of a new empowering cartography of places for Bali Island, which partly takes the form of their participation in the concealed geometry known as "four corners." The fourth corner of this underground economy is the Papua New Guinea Banking Corporation (PNGBC) whose money comes from a local cliff face known traditionally in local language as Tender. It was after the other three companies surfaced that the inside of this cliff face came on top (into the surface world) so as to become the new national bank of Papua New Guinea.

I was told that when underground power came outside, *ol masta* changed its name so that it was no longer called Bimbimi, Ambueteketeh, Chiori, or Tender. White men changed its character so that it became a company that seemed to belong exclusively to them. They did this so as to cover up all the meanings and all the roads to wealth and power. Dakoa believes that the subterranean secrets of Bali are not totally obliterated or concealed by the public domains of meanings that whites put into circulation but rather that Bali's power and wealth is secretly captured and disclosed as a cryptic message in the advertisements, names, and meanings of corporate capitalism. Thus underground masters have pointed out to Dakoa how the cliff face known as Tender has its name printed on monetary notes circulating in Papua New Guinea because it secretly supplies those notes: "The name of this stone supplies money, it supplies it on top of the ground." Dakoa also asked me to look at a five-kina note, and he pointed to a very minute D above the word "Governor." This capital D was said to be D-supply, and along with the word "Governor" underneath, it marked secretly the fact that Dakoa would become the king of Papua New Guinea. The money issued from Tender was secretly circulating his name so as to make him into "the last king of the last country." Dakoa also claimed that the underground was protecting him by not fully revealing his name; it was hiding his importance by revealing him only as a very minute capital D. As Dakoa put it, "They are hiding it a little bit. They don't want it to come up clear too much and for us to get buggered up. They're hiding it."

With respect to the cliff face that supplied these notes, Dakoa explained how some of the ways whites talked about tender were similar to his cult's understandings of the site known as Tender. Discussions by whites about tendering something for public sale are seized upon as part of that movement of goods and wealth into the public domain that the cult seeks to enact. Such coincidences of meaning fascinate people and confirm followers' exegetical practices that posit the world as made up of two terrains of meaning, with a surface outside layer partly concealing but also partly revealing an underground inside layer. The underground objectifies and mediates hermeneutic practices that posit the world as doubled over in allegory and secrecy. These hermeneutic practices are also confirmed by the interpretive techniques of Christianity that make use of biblical allegories and parables. The cult's measured forms of disclosure are also confirmed by the acronyms employed in Western advertising and by a government administration that has its own culture of abbreviations for positions of power, for it has its DC (district commissioner) and ADC (assistant district commissioner).

Dakoa has often told me how the large sum of money held by *ol masta* didn't belong to them but to Bali villagers, for it had originated from their ground, from the cliff face known as Tender. When I asked Dakoa why Bali villagers had not received this money, he replied, "Receive [*kis*] it for what reason? It can stay there and it can go out. It can supply, and it can go to all the banks. Later, we will receive it. Later, when we gather together. All of the banks, it [Tender] supplies them." Dakoa explained that Bali's money was under the control of *kandere,* who were using it to supply other banks and whites. Dakoa has been informed by underground masters that the Papua New Guinea Banking Corporation is a global bank and that Dakoa's name, along with those of his followers, resides with this bank as its true owners. The Banking Corporation is controlled secretly by Bali's *wowumu* and underground dead, who have warned cult followers not to boast of their cult's banking successes. When colonial kiaps counseled cult followers not to be too boastful of their company's successes, this was interpreted as whites warning followers about the concerns of American spirits. In silencing the boastful claims of the living, the underground leads followers to live in concealed worlds of meaning where they know the true source of wealth as residing with them but are unable to reveal this. The underground here is a trope for objectifying and grounding meaning, but it is also a way of instituting a world of clandestine meanings that is lived in by cult followers as their alienation from others in the surface world. The underground becomes that concealed domain of truth and origins which separates followers from others. It is the source of a secret existence, of those hidden proud truths that followers reserve for themselves as part of a pact of solidarity that they share with each other and the ground. Dakoa quoted an Australian kiap as saying: "You cannot work the money to come up clear too much for *kandere* will hit you and he will hit me." The kiap reportedly said this in response to a plan by cult followers to collect money from the underground and then use it to fill a forty-five-gallon drum so that nonbelievers could be convinced of the power of followers' cult work. Dakoa interpreted this kiap as saying, "Hey, this is taboo. You cannot work it in the open, for they [in the underground] will cross you and they will cross me." Cult followers were also reportedly ordered to count any money they found and to keep a note of it on a blackboard. Dakoa claims that this warning by *kandere* not to reveal underground secrets led his cult to conceal its work more actively:

> We no longer worked it outside too much. We worked it and hid it, hid it and hid it. It is like this: when we work here, we hide it. When we work with trees [named trees that are *wowumu*], we hide it. When we work with the *pom* [cult sites for addressing the underground], we hide it, for it would not be good if all *kandere* became cross. We have given it up [being proud, being open about cult work]. We don't let it come up into the open.

Finally, cargo cults rework traditional elucidatory practices focused on the underground by racializing the dialectic between inside and outside, aboveground and underground, body and spirit, seen and unseen. The world of race relations with its separate dichotomized lifestyles, with its black and white worlds of meaning, gives rise to a search for similar dichotomized differences between other terrains of meaning that are grounded in positing a separation of the seen from the unseen. Here the different forms of knowledge underpinning race relations come to be reconstituted within an interpretative desire to map and read one explicit space of meaning in terms of another that is less revealed and more implicit. All sorts of tropes that involve some layering of meaning have this relationship dichotomized, spatialized, and racialized. Tropes that involve a private versus a public meaning, a hidden versus a visible meaning, will have this relationship reobjectified through the use of the black-white dichotomy to remap the topography of these different surfaces of meaning. Linguistic practices for doubling meanings, like those employed in allegory, acronyms, metaphor, and parables, become susceptible for incorporation into this domain of racialized differences, which grounds itself in the topographical relationship of a visible outside surface world of meaning versus an invisible, inside, underground world of meaning.

Note

1. *Wowumu* are known in *pisin* as *masalai* and *strong bilong graun* (strength of the ground). They are immortal beings with all kinds of strange bodies who have existed ever since the ground was first formed. They are known for their power to change their appearance and to even take on the form of a white man or woman.

9

From Totemic Space to Cyberspace

Transformations in Sepik River and Aboriginal Australian Myth, Knowledge, and Art

Eric Kline Silverman

In many respects, the European gaze over the indigenous peoples of Australia and Melanesia engendered modern anthropology and its early concerns with the essences of human sociality such as totemism, moieties, and gift exchange. Recently, though, there has been little systematic comparison between Aboriginal Australia and the Sepik River of Papua New Guinea. The present chapter redresses this lacuna by discussing "traditional" and "modern" modes of identity, embodiment, and knowledge. I particularly focus on the Eastern Iatmul village of Tambunum, middle Sepik River.

I begin with totemic space, landed personhood, gendered time, and the politics of disclosure. I then turn to tourist art, commercial music, literacy, copyright, acrylic paintings, and the Internet. In this way, I identify continuities between tradition and modernity that, moreover, increasingly express the paradoxes and anxieties of transcultural hybridity and, to paraphrase Clifford (1997), "ex-centric nativism."

Totemic Space and Selves

For Eastern Iatmul, the primordial universe was aquatic. When a procreative wind stirred the waters, dry land surfaced from beneath the waves, which contained the "totemic pit" *(tsagi wangu)*. Ancestor heroes emerged from this chthonic womb and generated the grounded cosmos through totemic toponymy along various migration "paths" *(yembi)*. Each patrilineal descent group corresponds to specific "paths" of names and a largely contiguous section of the cosmic landscape. But totemism is not solely a collective memory of cosmogony that is inscribed on the landscape, for it is also embodied in the very identities of living people who are named after totemic entities.

As I have recently discussed elsewhere (Silverman 1997a:114–117), Eastern Iatmul totemism *(tsagi)* resembles the Aboriginal dreamtime.[1] Both cosmologies refer to a prehuman era in which anthropomorphic and theriomorphic ancestral beings created the physical and moral landscapes. Both cosmologies have similar themes: onomastic topogenesis, ancestral travel, a landscape of tracks or "strings" (Rose 1992: 52), and spatialized time (e.g., Munn 1969; Williams 1986, chapter 2; Rose 1992; Morphy 1995). But there is an important distinction.

All cosmologies, of course, alter in accordance with the praxis of social life. But the dreamtime seems averred by Aborigines to be a "single, unchanging, timeless source" (Myers 1986:52; cf. Munn 1970: 144; Williams 1986:49–51)—an "everywhen" (Stanner 1956:205). By contrast, Eastern Iatmul rarely envision a fixed cosmos, a distinction that exists on the level of local ideology (see also Silverman 1996:42–45). In the oft-noted conservative worldview of the dreamtime, ultimate stasis underlies apparent historical change (e.g., Stanner 1963: 253–254; Maddock 1972; Morton 1989:289–292). Eastern Iatmul, however, view their cosmology in terms of pluralism, disjunction, and contradiction. Hence, the totemic position of Europeans was less of a conceptual puzzle than it was for the fixed, Aboriginal dreamtime (Sharp 1952; Worsley 1955, 1967).[2]

In Tambunum, the identification between persons and their totemic namesakes is "consubstantial" (Harrison 1990:48). Since names were instantiated at specific places during mythic migrations, persons also identify with topographic features, broader spatiotemporal "paths" across the landscape, and other selves—past, contemporary, future—whose patronymics derive from the same ancestral travels. These totemic, mythic, and spatial identifications instance diffuse or "partible" personhood (Strathern 1988). This way, as Weiner (1991:196–198) argues for Papua New Guinea and Australia, human lives are iterative *and* creative, at once tracing the paths of past beings *and* leaving traces from their own unique movements and actions (see also Wagner 1986:19–23).

Aboriginal Australians also homologize personhood, totemism, and land (e.g., Munn 1970, 1973a, 1973b; Myers 1986; Williams 1986; Morton 1987, 1989; Layton 1995; Morphy 1995). But here, too, there is a key difference. Many Aboriginal cultures "ground" personhood through conception, which is attributed to totemic beings—unborn children, spirit-children, and so on—who inhabit specific locations (Stanner 1965:232; Montagu 1974; Tonkinson 1978; Williams 1986: 31; Morton 1989). In Tambunum, totemic crocodile spirits *(waiwainjiimot)* are said to determine human pregnancy. Although these beings may be associated with specific locations, conception is not similarly spatialized. Instead, the Eastern Iatmul anchor personhood to the landscape through patrilineal names and associated totemic "paths." In the Sepik, then, names mediate between identity and the landscape, whereas in Aboriginal Australia personhood is directly tied to the ground. Likewise, the dreamtime is an immediate and omniscient "presence" in Aboriginal life (e.g., Rose 1992:205) while, for Eastern Iatmul, mythic-historic power suffuses the world through names.

For Eastern Iatmul, too, topographic features are important links to the past only insofar as they have totemic names, which themselves embody ancestral potency. For Australian Aborigines, the landscape itself has "spiritual charisma" (Berndt 1984:177; Rose 1992:46; Swain 1993). As a result, the dreamtime is often said to exemplify the ecological "wisdom" of indigenous peoples—a claim that is frequently deployed as a critique of European resource extraction (e.g., Rose 1992; see also Sackett 1991). Eastern Iatmul, however, like the Wola of the Southern Highlands (Sillitoe 1993), are deeply ambivalent about their environment, especially the Sepik River. It is so vast and swift, so powerful and (re)generative, so dangerous and eroding, that its waters will prevail over the detritus of human activity.

Disputed Spaces and Selves

The relationship between identity, cosmology, and totemic "place" is particularly evident in land disputes. Australia, of course, unlike Papua New Guinea, was a "settler" rather than a "conquered" colony. Through the doctrine of *terra nullius* (land inhabited/owned by nobody) and the imposition of English common law on the Australian landscape, Aboriginal legal principles were erased outright. However, recent legal challenges and legislative actions have eroded *terra nullius* by affirming native land title as a legally protected "interest" that coexists with common law tenure holdings such as national parks, Crown possessions, and pastoral leases (Tehan 1997; see also Gray 1993; Tully 1994). These include the 1992 High Court decision in *Mabo v. State of Queensland,* 1993 Commonwealth *Native Title Act,* 1996 Wik decision, and the Native Title Amendment Bill of 1998.[3] Australian Aborigines, as they pursue land reclamation, use dreamtime knowledge and mythic cartography to negotiate with the state (see Layton 1995; Whittaker 1994).

In the Sepik, totemic knowledge can also provide a foundation for legal action. But the colonial history of the Sepik, largely a matter of outmigratory labor rather than land alienation, was vastly different from the post-1788 Aboriginal experience. Hence these cases have so far mainly concerned village-level disputes. Here is one example.

In 1988 Tambunum neared completion of a tourist guesthouse. The project was negotiated between Australian entrepreneurs and a group of elder men who are generally recognized to be the legitimate "voice" of the patriclan that claims the guesthouse location. These men also affixed their signatures and other authorial inscriptions onto a legal contract. The legitimacy of this written document, however, was called into question by a junior man who was excluded from the deliberations and contractual agreement. His express goal during the ensuing totemic debate was not material or cash benefits but the mere public acknowledgment that his mythic-historic ancestors created the guesthouse location (Silverman 1997a:103–104).

The guesthouse is built on a point of land named Agumurl, which is an important spatiotemporal node in the mythic history of the Shui Aimasa patriclan. Agumurl, a location that is now defined by the intersection of tourism and totemism, is claimed by the hereditary "father" of the Shui Aimasa patriclan, an aging and erudite man named Agumoimbnage. The phonemic similarity between the names of the man and the place are, in this context, not insignificant. When the junior rival argued that his totemic ancestors created the location and bestowed a different name than Agumurl, he effectively erased Agumoimbnage's totemic identity by denying the existence of this topographic personification.

In scale and urgency, this Eastern Iatmul debate hardly compares to the mining and logging disputes elsewhere in Papua New Guinea and Australia.[4] Nevertheless, it illustrates a central motif of premodern and contemporary social life in both regions: the relationship between cosmology, topogenesis, and personal identity.

Embodied Cosmos, Gendered Time

Eastern Iatmul and Aboriginal Australians also tie images of the body to their respective cosmologies. In both regions, as Weiner (1995a) elegantly shows for Papuan mythology, embodiment is a mode of thought that intertwines sexuality, space, and movement, often through metaphors of detachment and incorporation that evince Strathern's (1988) notion of cross-sexed or androgynous gender.[5] Cosmological temporality, too, is embodied, especially when mythic and ritual images of masculine stasis are encompassed by feminine dissolution.

For Eastern Iatmul, planting is a reproductive metaphor that transforms female fertility into the masculine realm of totemism and ritual. Mythic histories and genealogies enumerate long lists of locations where male ancestors interchangeably established villages *(ngepma)* and planted trees, especially coconut palms *(tupma)*. This association of male creation with landed social life contrasts with the undifferentiated and aquatic state of the primordial cosmos. Progressive or successive cosmological time, we could say, unfolds as an imposition of masculine structure onto feminine water.

In Tambunum, bones are said to derive from paternal semen, whereas the surrounding soft and fleshy parts of the body gel from maternal blood. The "backbone" of the human skeleton is explicitly likened to patriliny: the spine and pelvis are respectively labeled the "father bone" *(nyait ava)* and the "grandfather bone" *(nggwail ava)*. Together, the compound term *nyai-nggwail* refers to a patriline's totemic ancestors, names, and sacra. Social structure is also vegetative in addition to somatic. Patrilineal groups are imaged as tree trunks, branches, shoots, rhizomes, various types of root systems, and seedlings (see also Bateson 1936:94, 249; Wassmann 1991:72, 179; Rumsey, chapter 4 above). Women, through marriage, birth, and patrilocal residence, are likened to vines that creep between trees, as well as to birds and pollinating butterflies. Here we can clearly see the relationship between cosmology, embodiment, sexual reproduction, and the "dehiscence and caducity"—the fertile "bursting" and reproductive dropping off of a plant's germinal organs (Weiner 1995a). This way, too, the masculine structure of social life is enveloped by images of the feminine.

Land has multiple cosmological embodiments. As a single-sexed entity, land is a male crocodile spirit. It is also a floating maternal grass island *(agwi)*. But, in some contexts, land is a heterosexual union: a feminine island rests atop a masculine crocodile (Silverman 1996). Land can, however, also be cross-sexed when, as Wassmann (1991:98) notes, the crocodile and island are totemically equivalent. In one ritual, the crocodilian creature brandishes a male canoe paddle and pursues the feminine island, who is pregnant with eggs of dry land, in order to direct and contain her fertility. Male landed creation, in most of these cosmological figurations, is in some manner tied to female fertility.

Yet the things men create—houses, trees, and villages—are continuously threatened by the endless erosion of the female river (Silverman 1997a). In this sense, the alpha and omega of the Eastern Iatmul cosmos is feminine water rather than the masculine word of totemism. As the river flows, it regresses male social time back toward the pretotemic, womblike, aquatic state of the cosmos.[6] What can men do to resist this watery fate? Simply rebuild houses, stage rituals, chant totemic names, and, like their ancestral counterparts, plant trees.

At the beginning of a funerary rite, for example, men erect a patriclan "father tree" *(nyait mi)* outside the cult house. This image symbolizes the androcentric genealogical and totemic continuity of the clan. It opposes the somatic decay of death, which is obliquely associated with femininity. But the masculine "father tree" incorporates a stalk of totemic bamboo, which symbolizes the secret flutes *(wainjiimot)* of the male cult whose ritual utterances, as it were, proclaim men's exclusive control over magical fertility and sociocosmic reproduction. Men, however, purloined the flutes from women in the primal past. The "father tree" is thus androgynous: phallic uterus and uterine phallus. It also defines masculinity in terms of the reproductive powers of the female body. Furthermore, the "father tree" is an arboreal affirmation of masculine stasis amid a feminine river that threatens to encompass male ancestral creation and the illusion of structure in its waters. Yet the feminine ultimately prevails, since the names of the flute melodies, and the mellifluous sounds themselves, evoke the flow of riverine tides and seasonal floods.

The mythic importance of sexuality, gender, and bodily detachment and incorporation is particularly evident in the myth of sago. The origins of this consummate Sepik repast lay on the body of an old, repulsive woman who plucked fetid boils from her skin and threw them onto the ground. These disembodied sores spawned sago palms. But the pith of these primal trees resisted transformation into edible food until after an act of copulation atop the sago-producing apparatus. Once the genital fluids of heterosexuality dripped into the starchy mixture, humans were able to cook and consume nutritive sago. In local ideation, sago is a preeminent symbol of maternal nurture, the source of vitality for men's bodies and Eastern Iatmul culture. Yet this nourishment derived from an anti-maternal figure and an act of sexuality that otherwise depletes men of their strength and hastens somatic decay. Similarly, male ritual revolves around sacra that were once owned by ancestresses. And men can only oppose but never triumph over the watery dissolution of the river and aquatic time.

The dreamtime also envisions cosmic creation through idioms of gender and everted human sexuality (Munn 1970:153–156; Morton 1989; Rose 1992:42; Morphy 1995:197; Weiner 1995a:54–57). Alimentary images of swallowing and regurgitation are common (Munn 1969; Hiatt 1975), as are notions of arboreal phalli and chthonic wombs (Morton 1987:106). Aboriginal Australians, too, often define masculinity in terms of disembodied female reproductive powers, which are claimed by men and incorporated into their somatic, mythic, and ritual bodies (Hiatt 1971; Morton 1987; Shapiro 1989). But as Morton (1987:115–116) argues, largely after Munn (1970), Aboriginal cosmologies also cycle bodies between various states of being—corporeal and ancestral, female and male, ritual and parturient.

Likewise, Aboriginal cosmologies inscribe androgynous procreation onto the landscape. In the Roper River area, for example, defloration formerly occurred with a ritual boomerang, "its shape so elusively suggestive of both phallus and vagina, each imperceptibly turning into the other as result of the obtuse open curves of the boomerang" (Weiner 1995a:55–56). These androgynous sexual and procreative objects, incorporated within the human body, were also etched with cartographic designs that traced the dreamtime journeys of beings who created the landscape.

Aboriginal cosmological time, much like totemic temporality in the Sepik, juxtaposes masculine land with feminine water, erosion, and undifferentiation (Stanner 1963:270; Myers 1986:52). Indeed, time is embodied. Munn (1969) identifies conceptual linkages between death, menstruation, sexuality, seaward flood waters and inland river tides, and "the alternation between the wet season (swallowing) and the dry season (vomiting)." In the end, as it were, it often appears that the feminine prevails, much as it does in the Sepik. In Yarralin cosmology, where death is likened to a feminine "washing out" (Rose 1992:209), seasonal rains cleanse the maternal earth by "erasing" the traces of temporal events, and vast cycles of cosmological dreamtime floods wash over ordinary temporality with eternity (Rose 1992:217 and chapter 5 above).

Swain (1993:46–48), too, suggests a form of embodied Aboriginal time that is rooted in menstrual and lunar rhythms. Yet I disagree with Swain that Aboriginal ritual foregrounds the body in order to subsume it under the fecundity of place (see also Lattas 1996; Munn 1996). Rather, space and body interpenetrate through a mode of embodied thought wherein, as Weiner (1995a:29) suggests, the prevailing image is of "flows which are contained, halted, or momentarily encapsulated," from which new forms—persons, groups, ancestors—"emerge which swallow, halt, or encapsulate the other ones."

Knowledge Disclosed and Concealed

In Tambunum, the esoteric nature of totemism is maintained by the sheer number of polysyllabic names—estimated by Bateson (1936:222) to be in the tens of thousands—and a highly metaphoric language known only to ritual specialists (Bateson 1932:404, 417; Wassmann 1991:63–67). Semantic complexity is locally understood through a stratigraphic metaphor. Each totemic name actually consists of a "large name" *(numa tsa)* linked to a "little name" *(mak tsa)*. For the most part, Eastern Iatmul are hesitant about uttering the names of other descent groups without express permission. But while most "large names" are nonetheless public knowledge, the public disclosure of "small names" is carefully moderated, since they often embody considerable magical potency.

Public names and knowledge are known as *aiwat nyangiit* or "external speech," while esoterica is *attndasiikiit nyangiit* or "underneath/hidden speech." In this spatial ontology, the surface of knowledge and reality appears to be largely epiphenomenal when compared to the underlying realm of mystical secrets, occult spirits, and hidden relationships between seemingly disconnected totemic entities (see also Bateson 1936:237; Wassmann 1991:222–223; Silverman 1997a:109). On the surface, as Wassmann (1991:169, 171–173) claims, each clan's chants and songs denote a bewildering variety of totems. Yet these outer forms are merely protean "envelopes"—a deceptive "non-reality" (Wassmann 1991:170)—for a small number of elementary primal beings (see also Harrison 1990:56). In the neo-Platonism of Iatmul thought, differences in form often pertain to the world of appearances rather than to the underlying world of totemic essences.[7]

In Tambunum, totemic memory is likened to a basket that, like knowledge itself, exhibits an outer surface that conceals an inner "truth." Indeed, totemic specialists may chant the names of a descent group's ancestral basket *(kumbi)* at the beginning of funerary rites in order "to open" their collective memory, thus ensuring the melodious and unerring "flow" of names during the ceremony (see also Wassmann 1991:65). These metaphors for memory and knowledge resemble somatic images of the body—uterine enclosure, parturient flow, surface and interior, and, in the case of totemic chants, an outward phallic penetration of sonic space that assures the internal fecundity of social groups and female bodies.

A layered conception of names and occult knowledge is common in Papua New Guinea. Each grade of the male cult in Telefolmin, for example, reveals knowledge that calls into question the "doxa" of earlier stages (Jorgensen 1980, 1990a, 1990b). This is similar to the inside/outside arrangement of knowledge in many Australian Aboriginal cultures (e.g., Morphy 1991; Keen 1994), a distinction that is also glossed as subject/object (Munn 1970; Morton 1989), proximal/distal (Munn 1964:97, 1973b), noumenal/phenomenal (Myers 1986:49; Meggitt 1987:120), and Dreaming/"sensory presence" (Myers 1989:168–169).

In many Aboriginal and Melanesian cultures, the epistemic contrast between layers of knowledge is often relational rather than absolute. Any "truth" or conventional meaning is defined in accordance with other "truths" or "facts," some of which may not yet be known but which are anticipated to exist in the very structure of knowledge itself.

New stories continuously encompass—or "swallow," to invoke Weiner —former myths and ritual secrets. Bodies of knowledge have transforming, procreative contours, such that any disclosure can be only partial since "the supremely creative act" (Weiner 1995b:6) is to reveal ruptures in social life rather than to forge continuous and cumulative descriptive narratives.

Writing, Knowledge, and Artistic Innovation

Next, I shift from localized realms of identity and knowledge to the broader spacetime of modernity and its transcultural encounters. I begin with literacy, which, as discussed by Gewertz and Errington (1991, chapter 5) and Kulick and Stroud (1990), is a "modern" practice in the Sepik that is nonetheless unable to write over the traditional politics of knowledge.

In Tambunum, reading is a source of cultural instauration through books such as Mead's *Letters from the Field* and Bateson's *Naven*. Writing is understood to entail a sense of permanence and authority that is lacking in oral modes of knowledge and memory. In an ongoing land dispute with another village, for example, Eastern Iatmul introduced into the court a letter written by Mead in the 1960s as formal "evidence." Literacy is also linked to national educational goals and thus citizenship in the nation-state. But while there are no efforts to thwart the literate preservation of magic, genealogies, and names, these inscriptions can prove contentious when the written—hence, durable—document is understood to be a potential form of public memory that could silence rival claims to, say, totemic prestige. In part, this accounts for the dispute over the guesthouse contract already discussed and, for that matter, the "accuracy" of my own ethnographic writings.

Literacy is not restricted solely to alphanumeric writing. Broader instances of "graphicalization" (O'Hanlon 1995) are particularly evident on what, for heuristic purposes, I call tourist art. Both traditional and touristic motifs evoke general, often ambiguous, cultural themes —layers of meanings, as it were—rather than specific denotata. But contemporary art often incorporates words and graphic marks that have a narrower range of meanings. For example, young men in 1994 dipped their hands into paint and imprinted bodily signatures throughout the interior of a new men's house in Timbunke, the elder-brother

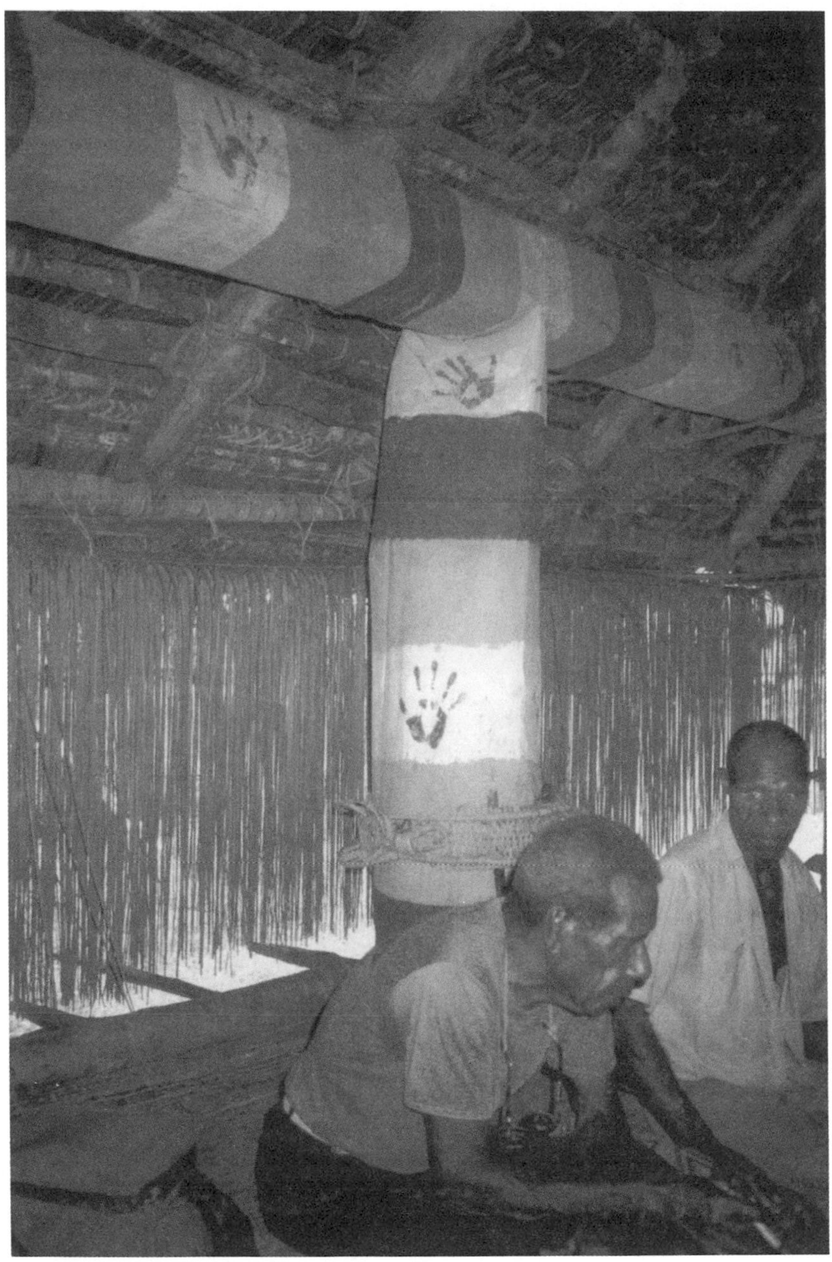

Figure 9-1. Sepik River men's house. (Photograph courtesy of author)

village of Tambunum (figure 9-1). Elder men attributed these graphic designs to a wider shift in the aspirations and outlook on the part of their juniors. As such, these decorative motifs seemed to express an emergent yet muted sense of individuality. Previously, cult house ornamentation evoked the totemic and mythic patrimony of descent groups. Yet these graphical inscriptions connoted anonymity *and* unique, bounded selfhood.

Literate and graphic inscriptions on Iatmul tourist art often express (post)colonial regional and national identities (Silverman 1999). Women weave "PS" into their baskets, an acronym for the Melanesian Pidgin (Tok Pisin) phrase "Pikinini Sepik" or "Child of the Sepik." Men craft variations of the national emblem, beneath which they often engrave biblical slogans. This way, tourist art uses literacy to denote citizenship, regionalism, and Christianity. Commercial recordings of popular music, too, often express regional ethnicity and a Christian sense of national identity (Webb 1993a).

Eastern Iatmul also inscribe their baptismal names on tourist works that, unlike totemic monikers, betoken "modern" individuality. As readers, too, no less than as writers, Eastern Iatmul express egocentric personhood when they browse art catalogs published by museums, galleries, and tourist agencies in the pursuit of novel and individualized artistic innovation. This way, a long-forgotten mask style, when espied in a museum guide, reappeared in the village repertoire, now in the context of tourism. The cultural instauration of tourist art through literate practices thus poses interesting questions about authenticity (see Steiner 1994; Silverman 1997b).

An elegant testimony to transnational routing in the Sepik can be seen in the two T-shirt designs drawn by village men.[8] In the first design (figure 9-2), carvers in Tambunum are "diwai man," a phrase that, in its literal translation as "wood men," ties contemporary Eastern Iatmul identity to literacy, the Tok Pisin lingua franca, and tourist art. The latter is also evident, in embodied crocodilian form that recalls the local cosmology, on the second design (figure 9-3), where a crocodile, appropriately clad in a woven *laplap,* grasps premodern carving tools affixed with steel blades. On second reflection, the literate phrase "wood men" evokes totemic polysemy through subtle reference to the arboreal symbolism of patriliny and male bodies (see above). These T-shirts, then, signify hybrid identity by juxtaposing a totemic tradition and a literate modernity.

There are many similarities between Eastern Iatmul tourist art and Aboriginal acrylic paintings. Both, for example, emphasize individual innovation and style (Myers 1989:183–184). Yet there are also key difference. Yirrkala artists, when they model their bark paintings after book reproductions, are drawn to "works by men who have gained repute" (Williams 1976:281). Sepik carvers, however, do not have widespread reputations, since the connoisseur's gaze neglects tourist art.[9] Second, while Yirrkala people have learned from missionaries that Euro-Australians desire paintings that "have a story" (Williams 1976:

Figure 9-2. Tam's Diwai Man. (Drawing by Simon Nagu. Reproduced with permission)

277), no set of cross-cultural aesthetic criteria has emerged for Sepik tourist art. Third, Yirrkala people restrict the use of reproductions as templates for new paintings to kin groups in accordance with custodial rights over myth (Williams 1976:281). Yet, for Eastern Iatmul, artistic form is subordinated by totemic name, and thus different groups rarely

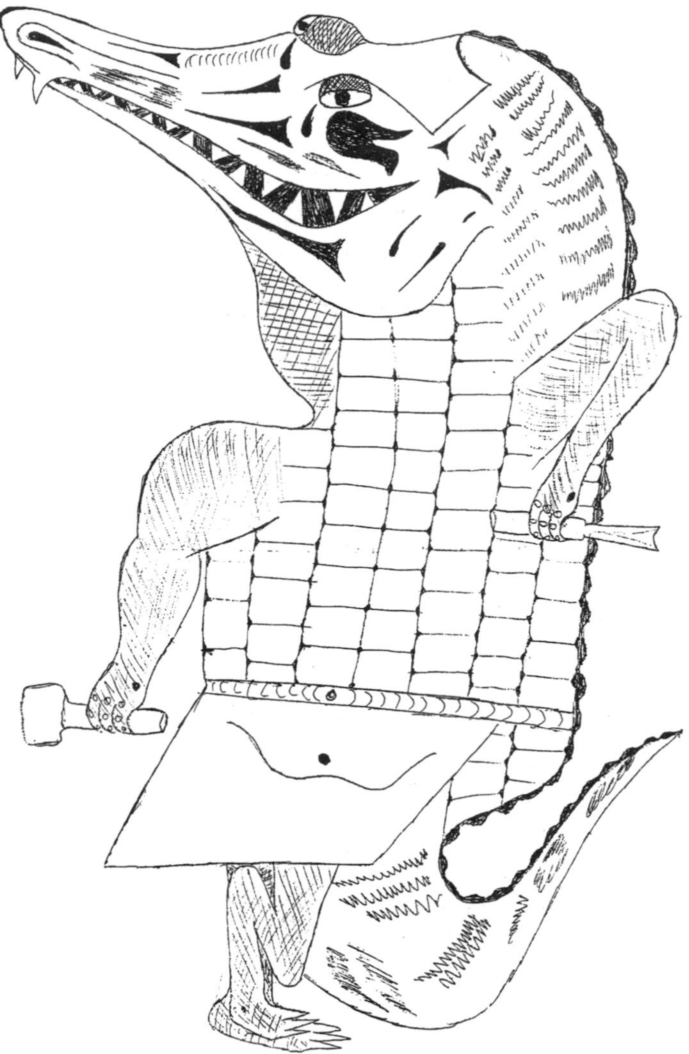

Figure 9-3. Crocodile in *laplap*. (Drawing by Simon Nagu. Reproduced with permission)

compete for rights to carve the "same" objects. Finally, some Aboriginal communities also restrict reproductive rights over paintings of nocturnal dreams (Price-Williams and Gaines 1994:384; Kimber 1995). But this, too, does not occur in Tambunum, where nearly everybody seems to carve a popular mask that derived from one man's oneiric imagery in the 1970s.[10] Non-urban Aboriginal artists tend to paint over the disjunctions and accoutrements of modernity. "Despite the fact of living in such close proximity to the dominant white world . . . Pintupi painting is remarkable in that it incorporates very little of the immediate world that is shaping their lives" (Myers 1989:165; Williams 1976:283). Conversely, Sepik River dwellers have enthusiastically integrated endogenous motifs into their art. In the early twentieth century, crucifixions and Kaiser Wilhelm were incised in the Upper Sepik on bamboo containers (Abramson 1976). Similarly, Iatmul often display European plates instead of shells on funerary effigies and spirit costumes (Bateson 1936, plate 27; Silverman 1999). These incorporations recall the prevalence of bodily encompassment in the local cosmology, no less the subordination of form to name, and Mead's (1970:20) comment that Iatmul villages have "an absorptive and retentive ability in excess of their powers of integration."

I have suggested that, while Eastern Iatmul tourist carvings retain aesthetic ambiguity, they also display a semantic shift toward specificity through literacy, "graphicalization," and onomastic and stylistic signatures. In Pintupi painting, by contrast, increased regularity in the distribution of design elements, a response to Western notions of "beauty," corresponds to "a reduction in overt semanticity" (Myers 1989:185). Nevertheless, Pintupi paintings continue to refer to dreamtime locations, which is an important aesthetic criterion both for the artists as "truth" and for Western connoisseurs as authenticity. In a sense, then, Pintupi paintings represent an aesthetics of miscommunication between local artist and European viewer.

Similarly, Dunbar-Hall (1997) argues that the Western appreciation of Aboriginal rock music focuses on individual songs. But each album/CD as a whole is a unit of meaning that is unable to be "heard" in the absence of knowledge about local groupings and the vernacular.[11] In this sense, contemporary Aboriginal music resembles yet "sounds" against the dominant aesthetic. Likewise, Biddle (1996) argues that *kuruwarri* motifs in Warlpiri acrylic paintings are a form of "redressive writing" rather than protoliteracy (Munn 1973a). They ensure "against an undifferentiated writing subject" (Biddle 1996:26), which is assumed by European-style literacy. Furthermore, "the writing of *kuruwarri* may be having as silencing an effect on Europeans as print literacy has had on Aborigines" (Biddle 1996:30). If Eastern Iatmul write literacy on tourist art in order to incorporate modernity, Warlpiri "write" anti-literacy on acrylic paintings in order to resist modernity.[12]

Copyrighting Art, Controlling Knowledge

The control of "traditional" knowledge in the context of "modernity" is not, for Papua New Guineans and Aboriginal Australians, simply a matter of writing. In Papua New Guinea, the question of legal copyright has been posed mainly for commercial recordings of music and songs (Niles 1996). This extends to the use of localized instruments such as bamboo beaters by musicians from other regions of the country (Niles 1996:52). But if the political and legal apparatus of Papua New Guinea has displayed limited explicit concern with visual art,[13] jural entitlement to motifs and forms is salient on the local level. Many men in Tambunum draw on the aesthetic traditions of non-Iatmul and even non-Sepik cultures in order to create novel carvings (Silverman 1999). In most cases, geographic distance militates against any potential dispute. One man, however, requested and received express permission from non-Iatmul (Biwat River) affines to reproduce their characteristic masks for tourists. Within the village, "copyright" infringement occasionally occurs when someone carves and sells a mythic-historic personage from another group. But these disputes, which are unceremoniously resolved by cash remuneration, are infrequent, since names rather than visual forms generally differentiate between totemic beings.

In Australia, the legal status of Aboriginal art under copyright law is a crucial and ongoing quandary. The non-Aboriginal dissemination and commercialization of Aboriginal artistic styles is accelerating and hugely profitable (Puri 1992:5). "Mechanical reproduction," to use Walter Benjamin's felicitous phrase, now includes the World Wide Web. For some, Aboriginal control over this traffic in images will enable economic autonomy and curb the "trivialization" of local cultures (e.g., Golvan 1992a). For others, though, any public dissemination of Aboriginal art is tantamount to religious ethnocide.[14]

The legal debate over the status of Aboriginal and Aboriginal-like images is tied to the wider dispute over land. Formerly, a sense of aesthetic *terra nullius* prevailed. Aboriginal art was timeless and anonymous. Artists were "conduits" for tradition rather than "fonts" of creativity. Consequently, Aboriginal art and artists did not meet the requisite notions of psychology, personhood, and originality that were the basis for Western copyright law (Sherman 1994). The *Mabo* decision, however, suggested the legal recognition of Aboriginal forms of intellectual "property" (see Puri 1993; Pannell 1994). Nevertheless, common law protection of Aboriginal art and knowledge will require modification of existing concepts that are central to copyright law—e.g., ownership, authorship, originality (Puri 1993), universality, and Enlightenment rationality (Gray 1995)—or comprehensive *sui generis* legislation (Blakeney 1995).[15]

The application of Australian copyright law to Aboriginal art is the result of several noted legal cases (see also Maddock 1988; Golvan 1992a, 1992b; Onus 1990a; Puri 1992:6–7; Johnson 1996).[16] In *Bulun Bulun v. Nejlam Pty Ltd.*, Johnny Bulun Bulun sought injunction against further reproduction and distribution of T-shirts that bore the unapproved reproduction of one of his paintings. Although the case was settled out of court, "unauthorised reproductions of authentic Aboriginal designs on garments, which had been endemic in 1988, ceased to be found in tourist shops" (Golvan 1992a:6). But if the right to reproduce "authentic" Aboriginal images for external consumption was henceforth authenticated by Australian law, ironically, "most tourist shops today are replete with examples of T-shirt designs which may appear to be works of Aboriginal art, but are in fact caricatures of such—namely, the x-ray koala!" (Golvan 1992a:6).[17]

Bulun Bulun's deposition cited the close relationship between art, "custom," and the land (Golvan 1992a:5). In fact, both traditional and contemporary Aboriginal artworks, visual and musical, are often categorized by Aborigines and non-Aborigines as the equivalent of legal deeds to land (Moyle 1983; Craig 1984; Megaw 1990; Pannell 1994). A famous example is the bark petition sent to the House of Representatives in 1963 by Yolngu of Yirrkala. The vernacular text and English translation are bordered by clan-specific designs that pertain to land that was threatened by mining operations. As Morphy (1983:115) writes:

> The genius of the bark petition was that it introduced an Aboriginal symbol into Parliamentary discourse, making it harder for Europeans to respond in terms of their own cultural precedents. Peti-

> tions framed in parliamentary language can be dealt with through parliamentary procedures. Petitions framed with bark paintings add a new element.

It was an element, too, as Morphy notes, "likely to be taken up by the media." Here, the public dissemination of "traditional" art, despite the "modern" context, was an intentional strategy that ensured an "authentic" continuity between persons and land.

Another prominent pre-*Mabo* copyright case was *Yumbulul v. Reserve Bank of Australia* (1991). This dispute centered on the reproduction of Terry Dhurritjini Yumbulul's funerary Morning Star Pole on the plastic 1988 bicentennial commemorative ten-dollar banknote. The Galpu descent group granted Yumbulul "traditional" rights to craft and paint one of these ceremonial objects, which he sold to the Australian Museum for public display. He also licensed reproduction rights to the Aboriginal Artists Agency, which was subsequently purchased by the Reserve Bank of Australia and depicted on the commemorative note. The local descent group censured Yumbulul for exceeding custodial rights over the design and for besmirching its sacred ethos with commercial rather than educational enterprise. As a result, Yumbulul brought suit against the Agency and Reserve Bank for copyright infringement, alleging that he would not have entered into the licensing agreements had he been counseled fully on the contractual implications. The court, in ruling for the defendants, judged Yumbulul's design to be sufficiently "original" for him to be its legal owner and thus fully entitled to enter into commercial licensing agreements —which, having done so, he was bound to honor. Furthermore, the court was unable to recognize the other traditional custodians of the design as rightful owners.

In this case, the courts evaded the issue of copyright. But as Golvan (1992a:6) noted, the court "was concerned that the traditional Aboriginal rights attaching to the reproduction of the art work were not protected under existing law." Golvan (1992a:7, 1992b) proposed "the creation of a right attaching to a tribe as represented by the relevant tribal custodians, being rights which might sit alongside the individual rights of artists." After *Mabo,* Golvan's suggestion gained legal currency. As a footnote to this case, Yumbulul's painted designs are now sold over the Internet on T-shirts.[18] The Web site, however, makes no mention of the Morning Star Pole controversy.

Authenticity and the World Wide Web

Many "urban" Aboriginal artists define themselves on the basis of a diffuse sense of Aboriginality. They "use imagery to which they had no right under traditional Aboriginal customary law; they felt that it was sufficient that they were Aborigines" (Ellinson 1994: 341; see also Rowse 1993, chapter 4). While this aesthetic hybridity violates a basic tenet of localized Aboriginal identity (Foley 1990; Croft 1990), it also betokens a wider sense of emergent Aboriginality that claims "ownership" over an otherwise enervating history of dislocation (Onus 1990b; Scott-Mundine 1990; Anderson 1990a; see also Fourmile 1994). This debate over identity recalls the "unauthorized" borrowing of traditional instruments across provinces in Papua New Guinea, and intersects with broader notions of cultural authenticity.

The relationship between cultural hybridity and the politics of cultural assertion is nicely framed by three recent musical events. *Tabaran* is a popular musical CD collaboration between the Melbourne band Not Drowning, Waving and musicians from Rabaul. The project, according to Webb (1993b), explicitly embraces the market allure of Tolai exoticism. Yet it also seeks to "instruct" listeners about an unfamiliar language, culture and musical tradition.[19] A similar combination of commercialism, didacticism, and self-representation also surrounded the reception of the popular Aboriginal group Yothu Yindi, which was "a strong indigenous Australian challenge to the appropriation of the didgeridoo by British and European World Music fusion groups" (Mitchell 1992:11). Yet these musical voices, too, both accede to hegemonic images of Otherness (and pan-Australian identity) yet define an authentic Aboriginal alterity (see Mitchell 1996, chapter 5). Indeed, Yothu Yindi's Web site[20] maintains links to sources of "authentic" Aboriginal culture and the Rainforest Action Network, while striving for indigenous autonomy. But it also sells Yidakis (didgeridoos) and painted "fine art prints."

For the most part, artistic forms from Papua New Guinea have not, like the didgeridoo (see Nuenfeldt 1993, 1997), been expropriated by the New Age movement. Nor have they been widely integrated in "alternative" musical works that seek to de-center dominant Euro-American genres. An important exception is *Voices of the Rainforest,* a 1991 CD/cassette issued by Rykodisc that records music and ambient sounds from the Kaluli of Bosavi. This compact disc, the first devoted entirely to indigenous Papua New Guinean music, is part of the long-standing collaboration between Steven Feld, an anthropologist and ethnomusicologist whose work is doubtless known to readers of this volume, and Mickey Hart, a drummer of the former Grateful Dead. *Voices of the Rainforest* portrays an "acoustic ecology" that no longer exists for Kaluli, one devoid of the sonic encroachment of "modernity." But, according to Feld (1991), this seemingly "inauthentic" soundscape is increasingly incorporated into the nostalgic wonder of Kaluli themselves, no less himself and others concerned with cultural, environmental, and musical diversity, such as Hart's musical series "The World" and the Rainforest Action Network. The latter, we have seen, is also linked, at least in cyberspace, to Yothu Yindi. Ultimately, as Feld (1991:132) recognizes, *Voices of the Rainforest* is a soundscape of "various anxieties" that arise from the politics of cultural representation at the dissolving boundary between the global and local.

The same anxieties beset the enormously popular acrylic paintings of contemporary Aboriginal communities, works that have engendered a vast interdisciplinary corpus of theory (see Myers 1989, 1991, 1994).[21] One particular concern has been the notion of "authenticity." In what art category, specifically, should these works be assigned—modern, primitive, traditional, folk, tribal, and so forth? The issue is not merely academic, as several European gallery and museum exhibitions have refused to include contemporary Aboriginal paintings on the basis of categorical dissonance (Raabe 1995).

There is no such scholarly discourse for Sepik River tourist art, which, unlike Aboriginal paintings, remains largely confined to the moral categories "primitive" or "tourist." If the former is pristine yet extinct, the latter is inauthentic and degenerative. Hence, these works lie outside the spaces of lucrative connoisseurship *and* theory. As I intimated earlier, however, standardized categorization schemes, which are the object of ongoing critique in the discourse over acrylic paintings, are no less problematic for Sepik River tourist art. It is unclear, for example, how we should categorize, if at all, masks that are (re)discovered in museum catalogs.[22] Museums, too, shun these objects (but see Lewis 1990). The exhibition "Contemporary Art of Papua New Guinea," curated by Pamela Rosi for Monmouth College, mainly featured works created in association with the National Arts School.[23]

But, as I have suggested, Sepik tourist art evinces the same qualities that one reviewer (Dissanayake 1988:47) found so compelling about the exhibition: "deeply felt reactions to the difficulties and dissonances of clashing cultures and competing values."

The "high art" reception of non-touristic Aboriginal paintings has canonized the painted dot or "pointillist" style (Adams 1996). Yet tourists and buyers have fostered no comparable set of aesthetic principles for Sepik River art. Nonetheless, Eastern Iatmul are adept at conjuring images of artifactual antiquity, rarity, and ritual secrecy, fictions that are lent visual force by "aging" techniques such as smoking and soaking. The authenticating value of oldness derives solely from Western "taste" and, more recently, Papua New Guinean export regulations.[24] Furthermore, many buyers and tour guides implore Eastern Iatmul carvers, no less Aboriginal painters (Taylor 1996:41–47), to adhere strictly to their "traditional," localized repertoire. (But as I noted earlier, fidelity to images always was a fluid matter.) For the most part, however, these are minor concerns since there is no discursive space responsible for the "reception" of contemporary Sepik art on the order of Aboriginal acrylic paintings and music.

Both Aboriginal and Sepik River art is created today explicitly for external consumption. This motivation is often marked, in the case of the former, under the rubric of cultural revival and artistic innovation. But galleries that display Sepik River art often reproduce Hobbesian and Rousseauistic fictions of primitivism. (Some of these fictions, as I mentioned above, can admittedly be traced to the carvers themselves.) An apt example is the presence of Sepik art in a "trendy" New York City (SoHo) store called Evolution that otherwise specializes in skeletons and fossils. Many authenticating fictions for Sepik River art resemble the appropriation of the didgeridoo by New Age exponents. Contemporary Sepik River art is rarely presented as an expression of contemporary identity. Indeed, the evocation of "tribal ritual" to authenticate these works is paralleled by the widespread claim that Aboriginal art is the oldest artistic and cultural tradition on earth. But while the latter stresses temporal continuity, the former evokes timelessness.

The World Wide Web contains scores of online sites that sell Aboriginal and Sepik River art, as well as relevant bibliographies, media releases, organizations, museums, government agencies, and course syllabi. Aboriginal and Sepik art works are commonly legitimated with phrases such as "fine tribal art," "authentic aboriginal art," "genuine," "high quality craftwork," "certificates of authenticity," depictions of the Aboriginal flag, and so forth. At the Web site for the Jungle Outpost, Black Hills Reptile Gardens, we are encouraged to "start your own 'Tribe' with a piece of Tribal Art from New Guinea." Elsewhere, we can purchase coasters, ties, and computer mouse pads decorated with "authentic" Aboriginal designs, even a Dreaming Swatch timepiece painted by Bridget Mutji.[25] Cyberspace is becoming simply the latest discursive space for contesting, asserting, creating, exploiting, falsifying, and experimenting with cultural authenticity.

Conclusion

Contemporary Aboriginal art is part of the wider negotiations over Aboriginality (e.g., Keefe 1988, 1992; Tonkinson 1990; Hollinsworth 1992; Lattas 1992a; Muecke 1992; James 1993). This contemporary debate, in its focus on space, place, and, according to Lattas (1992b, 1993), embodiment, transforms "tradition" into the discourses of modernity, which includes the World Wide Web. For some critics, commercial Aboriginal art delegitimates and negates Aboriginal identity through crass commodification. These works perpetuate "difference" within a nation-state regime that consigns assertions of Aboriginality to ethnic decor,[26] and erodes the integrity of Aboriginal religion through the unrestricted dissemination of sacred knowledge. They assent to the Euro-Australian usurpation of fictitious images of Aboriginality that, like the boomerang (Jones 1992), are circulated as signs of pan-Australian identity (see Lattas 1992a).[27] And, finally, the widespread admiration of these works enables Euro-Australians to absolve themselves of collective culpability for history—a history, moreover, that silences Aboriginal agency (Briscoe 1993).

There is, however, an opposing view of contemporary Aboriginal art that, in concert with my own interpretations of Sepik River tourist art, sees these works as engendering cultural identity. A splendid example is Taylor's (1990) analysis of contemporary transformations of the Rainbow Serpent in western Arnhem Land.[28] This dreamtime being has two manifestations: Yingara, who is associated with the first yet nonlocalized creative act, and Ngalyod, who is linked to specific locations. Men who migrate to towns from their clan lands tend to paint Yingara rather than Ngalyod, thus fostering a novel, regional sense of "corporate unity" that is not, like Ngalyod and traditional identity, tied to specific locales.

Similarly, one can view market-oriented Aboriginal art as subversively "slipping" Aboriginal values and concepts past otherwise resistant white Australians (Taylor 1988), thereby contesting what Wendt (1996) called the "whitefication of the colonised by a colonial education system" (see also Anderson 1993:148). Contemporary works, too, lend Aborigines "voice" within the museum and heritage communities (Hemming 1994; Anderson 1990b) and become legal assertions of topographic custodianship (see also Faulstich 1993; Stratton 1994). Finally, the status and meaning of Aboriginal painting, by virtue of the discourse that it has generated, is itself a political statement on the centrality of Aboriginality in contemporary Australia. In many respects, I have tried to suggest a similar positioning for Sepik River tourist art, despite the lack of a corresponding body of theory. As such, these works can be "read" against wider, emergent constructions of Melanesian personhood and nation (e.g., Foster 1995; Errington and Gewertz 1996; Otto and Thomas 1997).

Sepik and Aboriginal art, by drawing on enduring tropes of primordialism as well as recent concepts of hybridity, will gain controversy no less imperative in the year 2000 when, with millennial import, Australia hosts the Olympic Games. This will serve as an apt stage for Australian Aborigines and South Pacific Islanders to continue to craft, and to have crafted for them, images of "traditional" and "modern" cultural identities. In many respects, the future of these images lies in transnational spectacles of bodies, myths, and artistry such as the Olympics and cyberspace.

Notes

Fieldwork in 1988–1990 was graciously funded by a Fulbright award and the Institute for Intercultural Studies; the Wenner-Gren Foundation for Anthropological Research and DePauw University generously enabled a return visit in 1994. I am also indebted to Jimmy Weiner and Alan Rumsey for kindly extending an invitation to participate in the conference "From Myth to Minerals." Finally, I thank Andrea, who, in her third trimester with Sam, tolerated the heat of a midwestern summer while I weathered cool antipodean breezes and warm collegiality.

1. Williams (1986, appendix 1) summarizes the history of the term "dream time," which was coined by Spencer and Gillen for the Aranda in 1896.

2. In other Sepik societies, such as Manambu (Harrison 1990:76–80) and Chambri (Errington and Gewertz 1985, 1986; Gewertz and Errington 1991), the totemic origin of Europeans is politicized.

3. The implications of these events, and the case-by-case specifics of "co-existence," are mired in litigation and debate, much of which is readily accessible on the Internet. See, for examples, the homepages of the Native Title Research Unit, Australian Institute of Aboriginal and Torres Strait Islanders Studies (http://www.aiatsis.gove.au/ntru_abt.htm), Aboriginal and Torres Strait Islander Commission (http://www.atsic.gov.au), and National Indigenous Working Group on Native Title (http://www.edime.com/nativetitle/main.htm).

4. See the companion volume, *Mining and Indigenous Lifeworlds in Australia and Papua New Guinea,* edited by A. Rumsey and J. Weiner.

5. Strathern's (1988) insights into Melanesian gender have yet to be fully applied to dreamtime androgyny—itself an unexamined topic, according to Swain (1993:193–194).

6. For gendered temporalities elsewhere in Melanesia, see Weiner (1984; 1988, chapter 3; 1995a) and the citations in Silverman (1997a).

7. This, according to Wassmann (1991:218), explains Bateson's (1932:444–447) observation that Iatmul totems are not discrete biological species.

8. No less in the actual "routes" of these shirts, which were made in the United States and shipped to the Sepik by way of the *Melanesian Discoverer* tourist ship.

9. Some galleries, however, in the hope (I suspect) of authenticating Sepik art for an emerging market of connoisseurs, do foreground individual artists (for example, Alcheringa Gallery, http://www3.islandnet.com/bema/museums/ag/ag_frame.html).

10. In Darling Harbor, one such carving was fantastically described as "Ancestral Mask, used as part of the animistic worship of ancestral spirits."

11. A similar difference in "ways of listening" is discussed by Browne (1990:118) for Aboriginal radio. An interesting project would be to compare images of "modern" identity in tourist art and new media technologies such as video, television, and advertising (see Sullivan 1993; Langton 1994; Michaels 1994; Hayward 1995; Errington and Gewertz 1996; Gewertz and Errington 1996; Foster 1996/1997; Dussart 1997). In this regard, Ginsburg (1993:571–572) mentions two paintings by a Warlpiri woman, Jeannie Nungarrayi Egan, that contrast "hegemonic" and "democratic" telecommunication linkages between Aboriginal communities and government centers.

12. Resistance, too, can be seen in "the refusal by Maruku Arts and Crafts at Uluru National Park to 'scale down' spears to make their art portable" (Puri 1992:8); for a Sepik contrast, see Gewertz and Errington (1991:49–54).

13. This may shortly change pursuant to Papua New Guinea having signed the General Agreement on Tariffs and Trade (GATT).

14. In one noted case, Australian courts granted "breach of confidentiality" injunctions on behalf of the Pitjantjatjara Council against further publication of Mountford's 1940 book, *Nomads of the Australian Desert.* As an unintended result, the book is now a collector's item that fetches hundreds of dollars. See also Pockley (1998) for an interactive, online doctoral dissertation that focuses on the discourse of public images of Aborigines.

15. Golvan (1992c) suggests incorporating the protection of Aboriginal art under the 1984 Aboriginal and Torres Strait Islander Heritage Act.

16. Vivien Johnson, author of the Copyrites exhibition catalog (Johnson 1996), maintains a "House of Aboriginality" Web site, now available on CD-ROM, that depicts instances of Aboriginal imagery in popular culture. This is part of a ongoing project to identify and halt images that violate Aboriginal custodianship and legal copyright. (http://www.mq.edu.au/house_of_aboriginality).

17. A similar condition prevails outside of Australia. A recent catalog by REI, a popular American outfitter for outdoor equipment, included a "Kirra Boomerang . . . Aussie-style . . . Colorfully hand-painted with legendary Australian images . . . Made in USA" (at the time of writing, it can be seen on the Internet at http://www.rei.com/shopping/store3/OUTDOOR_ACCESSORIES/GAMES/GAMES/bud/621398.html).

18. http://www.squirrel.com.au/business/yumbulul/designs.html.

19. Another example of transnational routing is the 1993 video documentary *Tabaran,* which was filmed by Mark Worth and screened on Australia's SBS-TV (see Hayward 1993). Worth was the first Australian manager of the tourist guesthouse in Tambunum!

20. http://www.yothuyindi.com.

21. See also Megaw (1982, 1990); Marrie (1985); Jones (1988); Michaels (1988); Fry and Willis (1989); Rubinstein (1989); Taylor (1989); Altman and Taylor (1990); Benjamin (1990); Megaw and Megaw (1993); ATSIC (1997).

22. Elsewhere, I discuss the concepts of authenticity and categorization by contrasting Sepik River tourist art with the "master carvings" of the Papua New Guinea Sculpture Garden at Stanford University (Silverman 1997b).

23. For a virtual gallery that displays some of these works, see http://www.pmc.edu/club.html. Relatedly, see Baker (1980); Simons (1993); Cochrane Simons and Stevenson (1990); and the October 1995 issue of Art and Asia Pacific.

24. In West Africa (Steiner 1994:102), "authentic art" is precontact for Europeans but postcontact for African traders.

25. See, respectively, http://reptile-gardens.com, http://www.larkfield.com.au, and http//www.swatch.com/gallery/gabrimut.htm.

26. A few days before the conference at which this research was first reported, I noticed the decorative placement of Sepik tourist art inside the front doors of David Jones department store in Sydney.

27. A case in point is the debate over the Aboriginal painter Eddie Burrup,

who was recently unveiled to be Elizabeth Durack, of Irish descent. Was this an outrageous and calculated act of cultural appropriation? Did it instead confirm the ascendance of the "work" over the artist? The debate is compounded by the fact that "Burrup" continues to paint.

28. The Rainbow Serpent is one cultural motif that has been compared between the Sepik and Australia (Mead 1933–1934; Brumbaugh 1987).

10
The Object in View
Aborigines, Melanesians, and Museums

Lissant Bolton

There is a cartoon by the *New Yorker* cartoonist Charles Barsotti that shows a man in a suit and tie standing before a glass display case, looking with respectful awe at the single small pot within it. The caption reads, "The wonder of it all" (figure 10-1). This cartoon sums up something that I greatly value about museums: the way in which objects can open horizons of knowledge and imagination that are rich and moving. Through the practices of collection and public exhibition, museums have developed a discipline of looking—a way of retrieving meaning from objects. This meaning is comprehended imaginatively by each viewer and often depends on the object as a conceptual opening through which the viewer can pass to apprehend another time or another place. Museums, in this sense, are about the pleasure of eye and mind, and as Barsotti suggests, such seeing and imagining often incorporate awe and wonder at the object, at other times and other places.

The discipline of looking is a particular cultural practice, one that has crossed many national boundaries but belongs to a specific Euro-American tradition. Its distinctive character is that it depends on the disconnection of objects from the contexts in which they were made and used. It is because the objects are disconnected that they can represent, and thus become a way to imagine, those contexts. The objects become, as Roy Wagner puts it, "strategic relics" (1981:28).

Different traditions of museology place different constraints on this

Figure 10-1. "The Wonder of It All." (Cartoon by Charles Barsotti, 1986. The New Yorker Collection from cartoonbank.com. Reproduced with the permission of The New Yorker)

process of imagination. Art museums usually provide a minimum of information and context for the object, allowing visitors free rein in their engagement with the object (albeit as art). In art museums the "wonder of it all" approach predominates. The practices of ethnographic and history museums are different. The principle by which ethnographic collecting operates is that objects are collected on the assumption, or with the intention, that their significance in the situation in which they were collected will be retained. As a consequence ethnographic museums usually impose a particular set of meanings on objects through label text and illustrations, presenting these meanings not as interpretation but as fact.

Changing theoretical developments in anthropology and related disciplines have been influential in altering understandings of museum collection and display. In recent years debates about the connection between object and meaning have become part of the discourse of museology and museum anthropology. As these disciplines have become increasingly sophisticated, the idea that the meaning of the objects to their original makers and users can be retained in any straightforward sense has been called into question. The small pot in Barsotti's cartoon is accorded honor by being placed alone in its glass case, an invitation to the viewer to look at it with awe. Its journey across time and space from its maker to the case gives it a significance as a survivor, which it could not have had to its maker. The meaning of objects is affected by their context: as objects are moved from context to context, their significance changes. The way in which the meaning of objects is affected by their immediate context is an increasingly recognized problem in ethnographic collection management and display.

With the development of these ideas has come also the recognition that such meanings are rarely without moral and political dimensions. Objects are collected and displayed in specific political and intellectual environments. Much early ethnographic collecting was made with the assumption that objects and information were all that would remain of certain communities. The objects were to represent a people and a way of life that would soon no longer exist. The earliest recommendation that an Australian institution collect ethnographic material, for example, seems to have been George Bennet's 1832 suggestion that the Australian Museum collect artifacts and skulls "as lasting memorials of an extinct population" (cited in Specht 1979:141). Bennet assumes that the settler community had a moral and intellectual right to document the very people whose society their own was understood to be destroying.

There is also often an explicit political purpose in the display of ethnographic collections. Flora Kaplan's edited volume *Museums and the Making of "Ourselves"* demonstrates how, for newly independent nations, the gathering of objects can contribute to a notion of national unity. In her introduction Kaplan argues: "Each country uses its museums to represent and reconstitute itself anew in each generation" (1994:4). Thus Emmanuel Kasaherou, then director of the Musée Territorial de Noumea, wrote about the development of the Jean-Marie Tjibaou Cultural Centre, a French colonial initiative that opened in Noumea in 1998, that it was being built "to use our past Kanak roots as a base from which to develop a new evolving culture which includes the whole population of the country" (1995:32).

Although such changing theoretical developments have been influential in altering understandings of museum collection and display, by far the most important factor in bringing changes to ethnographic museum practice has been the influence of indigenous communities. In the last two decades indigenous Australians and Melanesians, among others, have entered museums and brought with them a series of ideas about the meaning of objects that have unsettled and irretrievably altered the ways in which ethnographic collections can be imagined and understood. This impact is not singular in its effect. The engagement between indigenous communities and museums has taken many forms and had many consequences.

This chapter looks at some of the alterations to museum practice introduced by indigenous involvement by considering the way indigenous Australians and Melanesians have engaged with the idea, and the reality, of museums. I have a specific relationship to this material. Raised in the Euro-American tradition of museum-going and thereby educated to perceive the wonder of it all, I have spent a good deal of my working life in museums. I was an ethnographic collection manager at the Australian Museum in Sydney for many years, my employment spanning the period during which that museum began to employ and to refer to indigenous Australians in dealing with its Aboriginal collections. In 1989 I also became a voluntary staff member and adviser to the Vanuatu Cultural Centre. I was brought up, so to speak, in a Western professional museum context and have learned another perspective through interaction in the museum with indigenous Australians and Melanesians. The changes and the debates that I discuss here are matters in which I have myself participated to some extent, and my participation has inevitably colored my understanding of these processes.

The diversity of indigenous perspectives on museums can be illustrated with two quotations. The first is from the recommendations of the UNESCO regional seminar held in Adelaide in 1978, at which indigenous Australians spoke forcefully about their desire for access to public collections of Aboriginal material culture in Australia. They argued for "the important role that owners and leaders of particular cultural traditions can have in giving life to existing collections of lifeless objects" (Edwards and Stewart 1980:13). The second quotation comes from Lawrence Foana'ota, director of the Solomon Islands Museum: "Some people . . . still regard [the museum] as a dumping place for old, meaningless, and dead objects that no longer have any value or use to the communities in the provinces" (1994:100). Both statements suggest that objects have no life when they are disconnected from the people who can give them meaning. The Adelaide recommendation urges a reconnection to resuscitate the objects, while the Solomon Islanders described by Foana'ota see the museum as a place to put objects that are past their use-by date, objects that have no further significance to their makers and users.

The assumption of settler superiority and authority set out in George Bennet's suggestion that the Australian Museum collect Aboriginal material as "lasting memorials" was the assumption behind ethnographic collecting in Australia for many decades. For indigenous Australians, instituting some form of control over how museums use collections of Aboriginal material has been of considerable importance in asserting the vigor of their population and in reversing the assumption of colonial authority. A turning point was the Adelaide UNESCO seminar, which was co-organized with the recently founded Aboriginal Arts Board. The seminar itself arose out of changes in the political and social climate in Australia and was fueled in part by the referendum of 1967. Indigenous delegates claimed the right of Aboriginal people to influence the management of objects used to represent their communities and the presentation of their knowledge and practice in exhibitions. They focused on the need for the employment of Aboriginal staff to manage Aboriginal collections and for greater indigenous involvement in the development of exhibition and education programs, and they raised concerns about the management of secret/sacred or restricted objects and the management and reburial of collections of Aboriginal human remains. Jim Specht, who attended the seminar for the Australian Museum, says that indigenous participants "repeatedly criticised Australian museums and their boards of management for their insensitivity, arrogance and exclusiveness" (Specht and MacLulich 1996:31). The proceedings include a long list of recommendations (Edwards and Stewart 1980).

Crucial to the Adelaide seminar, and to the ongoing transformations that have developed from and beyond it, is the concept of cultural property. In popular usage today, the idea of "culture" is often framed primarily in terms of ownership and rights. The relationship between indigenous people and museums is politicized by ideas about culture as ownership, and these ideas are embodied in the term "cultural property." This term developed within UNESCO, and it is defined, somewhat laboriously, by the 1970 UNESCO *Convention on the Means of Prohibiting and Preventing the Illicit Import, Export, and Transfer of Ownership of Cultural Property.*[1] UNESCO defines cultural property at the level of the state and refers to it as property designated as important by the state itself. As this term has come into common use, however, at least in museums, it usually operates with reference to much smaller groups, which are usually designated as "traditional owners." Cultural property is spoken of as belonging to traditional owners—that is, to the makers and users of the object or to their descendants, descent being loosely defined so that it can refer to a specific family or an entire ethnic group.

This idea of cultural property has had a significant impact at a conceptual level within Australia. It challenges the settler assumption of a moral and intellectual right to speak about the knowledge and practice of indigenous peoples. Instead, it allows that the descendants of the makers and users of ethnographic objects have a moral right to determine the meaning and often, in consequence, the use of those objects—or at the very least to prohibit certain meanings and uses. This moral right applies even where the legal ownership of the objects lies in other hands—specifically, in the hands of public institutions. That is to say, the right is often observed by museums in their practices of collection management and display, even where it has not yet been formally enshrined in the institution's policies. The relationship between acceptance of the idea of cultural property and the adoption of formal policies that acknowledge it is a complex one.

For most objects in ethnographic collections, details of provenance and producer are not known, and therefore the concept of cultural property is applied generally, the right to speak about objects being allocated to all the people who could be classified as belonging to the group from which the makers and users come. In the Australian context, this means that any indigenous Australian is understood to have a greater right to speak about any Aboriginal object than any non-indigenous Australian. The consequences of such an approach are profound. The political and emotional needs of indigenous Australians with respect to objects have a very considerable force. Museum collections have become one of the loci of Aboriginal reclamation of a traditionally derived identity and, more specifically, of the reclamation of cultural autonomy.

Australian museums have by now accepted most of the recommendations from the Adelaide seminar and have made many changes in the way they operate. All museums in Australia now recognize the moral rights of traditional owners with respect to collections of secret objects. Respecting Aboriginal sensitivities about this material, no museum now displays, or allows research access to, Aboriginal secret material, even when very little is known about the individual objects. This development involves a radical alteration in museum practice, since the objects are no longer available for display or for other kinds of research. Most museums have further accepted the principle that if specific traditional owners can be identified, a secret object should be returned, in actual and legal transfer. These returns are made possible where there has been no radical break in the meaning of these objects to their owners—where the meaning of the specific object is remembered. That is to say, while the significance of the object is altered by its sojourn in a museum storeroom, to its owners it holds continuing significance, which can be taken up again upon its return to them.

All major museums now employ Aboriginal staff, so much so that in some instances, such as that of the Museum of Victoria, the majority of the Indigenous Studies Department staff are Aboriginal. Most museums defer to Aboriginal consultative or advisory committees in making decisions about exhibition and education programs, as well as about collection management. No museum in Australia now displays or allows research access to Aboriginal human remains or secret or restricted material, and significant numbers of objects in both categories have been returned to their traditional owners.[2] This transformation has been formalized in the Museums Australia policy statement *Previous Possessions, New Obligations* (1996), a document intended to guide museums in framing their own procedures for dealing with indigenous Australians. In the introduction, the president of Museums Australia, Des Griffin, declares: "This . . . policy is intended to recognize the fact that Aboriginal and Torres Strait Islander peoples have a right to be involved in all aspects of care, management and presentation of their culture" (1996:2).

As well as becoming involved in state museums, many Aboriginal communities, especially those in rural southeastern Australia, have also set up their own small museums and cultural centers, which range from displays in Aboriginal community offices to purpose-built small museums such as the one in Shepparton in Victoria. A number of communities have modified existing buildings for the display of Aboriginal material, such as the Nungera Museum at Maclean in northern New South Wales, which was established in an old bank building in the mid-1980s. In 1998, for example, there were in New South Wales eight community museums and another four shopfront displays set up in community offices and the like; an Aboriginal center at Wallaga Lake, which operates tours and other programs for the tourist market; and a center at Foster concerned with issues of archaeological heritage. Aboriginal community museums are established through the medium of Aboriginal land councils or other incorporated bodies, and are funded from state and federal funding bodies. The Aboriginal and Torres Strait Islander Commission is a strong source of funding support for such projects.

Until the last few years, Aboriginal communities in northern and western Australia took a different approach to museums. In a context in which objects are still being made and used, local priorities have focused on the storage and protection of important objects, leading to the foundation of Keeping Places, where objects are kept until needed for use. Over the last three or four years, however, Margaret West, of the Northern Territory Museum, reports (personal communication 1998) that there has been a trend toward the development of more-conventional museums with conservative, object-based displays. The Djomi Museum at Maningrida, the Bukularrnggay Museum at Yirrkala, and a Wadeye community museum at Port Keats have all been assisted by the Regional Museums Program of the Northern Territory Museum to develop exhibitions designed largely for visitors. West comments that in all cases the local community concentrates their interest not on the objects but on photographs, both archival photographs and photos of living people. Local people are not, she says, as interested in looking at objects that are still being made in the community. In the case of both the museum at Port Keats and the one at Bathurst Island, collections focus as much on repatriated archival material such as photographs and publications as on objects. Both of these museums were founded with the assistance of church groups, and they have a historical emphasis and act as a community resource center.

Major state museums provide training and support services to all such regional initiatives, partly as a result of financial assistance to them from the Aboriginal and Torres Strait Islander Commission. The Australian Museum, for example, now has an Aboriginal Heritage

Unit with two indigenous Australian staff who visit and assist New South Wales Aboriginal communities involved in cultural preservation and provide various training options for community members involved in regional museums and cultural centers. One of the problems that indigenous community museums of this kind face is that there are few objects known to derive from these areas in either public or private collections. Most state museums have established loan programs, which enable objects to be returned to the region and community from which they are understood to come on temporary or semi-permanent loan. This process returns objects not only to communities but also, significantly, to a place.

Of course, by no means all members of Aboriginal communities are interested in local museums and cultural centers. Such small museums are often the result of the driving interest of one or several community members, and if that person or group withdraws from the project for some reason, support from the wider community is often not sufficient to sustain it. The Nungera Museum at Maclean, for example, was largely the initiative of a woman named Joyce Clague, and when she ceased to be involved in the project, the museum died. The fluctuations of interest in community museums may also reflect a political reality: the establishment of a museum and the return to it of Aboriginal objects deriving from the local region asserts Aboriginal control over Aboriginal identity. These actions do not involve ongoing engagement with either the museum or the objects, and contemporary museological preoccupation with conservation, research, and display may be of little interest to the local community. The meaning of the objects has to do with their ownership and control and location, and once they are obtained, their individual significance may often not be important.

Within major museums, Aboriginal staff and advisers also sometimes redirect attention away from the existing ethnographic collections. One of the objections that indigenous Australians have consistently made against museums has been that Aboriginal society is presented as if it were timeless, as if it existed in a nonspecific ethnographic present on which the European incursion has made little impact. Many museums were founded to capture the disintegrating image of this timeless present, and for this reason, most museums refused to collect objects that obviously incorporated European goods and concepts. Indigenous Australians have consistently pressed museums to present images of their contemporary concerns and preoccupations. One of the Adelaide seminar recommendations encourages established museums and art galleries to "mount exhibitions and special displays detailing contemporary Aboriginal and Torres Strait Island issues and aspirations and Aboriginal cultural and social history of the recent past" (1980:13). The 1996 Museums Australia policy document sets out this same emphasis on contemporary Aboriginal experience in more forceful language: "Aboriginal and Torres Strait Islander cultures must be presented as vital, living, diverse and changing" (1996: 8, point 4.3).

These objectives achieved one expression in an exhibition that opened at the Australian Museum in March 1997, "Indigenous Australians: Australia's First Peoples." This exhibition was designed largely by Aboriginal people; both museum staff and members of New South Wales Aboriginal communities were consulted on the exhibition's content, which focused primarily on the postcontact history of Aboriginal people and on such issues as stolen children. The museum's important ethnographic collections do not feature to any significant extent in the displays. Far more important to NSW Aboriginal people is the opportunity to present their own image of themselves in an institution that formerly presented only its account of their lives and concerns.

Developments at the Museum of Victoria follow a similar trend. The Indigenous Cultures Program in this museum operates a number of projects not directly related to material culture. These include community language workshops and family history and photographic research programs. Gaye Sculthorpe, head curator of the Museum of Victoria Indigenous Cultures Program, says that there is less Aboriginal community interest in objects than in these other programs. Many Aboriginal objects deriving from what is now Victoria are, however, on loan to Aboriginal community museums within the state. Displays at the Museum of Victoria itself are concerned especially with twentieth-century Aboriginal history, and object acquisitions reflect this focus. In 1996, for example, the museum acquired a truck used by a boxing troupe that comprised Aboriginal and non-Aboriginal boxers.[3]

Until after World War II, expatriate concern about the disappearance of Melanesian local knowledge and practice led to the making of collections for European and Australian museums rather than to the founding of museums in the region. Only gradually, as these places took on a coherent image as distinct entities (as colonies and incipient nations), did regional museums appear. A museum was founded in Papua New Guinea in 1954, in Vanuatu in 1956, and in the Solomon Islands in 1969. The exception is the New Caledonian Museum, founded in 1863. All these institutions were founded by expatriates and were staffed mainly by expatriates until after each country achieved independence. As in Australia, the indigenous community did not begin to enter these museums as staff, or even as visitors, until the late 1970s. In Melanesia, the employment of local staff in the museum was part of the process of acting upon independence.

Melanesian museums, like those in Australia, have become a focal point for the negotiation of ideas about culture and cultural heritage. But the concept of culture has entirely different political implications in Papua New Guinea, the Solomons, and Vanuatu than for indigenous Australians. Independence restored political autonomy at a time when many rural Melanesians were living in a way that was consistent with their precolonial knowledge and practice. They suffered less of a radical break with their past, even though much has changed. Although developments such as the growth of urban and political elites are creating increasing rural alienation, indigenous culture is not at present a locus of political protest. Melanesians are not asserting their identity in opposition to the state by claiming the objects in the national museum as their own cultural property, nor is there any protest against the presentation of local knowledge and practice through exhibitions. Museums are a focus for the presentation and negotiation of ideas about cultural identity at a state level, but they are generally not important to the wider population.

This situation has come about partly because of the way in which the idea of "custom" has been formulated in the Melanesian nations. In common usage the terms used in the Melanesian pidgins—*kastam* (PNG), *kastomu* (Solomon Islands), and *kastom* (Vanuatu)—are used to refer not to objects but to knowledge and practice, to dances, songs, stories, indigenous medicine and magic, and so on. Public occasions that celebrate custom tend to be arts festivals and regional shows of various descriptions, reinforcing this perception. Objects are not featured in these contexts except as body ornamentation and dance props. Most of the objects that continue to be made and used in village contexts are not objectified as "custom"; rather their meanings are a product of their immediate context.

If one problem facing Melanesian museum staff is the indifference of the wider population, another is the difficulty of reconciling local conditions and concerns with international museum practice. International organizations such as UNESCO and the International Council for Museums are active in the Pacific region, organizing and funding conferences and training courses for regional museum staff. Most Melanesian museum professionals have become skilled in the language of museum curatorship, but struggle to find ways to implement it with minimal resources of funding and equipment and in a context where international museum standards often make little sense. The Museum of Victoria's Gaye Sculthorpe commented recently that in Australia, Aboriginal museum staff are beginning to develop a new and distinctive style of indigenous curatorship (personal communication 1998). In some ways another style of indigenous curatorship is also developing in the Pacific. If Aboriginal curatorship is built on the principle of the reconnection between object and traditional owner, Melanesian curatorship is developing around the idea of an ongoing, uninterrupted connection.

In general, Melanesian museums hold few old objects in their collections. With the exception of the PNG Museum, which has acquired significant numbers of objects through repatriation, especially through the repatriation of the MacGregor Collection from the Queensland Museum, most items in their collections were acquired within the last three decades. Often the objects in the museum are the sorts of objects that are still being used, or are at least remembered, in the places from which they come. This means that those Melanesians who *are* interested in the museum see the objects in it as connected to recent or even present-day local knowledge and practice.

This idea of an ongoing connection is, for example, made explicit in attitudes and actions toward spirits and spiritual power. The idea that the objects in museums have dangerous spiritual powers that have to be controlled is widespread in Melanesia. In 1989 when I went to Vanuatu to catalog the Vanuatu Cultural Centre's collection, staff arranged for a renowned sorcerer, Aviu Koli, to perform a ritual to "kill" the power of the objects that my colleagues and I would be handling, lest we be endangered. The objects were alive with spiritual power that needed to be controlled. The center's staff told stories of the objects restless in their glass cases at night, stories told to me with a rueful uncertainty about whether they would or could be believed.

In this case, even if the specific meaning of objects to their original makers and users might not be known, a meaning was knowable by means of an occult insight that was itself part of local practice. At a meeting of Pacific region museum staff that I attended in 1995, this same issue caused delegates (especially those from Melanesia) considerable concern. They discussed at some length the danger that unrecognized spiritual power inherent in objects could and did cause curatorial staff in their own institutions and in museums elsewhere. Emmanuel Kasaherou, director of the Musée Territorial de Noumea, wrote in 1995: "Even today there are many Kanak people who are uneasy when viewing traditional objects with supposed magical powers which could be dangerous to the viewer. With these ways of looking at traditional objects, the purpose of the museum is hard to understand" (1995:31).

Melanesian museum staff are also often frustrated or bemused by the distinction that sets objects—material culture—apart from other aspects of local knowledge and practice. Another significant concern raised consistently at meetings of Pacific region museum staff is the management of sacred sites and other places of importance. Anthropological research increasingly recognizes the importance of places in the construction and remembering of knowledge and history in Melanesia. For regional museum staff this issue arises at a more practical level as they see places destroyed by logging and other forms of development. Thus Soroi Eoe, director of the Papua New Guinea Museum, writes:

> Museums should . . . serve as development catalysts by assisting governments to forge their development projects in ways that better serve the people of both today and tomorrow. . . . Particularly important is [museums'] involvement in multi- and bilateral aid programmes, which through mining, lumbering and drilling projects currently in operation in the Melanesian states . . . are responsible for the large-scale deforestation of enormous tracts of wilderness and the destruction of villages resulting in the displacement of their inhabitants. (Eoe 1991:3)

That heritage site management is a responsibility of the museums in PNG, the Solomon Islands, and Vanuatu[4] is a reflection of the degree to which museums in the region are responsible not just for objects but for cultural heritage preservation in general. The imperative to preserve objects can pale in significance when compared with the imperative to preserve places. The conflict between the development preoccupations of national governments and the museum's concern to sustain indigenous knowledge and practice causes great difficulty, and often a great deal of discouragement, for museum staff. In such a context, again, the preservation of individual objects can seem less critically important.

In other words, in Melanesia, as at the Museum of Victoria and other Australian museums, staff are initiating programs of cultural revival that are not directly focused on objects. The most locally active and successful Melanesian museum is the Vanuatu Cultural Centre, and its success seems to derive in significant measure from the fact that it does not emphasize object-oriented activities. Rather, the institution has concentrated on recording oral traditions using audiotape and videotape, on promoting arts festivals, and on the maintenance and revival of local languages and rituals. The museum's efforts in these areas have been achieved through the development of a group of voluntary extension workers, known as field-workers, rural ni-Vanuatu[5] who work in their own villages and districts to "document and revive" local knowledge and practice. Until the opening of a new museum building in Port Vila in 1995, the Cultural Centre paid far less attention to its collections and exhibitions than to these programs.[6]

When the new museum building was opened, museum staff allocated to several field-workers cases in which to set up displays. Each worked with friends or colleagues from his own area. They were given no instruction in exhibition theory or design and no direction about display content. They were merely given the assistance of a ni-Vanuatu carpenter, who could make supports and mounts for objects, and left to their own devices. Sometimes the field-workers chose to display newly made objects brought from the islands—in one case contemporary body decorations from a traditionalist enclave on Tanna, in another a newly revived form of textile, barkcloth from Erromango. Field-workers from Ambrym took fern-tree figures in the existing Cultural Centre collections and restored and repainted them.[7] The opening of the exhibition was immensely successful, with some thousands of visitors on opening day alone. Significantly, no labels were attached to these objects; instead, field-workers stood beside the displays to explain them. The museum became a kind of performance space in which ni-Vanuatu affirmed and expressed their contemporary knowledge and practice to each other.

The story of the opening exhibition of the new Vanuatu museum illustrates a further issue, which is the conflict between programs directed at local people and programs directed at tourists. Melanesian museums find it consistently difficult to provide resources for tourists while at the same time addressing a local audience. This conflict is evident at the most basic level, such as the arrangement of objects in exhibitions and the content of and language used in display labels. The opening exhibition in Vanuatu would have made almost no sense at all to any tourist who came in the door. There is no need to restate here debates about the relationship between tourism and the ongoing integrity of indigenous cultural practice; rather I will simply observe that these issues are of concern to Melanesian museums.

The concerns arise not least because, if programs of national development affect museums through issues of site preservation, they also affect them through the issue of tourism. Governments the world over are inclined to the misapprehension that museums can help to make money from tourists, and governments in Melanesia are no exception. Nelson Paulius, representing the PNG minister of culture and tourism, said to a 1989 gathering of Pacific region museum staff:

> International tourists who visit Papua New Guinea and other Pacific island nations are fascinated by, enjoy and wish to buy our colorful and artistic arts and crafts. . . . In Papua New Guinea, our Department of Culture and Tourism will continue to encourage provincial and local governments as well as cultural groups to establish museums and cultural centers which will facilitate the performance of songs and dances and preserve traditional artifacts. (Paulius 1991:11)

There have been some attempts in Melanesia, especially in PNG, to develop community museums and cultural centers in rural areas. Like Aboriginal community museums, these entities are often established because of the interest of one or two individuals and are dependent on the continuing interest of those individuals for their survival. Funding for these initiatives sometimes comes from national and provincial governments or from external funding agencies of various kinds. In many cases, these initiatives are designed with the intention of attracting, educating, and obtaining money from tourists, as Paulius suggests they should, but tourist numbers are rarely sufficient to sustain them, and many of them appear and disappear over a period of only a few years. Brief accounts of many of these appear in Eoe and Swadling's edited collection *Museums and Cultural Centres in the Pacific* (1991).

The situation in New Caledonia is somewhat different. One of the consequences of the signing of the Matignon-Oudinot Accords in 1988, by which France and New Caledonia agreed to move toward a referendum for independence in New Caledonia, was the foundation of the Agence de Dévelopement de la Culture Kanak (ADCK), an organization funded by the French government and created to develop and promote Kanak culture. The main project of the ADCK has been the development of the Jean-Marie Tjibaou Cultural Centre, a remarkable building designed by Renzo Piano and constructed at a cost of 320 million French francs, which opened in 1998. The ADCK has both French and Kanak staff, but it is distinctive in the region in producing publications that refer to the Kanak population as "they" rather than as "we." The emphasis of the center is on fusion, both of the old with the new and of the different cultural elements within New Caledonia. The Tjibaou Cultural Centre's Web site sets out as a goal of the institution

> to be the principal point of interchange with other cultures existing in New Caledonia, making it the "reference culture" by offering the Kanak inheritance as part of the general cultural heritage of the whole population of New Caledonia and, on this basis, proposing elements of common cultural reference in which artistic creation can take root.[8]

The Tjibaou Cultural Centre is also intended to be a cultural focus for the whole Pacific region, although the extraordinarily generous funding that supports the institution, as well as the European-influenced style of its programs, sets it apart from other museums in the region. It will be a very considerable tourist attraction in its own right. The relationship it might have with rural Kanak has yet to be established.

This approach by the Tjibaou Cultural Centre runs counter to developments in the rest of the region, most particularly in the matter of staffing. In Australia it is increasingly difficult for museums to employ other than indigenous Australians to work with Aboriginal collections, and although Melanesian museums sometimes employ non-Melanesian staff on contract, their policies are to employ local staff only. As already discussed, the emphasis on indigenous staffing has led to new models in the management of ethnographic collections in the region.

Indigenous interests in museums can best be summarized in terms of contemporaneity. Although by no means all members of their communities are interested in museums, where Aborigines and Melanesians do have this interest, their interest is in using the collections, and the institutions, to address contemporary issues. Aboriginal people assert autonomy and authority through the control of collections, using museums as a venue in which they can develop wider cultural programs. For Melanesians, museums are a vehicle through which they seek to preserve and promote local knowledge and practice. The orientation to the present is a component of what is happening in Barsotti's cartoon—the small pot in the drawing is a conceptual opening to a world that the viewer imagines and wonders at through his own present understandings and for his own present pleasure. The difference is in the attitude toward the objects themselves. Indigenous curators are interested, or not interested, in the objects in museums in the context of their present concerns. They are not necessarily interested in the objects in and of themselves.

The present director of the Vanuatu Cultural Centre, Ralph Regenvanu, expresses such ideas clearly, writing about the impact of a Swiss-French touring exhibition that was shown in Vanuatu in 1996. "Arts of Vanuatu" contained a selection of objects from the museums of Europe and was extremely successful. It was visited by more than one third of the population of Port Vila, Vanuatu's capital, a percentage that most Western museum directors can only dream about. Regenvanu emphasizes the degree to which the ni-Vanuatu interpreted the objects in the exhibition in terms of their present concerns: "It is the narrative, visual and material records of our traditional cultures which now provide the wellspring from which contemporary cultural identity in Vanuatu can be reassessed, contemporary artistic traditions strengthened and new and truly indigenous forms of expression created" (1997:11). Soroi Eoe, director of the PNG Museum, puts the same ideas in another form: "Museums should go to the people and take an active interest in their problems" (1991:2).

The new models of indigenous curatorship in Australia and Melanesia are a stimulating and important development within the wider disciplines of museum curatorship and museum anthropology. They contribute to the overturning of political injustices and improprieties and bring new meanings to the objects in museum collections. The fundamental change that these models bring, however, is a shift in focus away from objects themselves. This is a very important change, and it needs to be recognized and acknowledged. The discipline of looking, which involves wonder at the object itself, is becoming in this context a thing of the past. A tradition of Euro-American scholarship is not so much disappearing as becoming, in this arena, difficult to sustain. Barsotti's cartoon may itself be becoming a way to think about another time and another place.

Notes

Many people provided information for and commentary on this chapter. I would like to thank in particular Elizabeth Bonshek, Mark Busse, Philip Gordon, Klaus Neumann, Mike O'Hanlon, Gaye Sculthorpe, Jim Specht, and Margaret West for their assistance.

1. The UNESCO definition reads: "For the purposes of this convention, the term 'cultural property' means property which, on religious or secular grounds, is specifically designated by each State as being of importance for archaeology, pre-history, history, literature, art or science and which belongs to the following categories: . . . (f) Objects of ethnological interest."

2. The South Australian Museum is presently host to the federally funded National Skeletal Provenancing Project, which is directed by physical anthropologist Colin Pardoe. The aim of this project is to research unidentified Aboriginal human remains so that they can be returned to the correct social group for reburial.

3. Sculthorpe discusses the importance of presenting Aboriginal history in museums in her 1993 article "Interpreting Aboriginal History in a Museum Context."

4. Heritage site management is the responsibility of the Archaeology Department of the National Museum and Gallery in Papua New Guinea, the National Sites Survey of the Solomon Islands Museum, and the Vanuatu Cultural and Historical Sites Survey, a department of the Vanuatu Cultural Centre.

5. "Ni-Vanuatu" is the term used in Vanuatu to refer to the indigenous citizens of that country. Other constructions, such as "Vanuatuan," are never used.

6. A number of publications discuss the Vanuatu Cultural Centre projects. The *Oceania* special issue *Fieldwork, Fieldworkers* discusses the impact of the field-worker program on research in Vanuatu in a number of different disciplines (Bolton 1999). See also Sam 1996, Bolton 1996, and Rodman 1998.

7. This restoration caused horrified fascination among Australian Museum materials conservators, who were running a conservation training course for Cultural Centre staff at that time.

8. Quoted from the Jean-Marie Tjibaou Cultural Centre Web site, http://www.noumea.com/neacom/jmtjag.htm#A3.1.

Afterword

James F. Weiner

The Politics of the Secret, Chris Anderson's edited collection that appeared in 1995 (Anderson 1995), dealt mainly with the contemporary fate of the Central Australian *tjurunga,* the sacred, incised objects of the male cult. Among other things, the *tjurunga* was a corporeal extrusion of places within the Central Australian terrain, a material fragment of specific ancestral place that anchored the ritual re-creation of creative and procreative acts in Central Australian social life and cosmology.

Many of these *tjurunga* found their way into Australian and foreign museums and private collections throughout the world. Through this dilation and expansion of the *tjurunga*'s emplacements, and through the medium of the acrylic painting that catapulted Central Australian and Western Desert painting to the status of international emblem of Australian Aboriginality, people of the central desert have had to come to grips with the way in which their depicted mythic landscape has achieved an almost dendritic connection with the Western world of airways, television transmissions, and lines of commerce. What this immense dilation means for the status of Australian placedness and its mythic and objective expressions is in many ways what is addressed throughout this volume.

The dilemma of the *tjurunga* that escapes the emplacing control of its Aboriginal owners provides us with the image to make some closing remarks here. One of the two complementary themes running through this volume concerns the shapes and conduits into which knowledge itself is placed and emplaced and the manner in which this territorializing of knowledge results in the system of differences that make communication, exchange, and sociality possible. The second theme is the obverse of this process: where knowledge is emplaced and contained through a variety of discursive and metadiscursive techniques, discourse itself is also emplaced and localized, because knowing how and of what to speak is greatly a matter of one's spatial and territorial positioning. Talk itself, as the resource out of which origins and explanations are proffered and accepted, is inexorably local and emplaced, in the form of the poolings of words and images that we label myths. Let us then first consider the way knowledge is put into place.

We can begin by observing that the songs and myths that are the salient form of attachment to land and to the constitution of the person through terrain are not just texts "about" land or placedness. Rather they are the fundamental vocal and verbal dimensions of landedness, the form that this relation takes in people's embodied consciousness (just as in van Baal's formulation, myth was the form that the Marind-anim ancestor beings took in human language [Weiner 1995c]). In Papua New Guinea, where people for the most part have not experienced alienation from the land, one senses that this Proustian intimacy of place is still unbroken and continues to generate new vocal forms. Even if these contemporary lyrical manifestations are primarily young men singing string band songs about another province, there is still a certain experiential dimension of landedness tied to them.

An important theme of placedness, as Myers (1986), Feld (1990), Maschio (1994), Weiner (1991), and Bell (1998) have noted, is intimacy and sentiment. No one who has spent much time living with landed people can avoid encountering in great depth the kinds of emotional attachment and expressions that both accompany and constitute the connections we have described here. This intimacy and sentiment is surely an important component of what we could call *topogenesis,* or topogeny, as James Fox (1997b) has termed it, the creation of places. But along with this is its mirror opposite, which could be called *topothanatia*—the death, withdrawal, effacement, or covering over of places. The idea of intimacy becomes important in a different way when we consider how commonly in Australia (especially) and Papua New Guinea ritual restrictions prevent people from going to certain places.

How, then, can other people learn about these places, given that cosmologically vital things take place and are made visible there? They can learn about them only through the verbal accounts that people bring back for revelation in the public space. That is the mode of knowledge of place for people who do not have the immediate intimacy of ritual-productive-manipulative engagement. What happens then when that spatial apartness of knowledge is interfered with, when the process of keeping places—not just stories—secret is no longer possible? We then confront the apocalyptic attempts to reinsert the mythical "between" space and people's experience of it that we observe in the Melanesian cargo cult and in the Adjustment Movement in Arnhem Land, Australia, in the early 1960s (Berndt 1962).

As well as the birth and death of places, we have, in a system so predicated on the creative potential of movement, just as strong a concern with its opposite, stillness. Weiner (1991), Munn (1973b), Scoditti (1996), Young (1983), Kahn (1997), Feld (1997), and others who have worked on this nexus in Australia and Papua New Guinea have had to articulate aspects of both movement and stillness.

Stillness manifests itself in an important process of objectivation whereby the spatial and lineal dimensions of these knowledge regimes are their visible form. The Northern Territory of Australia has become famous for the manner in which iconographic designs, painted on bark, human bodies, or the ground itself, depict the spatial configuration of myth and its consequent power to convey key components of human relationality. Thus, in both Papua New Guinea and Australia, the process of miniaturization or replication *en petit* of a more encompassing world place is a vital component of making the world manipulable and subject to human representative agency. But these miniaturizations of place and track were not themselves static—they were objects that could move between people. In Central Australia, the *tjurunga ("churinga")* were the material incarnations not only of a specific ancestor but also of the reproductive power of that ancestor to produce human beings in particular places. In many cases, the creation of places in this part of the world is also importantly a sexual act that marks, divides, and creates a world in every respect, of which the most notable example is the Wagilak myth cycle of the Yolngu (formerly Murngin) people of northeastern Arnhem Land (Berndt 1951, 1952; Weiner 1995c).

This placing of sexual power is also the key to the Central Australian notion of reproductivity:

> On the birth of a child, or soon afterwards, the old men of the group determine its *tjurunga*, its other deathless body. . . . If the *tjurunga* is a huge immovable object, for instance a rock lying outside the sacred cave or a tree flourishing nearby, the old men of the group, on the birth of a child reincarnated from such a rock or tree, usually fashion another *tjurunga* for it from mulga wood; this is then engraved with the traditional patterns proper to the totem of the child, rubbed with fat and red ochre, and then put into the storehouse. (Strehlow 1947:94–95)

There are other mnemonic objects that are used by Australian and Melanesian peoples to model and manipulate their spatial world. Among the Iatmul, each clan possesses a *kirugu*, a sacred knotted cord, which is brought out and manipulated during totemic name debates. The knots in the cords are of two types, large ones, representing places along an ancestral migration, and smaller ones, standing for totemic names encompassed by the events sequentially mapped by the larger knots. The *kirugu* represents not just a sequence of places but the total migration of a people. The cord therefore maps not just a sequence of *topoi* but the movement that originally linked them in ancient times.

The passing on of these objects between people makes a mobile token out of the movements that originally created territory; this macrocosmic space moves from being the ground of creation, out of which humans arose, to the figure passing between humans, constituting their own sociality as ground out of these topological objects. They become places that move between people—a humanized form of convention, in which people move between places. In chapter 6, Anthony Redmond assigns to this process a more emphatic literalization as far as the Ngarinyin people are concerned: the features of the landscape are themselves not fixed but "travel, shake, tremble, and split." Rock fragments and enters the bodies of humans, becoming organs.

In these graphic mnemonic objects, we see, as Roy Wagner describes it in chapter 3, the folding of space into another form, a form that can articulate with the dimensions and range of human corporeality and manipulability. But, as Deborah Rose demonstrates in chapter 5, the practical consequence of this folding is its subsequent unfolding—of the Victoria River area of the Northern Territory in Australia, no site was ever distinct and separate; rather, "these structures are characterized by intersections, overlap, and crosscutting." Sites are always linked to other sites, and the care of a particular site unfolds into care of the country as a more encompassing ground of being. For both the Victoria River people and the Ngarinyin, "land and body are interpenetrating, polymorphic . . . sediments of experience which establish a foundational identity" (Redmond, chapter 6 above).

Those of us who have described a knowledge system that grows out of this intimate emplacement of language and production have all had to face the problem of how to explain, articulate, or imagine what happens when the analogic function that links place, memory, and verbal *topoi* is lost. In Australia, two recent Aboriginal sacred site controversies, Coronation Hill in Northern Territory and Hindmarsh Island in South Australia (the latter the subject of Weiner's chapter 7 in this volume and Bell's recent volume [1998]), drew attention to the contemporary struggle of Aboriginal people to reinscribe their territory with some sense of sacredness, particularly when that territory is perceived to be under threat by proposed commercial developments of various kinds.

But more than that, Peter Sutton makes a compelling case for the reterritorialization of the contemporary indigenous lifeworld in Australia. He argues convincingly that

> a specific kind of concrete productive/stewardship relation is in fact restored by the very processes of site protection, the opportunity to conduct land claims, the engagement in management of "heritage," ordinary land management on property held by collectivities of traditional owners, the distribution of royalties to traditional owners, the politics of incorporated landowner bodies, the taking of responsibility for nature conservation liaison with official government bodies such as National Parks and Wildlife Service on such estates, and so on. The religious superstructure is no longer free-floating or detached or lost from the reproduction of certain kinds of social groups, nor from the material conditions in which such groups evolve and are maintained, or even displaced by others like themselves. (Sutton, personal communication 1996)

Sutton is trying to characterize the new forms of relation to land and place in which Australian Aborigines are finding themselves enmeshed. The issue of how knowledge can be retained, kept in place, controlled under the increasing conditions of deterritorialization that characterizes the contemporary globalization of the world is the subject of Silverman's and Bolton's chapters (chapters 9 and 10).

What is thus also notable about this volume is that the contributors are not satisfied with characterizing some hypothetical precontact culture, but are intent on demonstrating the manner in which these regimes of mythologized space and restricted cultural knowledge continue to function and transform themselves under contemporary global conditions. The contributors successfully explicate the manner in which regimes of restricted knowledge serve to enhance and protect cultural property and the proprietorship over sites and territory; how myths evolve to explain and culturally appropriate important events pertaining to contact between indigenous and Western societies; how graphic designs and other culturally important iconic and iconographic processes provide conduits of cross-cultural appropriation between indigenous and non-indigenous societies in today's multicultural nation-states.

Speech that Places

In both Aboriginal Australia and Papua New Guinea:

1. Myth is a salient form, both linguistically and performatively, through which important and often restricted cultural knowledge is embodied and transmitted;
2. the events of myth commonly and importantly focus on the journeys or travels of central creator beings who performed place-making and place-naming acts upon the land in the context of these mythic events;
3. the relationship to places and to the naming-power of certain ritual and artistic acts is a focal identity-creating process within these Papua New Guinea and Australian Aboriginal societies.

As Pamela Stewart and Andrew Strathern point out in chapter 4, in both Australia and Papua New Guinea, the landscapes are saturated with "values and meanings that provide a rich material network of associations for identity constructions, from the personal and emotional to the social and politico-legal." The language of social and cultural constructionism now dominates the anthropological analysis of contemporary social life around the world, and it is an inescapable fact that the tasks of becoming a subject and of exercising human agency and autonomy are assumed to be the social challenges for all peoples, particularly indigenous groups in confrontation with various representatives of Euro-American liberal corporate society. Perhaps, however, it is salutary to remind ourselves how utterly unconstructed pre-Western Australian and Melanesian social identities were. As the Australian Ngarinyin told Redmond, "'We humans didn't make the world with our own hands.'"

This account deserves careful scrutiny, because it cannot be easily accommodated by the language of constructionism. Roy Wagner's analysis of Daribi myth (1978) provided the first full-length account from New Guinea of a mythology whose function was not to construct a world through the use of language but rather to partially reveal its contours. He noted that the Daribi made a twofold division between types of mythic narrative:

> *Namu po* belongs to the realm of human artifice, designating, as Daribi point out, stories made by human beings—what are often called "tales" in contradistinction to myths. . . . [In contrast, as] root causes, *po page* are not things that human beings can simply make up; they are given determinants, normally hidden, of that which is and can only be discerned through the transmission and learning of specific oral accounts. . . .
>
> *Namu po* is the revelation of someone's speech, advice, admonition *(po)* through the means of stories *(namu); po page* is the revelation of existing circumstances and their origins *(page)* through the means of speech *(po)*. Thus Daribi myth comprises a moral discourse *(namu po)* with cosmology and a cosmological discourse *(po page)* with the world of moral convention, each aspect of the whole being constituted through the obviation of the other. (Wagner 1978:57)

Similarly, the account of Pintupi knowledge that Myers gives arraigns it against the domain of what is deliberately "made" in human life:

> The Pintupi view is that one "follows up" The Dreaming, submitting receptively to a given order of things. . . . The Dreaming leaves something of itself, its subjectivity (from "inside"), at a place where it becomes part of the contemporary objective environment. . . .

> These figures and their objectifications are really the creations of human activity, although this connection to human historicity is denied in their projection outside of social space. These constructions are depersonalized, instead, as Law—their connection with the subjectivity and will of another. . . .
>
> "Knowledge" is experienced in precisely this fashion. Pintupi culture recognizes it as something which a man is "given" and which he "holds" in his stomach, "inside," with his "spirit" *(kurrunpa)*. It passes from "outside" to "inside." (Myers 1986:241–242)

The dilemma for indigenous people today, confronted by the challenge of the Western nation-state, is to convey a sense of the vitality and creativity of their tradition without its seeming on the one hand contrived and fabricated and on the other an inflexible tradition or law that by definition cannot long be sustained without artificial support. How, then, do we confront Strehlow's startling characterization of Aranda tradition in the following 1947 passage?

> Since every feature of the landscape, prominent or otherwise, in Central Australia is already associated with one or the other of these myths, we can readily understand the attitude of utter apathy and the general mental stagnation that exist amongst the present generation of the natives as far as literary efforts of any kind whatever are concerned. The thoroughness of their forefathers has left to them not a single unoccupied scene which they could fill with the creatures of their own imagination. Tradition and the tyranny of the old men in the religious and cultural sphere have effectively stifled all creative impulse. . . . It is almost certain that native myths had ceased to be invented many centuries ago. (Strehlow 1947:6)

A response in another context many years later by Roy Wagner gives us the vital perspective:

> To "follow" the track is to infuse a microcosm with the existence and motion of its maker, and, by a certain analogy, any sensory enrichment of its iconography constitutes a similar reversal of abstraction. To perform these operations upon the collective, summative sense of "track," as the total lifeway and experience of a people, is to realize and vivify the making of that track as a creative act. (Wagner 1986:21–22)

In fact, Strehlow's own informants gave him the same account:

> The Ilbalintja men are always talking and boasting about their bandicoot *(gura)* ceremonies. But their ceremonies are utterly useless. Euros are to be found everywhere, and it is we who create them. The bandicoots have vanished long ago. Even we old men

> can remember eating bandicoot meat only when we were still mere boys. Where they have gone to since, I do not know. (Strehlow 1970:304–305)

Against what illusorily appears as the conventionalizing properties of important mythic accounts is the repetitively creative use of mythopoesis on the part of the indigenous people of Australia and New Guinea. Lattas provides an example of this in his description of how the Bali Islanders of East New Britain make a mythopoiea out of the pervasive acronymic tendency of the contemporary English language. What we are dealing with is an attempt to relocalize a type of language that is spoken all over the whole modern world: an encrypted, acronymic compression of language. Westerners employ this language consistently, a form of encrypted rationalization, or explanation in rational terms that is abbreviated. The computer world, of course, is its primary domain and means of proliferation. As Wagner has suggested, computers exist because of it, rather than its existing because of computers. The Bali Island man described by Lattas could look at this infolding of Western language and simply interpret it as what we as Westerners do as world activity.

To effect a translation of this interpretive act, to make ethnographic sense of this, is not just a matter of assigning glosses to the Bali Island man's utterances. One must also take regard of how he manages the conjuncture by appropriating acronymic language. This appropriation provides him with not just a set of English words, but also a far more expansive map of metaphoric and analogic figuration within English. Through this man's innovative reading of acronymic glosses in his new word-littered landscape, we see how in the compression of acronymic glosses, one can effect a spatial-causal connection between hitherto unconnected domains, agencies, and sources of power. Phrased in this way, the continuities with what we have conventionally called "magical thought" become more pronounced.

The great distances linked by myth, track, and song, the unfolding of a trope over a vast linear expanse, confront this opposite process, by which space keeps getting folded into smaller and smaller compartments—in the shape of the pearl shell, the *tjurunga,* the knotted cord, and other sacred objects, New Guineans and Australians demonstrated that acronymicity (if we may be permitted to coin such a barbarous-sounding neologism) was a fundamental dimension of this macrocosmic world of tracks and sites.

A consideration of the formidable length and expansiveness of tracks, paths, migratory lines of flight, the routes by which objects changed hands, and the consequent infolding of external languages, objects, myths, and names has far-reaching consequences for how we constitute cultural difference in this region. It leads us to consider that cultural alterity not only was not problematic but was essential to internal continuity and distinctiveness. Much of the ethnographic evidence collected indicates that Australian and Melanesian people were dealing with contact with colonial societies in purely local terms, as another chain in the varied connections that the contributors to this volume have mapped out. To put it another way, our comparative project as anthropologists is paralleled by an indigenous comparativism that was and continues to be part and parcel of cultural and linguistic articulation in this region. This "difference" made visible by this continuous activity of contrast-making was *not* something that can be reduced to degrees of distance, numbers of objects, enchained names along a site path, links along an Internet or within a string of business connections. It is rather the very gaps and proportions of meaning, space, and temporality that allow locality itself to emerge at all.

It is this internal differentiation that is most threatened by the notions of culture that Western nation-states bring to their encounter with indigenous people in regions such as this. It is no accident that the greatly increased centrality given to landedness in Australia has come just at the last phase of dispossession. What emerges, especially in the Wik legislation (the legislation in Australia that has modified the Native Title Act of 1993), is exactly the attempt to fix relations of landedness at a certain point of intercultural history in order to permanently "settle" the issue of Aboriginal compensation for land.

The regime of landedness implied in the New Guinea and Aboriginal models of track and trace defies fixing in one particular place: like the mnemonic objects and myths themselves, these models send out rhizome-like extrusions that reproduce the entire system of contrasts. But the language of indigenous identity and locality is more and more being phrased in terms of people rooted in landscapes in places like Australia, Canada, and New Zealand and is emerging in the still-developing state structures of Papua New Guinea. This imagery is influenced by the state's attempt in all these cases to both solve the problem of indigenousness and fix the problem of how to fold such an indigenous alternative back into what we take to be the relation between monoculturality and multiculturality in the social composition of the modern state.

We have suggested that under conditions of cultural articulation whereby foreign objects and languages are necessary to internal stability, the strategic recognition of "loss"—of knowledge, objects, myths—is part and parcel of the motivation to seek out and establish new paths and new connections. What happens under the pressure of monoculturally construed tradition, however, is that the nature of the poetic and the poesis of loss also becomes shifted. In the case of Hindmarsh Island there emerged a different poesis of loss. The claims of the proponent Ngarrindjeri women relaunched the whole reconstitution of knowledge and reconstitution of self from a position of absolute, rather than relative, loss.[1] Under the pressure of a Western system that focuses on the accretion and accumulation of data as a foundation of knowledge, loss of knowledge cannot serve as a constructive precondition for establishing action; it is viewed only in negative terms, as irreversible entropic destruction. In the case of Hindmarsh Island, the wider society contextualized the Ngarrindjeri's notions of lost knowledge in terms of the role of national perception of the progressive and irretrievable loss of Aboriginality itself.

Anthropologists who have worked in Australia will attest that what is lost in the first instance as a result of dispossession is knowledge of the places. What is apparently retained for a much longer period is the knowledge of the songs and the stories associated with these places. What people thus lose is the relationship between the stories and the particular portion of the ground, the content of the analogic armature that has been brought out in these papers. This was what the proponent Ngarrindjeri women attested to in the Hindmarsh Island case. "I knew the stories but it was only recently that I discovered where the stories adhered to topographically," to paraphrase the words of Doreen Kartinyeri, the spokesperson for the proponent women. If we wish to see the songs not just as something merely "about" land but as a form generated from that condition of intimacy, then Kartinyeri's statement is something we need to attend to very closely. This condition for dissident and proponent Ngarrindjeri women alike in the Hindmarsh Island case was a severely restricted range of movement resulting from the Mission station movement, which contained most of the Narrindjeri and other Lower Murray people onto Missions and cut them off from access to 80 percent of their traditional foraging grounds (see Clarke 1994). This containment certainly interfered with the nexus of verbal elaboration and memoriation in a much more profound way than anything happening in Papua New Guinea so far as a result of mineral exploration and logging.[2]

In these systems we have compared, it is not only the nodes or *topoi* that are different but also the relative emphasis on the land. We have begun with the notion of intimacy with actual places as an anchoring point. The visualizing of these places in the imagination attests to the veracity of the sequence of movements depicted in the songs, myths, or mnemonic objects, because one knows that the places are in this order. In the Iatmul case as presented by Wassmann, the sequence is an analogic movement through space—it is an order of *topoi* that one moves through and that is essentially discursive in nature, a practice integral to the politics of interclan competition and struggles among Iatmul men and their relation with women. It is a practice, as is Foi and Kaluli site poetry, that makes the discursive an essential component of landedness. Similarly, what is being struggled over in the Iatmul case is not just rights to use land. One recites the names of the villages in sequence, not staking a claim to the village but asserting possession of the rhetorical, nominal form of knowledge.

Because of the way loss is inscribed as an essential component of knowledge under these conditions, the nexus between verbal *topoi* and actual places is no less problematic in these cases than it is for people who were subject to a massive expropriation of their land. F. E. Williams was with the Keraki people of the Morehead area of Western Province in Papua New Guinea in the early 1930s. When he tried to get people to take him out and show him places, he had enormous difficulty. They told him, "These places must be out here somewhere because we know about the story and we know that it came back here" (see Chapter 1). Here an avowed loss of knowledge of the nexus between place and story was apparently part of the indigenous system, rather than a result of the intrusion of state expropriation.

As I've had reason to return to again and again in the past years, the Foi myth of the origin of pearl shells, the transactable *topos* of their emplaced reproductive world, details not how pearl shells originally *arrived* in Foi territory but explains how these shells were originary to the place of the Foi and were subsequently *lost* (see Weiner

1995c). To return one last time to the planned natural gas pipeline between Papua New Guinea and Australia: the famous Rai Coast cargo leader Yali, immortalized in Peter Lawrence's classic account *Road Belong Cargo,* envisioned that Heaven, the source of all material wealth, was located directly above the city of Sydney. Juillerat reports that the Yafar[3] word *hoofuk,* which means in general the inner, germinal, reproductive core or kernel of anything, is also the word for "cargo." It seems that in the way of many late-modern reversals, the cargo is now flowing in the opposite direction, from its mythical engrounded place in New Guinea to the Heaven-made factories and refineries of Australia. The convergence of apocalyptic millenarianism, new forms of conservative relocalizing and remythologizing practices in the West, and the sheer struggle over resource and territory in a shrinking world are posing a great challenge to anthropology's continuing task of describing and making visible the indigenous. The work within this volume leads us to conclude that the Melanesian/Australian region is one within which the anthropologically important issues of contemporary indigenousness, cultural property, the vesting of the future of indigenous communities in land rights, and control of their own regimes of knowledge transmission are visible in their most explicit and complex form. We hope the volume will be of value to all anthropologists and social scientists working with indigenous communities around the world, all of whom are confronted with the problems of how to characterize the continuity and viability of non-Western modes of knowledge formation and transmission under the pressures of global encroachment and challenge.

Notes

1. This is brought out in the companion volume to this collection, *Mining and Indigenous Lifeworlds in Australia and Papua New Guinea.*
2. But see Kirsch's chapter in Rumsey and Weiner (forthcoming).
3. West Sepik province, Papua New Guinea.

REFERENCES

Aboriginal and Torres Strait Islander Commission. 1997. Cultural industry strategy. http://www.atsic.gov.au.

Abramson, J. A. 1976. Style change in an Upper Sepik contact situation. In *Ethnic and tourist arts,* edited by N. H. H. Graburn, 249–265. Berkeley: University of California Press.

Adams, J. 1996. No dots, no dollars. *Art Monthly Australia* 93:20–22.

Altman, J., and L. Taylor, eds. 1990. *Marketing Aboriginal art in the 1990s.* Canberra: Aboriginal Studies Press.

Anderson, C. 1990a. Australian Aborigines and museums—A new relationship. *Curator* 33:165–179.

———. 1990b. The view from the bush. In *Marketing Aboriginal art in the 1990s,* edited by J. Altman and L. Taylor. Canberra: Aboriginal Studies Press.

———. 1993. The art of the sacred and the art of art: Contemporary Aboriginal painting in central Australia. In *Artistic heritage in a changing Pacific,* edited by P. J. C. Dark and R. G. Rose, 142–148. Honolulu: University of Hawai'i Press.

———, ed. 1995. *Politics of the secret.* Oceania Monograph, no. 45. Sydney: Oceania Publications.

Andrews, N. 1996. Illegal and pernicious practices: Inquiries into indigenous religious beliefs. In *Heritage and Native Title: Anthropological and legal perspectives,* edited by J. Finlayson and A. Jackson-Nakano. Canberra: Australian Institute of Aboriginal and Torres Strait Islander Studies, Native Title Research Unit.

Austin-Broos, D. 1994. Narratives of the encounter at Ntaria. *Oceania* 65 (2): 131–150.

Ayres, M. 1983. This side, that side: Locality and exogamous group definition in the Morehead area, southwestern Papua. Ph.D. diss., University of Chicago.

Baal, J. van. 1963. The cult of the Bull-Roarer in Australia and southern New Guinea. *Bijdragen tot de Taal-, Land- en Volkenkunde* 119:201–214.

———. 1966. *Dema: Description and analysis of Marind-anim culture (south New Guinea)*. The Hague: Martinus Niehoff.

Baker, C. 1980. *The innocent artists: Student art from Papua New Guinea.* Poole, U.K.: Blanford Press.

Baker, R. 1993. Traditional Aboriginal land use in the Borroloola region. In *Traditional ecological knowledge,* edited by N. Williams and G. Baines, 126–143. Canberra: Centre for Resource and Environmental Studies, Australian National University.

Ballard, C. 1993. Stimulating minds to fantasy? A critical etymology for Sahul. In *Sahul in review: Pleistocene archaeology in Australia, New Guinea, and Island Melanesia,* edited by M. A. Smith, M. Spriggs, and B. Fankhauser, 17–23. Occasional Papers in Prehistory, no. 24. Canberra: Department of Prehistory, Research School of Pacific Studies, Australian National University.

———. 1994. The centre cannot hold: Trade networks and sacred geography in the Papua New Guinea highlands. *Archaeology in Oceania* 29 (3): 130–148.

———. 1998. The sun by night: Huli sacred geography and myths of the time of darkness. In *Fluid ontologies,* edited by C. Ballard and L. Goldman, 67–86. Westport, Conn.: Bergin and Garvey.

Barth, F. 1975. *Ritual and knowledge among the Baktaman.* New Haven: Yale University Press.

———. 1987. *Cosmologies in the making.* Cambridge: Cambridge University Press.

Bateson, G. 1932. Social structure of the Iatmul people of the Sepik River. *Oceania* 2:245–291, 401–453.

———. 1936. *Naven: A survey of the problems suggested by a composite picture of the culture of a New Guinea tribe drawn from three points of view.* Cambridge: Cambridge University Press.

———. [1936] 1958. *Naven.* Stanford: Stanford University Press.

Beckett, J. 1975. Death in the family: Some Torres Straits ghost stories. In *Australian Aboriginal mythology,* edited by L. Hiatt, 163–182. Canberra: Australian Institute of Aboriginal Studies Press.

———. 1994. Aboriginal histories, Aboriginal myths: An introduction. *Oceania* 65 (2): 97–116.

Bell, D. 1998. *Ngarrindjeri Wurrawarrin.* Melbourne: Spinifex Press.

Bellman, B. 1984. *The language of secrecy: Symbols and metaphors in Poro ritual.* New Brunswick, N.J.: Rutgers University Press.

Benjamin, R. 1990. Aboriginal art: Exploitation or empowerment? *Art in America* 78, no. 7–8 (July): 73–81.

Bercovitch, E. 1989. Mortal insights: Victim and witch in the Nalumin imagination. In *The religious imagination in New Guinea,* edited by G. H.

Herdt and M. Stephen, 122–159. New Brunswick: Rutgers University Press.

Berndt, R. M. 1951. *Kunapipi: A study of an Australian Aboriginal cult.* Melbourne: Cheshire.

———. 1952. *Djanggawul.* Melbourne: Cheshire.

———. 1962. *An adjustment movement in Arnhem Land.* Cahiers de L'Homme: Paris and The Hague: Mouton.

———. 1984. Traditional morality as expressed through the medium of an Australian Aboriginal religion. In *Religion in Aboriginal Australia,* edited by M. Charlesworth, H. Murphy, D. Bell, and K. Maddock, 175–211. St. Lucia: University of Queensland Press.

Berndt, R., and C. Berndt. 1952. *The first Australians.* Sydney: Ure Smith.

———. 1993. *A world that was.* Melbourne: Melbourne University Press.

Biddle, J. L. 1996. When writing is not writing. *Australia Aboriginal Studies,* no. 1:21–33.

Biersack, A. 1996. The human condition and its transformations: Nature and society in the Paiela world. Paper presented at the annual meeting of the American Anthropological Association.

———, ed. 1995. *Papuan borderlands: Huli, Duna, and Ipili perspectives on the Papua New Guinea highlands.* Ann Arbor: University of Michigan Press.

Bird-David, N. 1992. Beyond "the hunting and gathering mode of subsistence": Culture-sensitive observations on the Nayaka and other modern hunter-gatherers. *Man* 27:19–44.

Blakeney, M. 1995. "Milpurrurru & Ors v. Indofurn Pty Ltd & Ors—Protecting expressions of Aboriginal folklore under copyright law." E Law: *Murdoch University Electronic Journal of Law* 2, no. 1 (April 1995). http://www.murdoch.edu.au/elaw/ issues/v2n1/blakeney.txt.

Blundell, V., and R. Layton. 1978. Marriage, myth, and models of exchange in the West Kimberleys. *Mankind* 11:231–245.

Bolton, L. 1996. Tahigogona's sisters: Women, mats, and landscape on Ambae. In *Arts of Vanuatu,* edited by J. Bonnemaison, C. Kaufman, K. Huffman, and D. Tyron. Bathurst: Crawford House Publishing.

———. 1997. A place containing many places: Museums and the use of objects to represent place in Melanesia. In *Anthro/aesthetics: The cultural construction of aesthetic objects,* edited by D. Losche. Special issue of Australian Journal of Anthropology 8 (1): 18–34.

———, ed. 1999. *Fieldwork and fieldworkers: Developments in Vanuatu research.* Special issue of Oceania 70 (1).

Bonnemaison, J. 1994. *The tree and the canoe: History and ethnography of Tanna.* Honolulu: University of Hawai'i Press.

Borsboom, A. 1998. Knowing the country: Mabo, Native Titles and "traditional" law in Aboriginal Australia. In *Pacific answers to Western hegemony,* edited by J. Wassmann, 311–333. Oxford: Berg.

Bosch, F. D. K. 1960. *The golden germ: An introduction to Indian symbolism.* The Hague: Mouton.

Bowman, D. 1995. Why the skillful use of fire is critical for the management of biodiversity in northern Australia. In *Country in flames: Proceedings of the 1994 symposium on biodiversity and fire in north Australia,* edited by D. Rose, 105–112. Canberra and Darwin: Biodiversity Unit, Department of the Environment, Sport, and Territories, and the North Australia Research Unit.

Bowman, D., and W. Panton. 1993. Decline of *Callitris intratropica* in the Northern Territory: Implications for pre- and post-colonisation fire regimes. *Journal of Biogeography* 20:373–381.

Bradley, J. 1995. Fire: Emotion and politics. A Yanyuwa case study. In *Country in flames: Proceedings of the 1994 symposium on biodiversity and fire in north Australia,* edited by D. Rose, 25–31. Canberra and Darwin: Biodiversity Unit, Department of the Environment, Sport, and Territories, and the North Australia Research Unit.

Bright, A. 1995. Burn grass. In *Country in flames: Proceedings of the 1994 symposium on biodiversity and fire in north Australia,* edited by D. Rose, 59–62. Canberra and Darwin: Biodiversity Unit, Department of the Environment, Sport, and Territories, and the North Australia Research Unit.

Briscoe, G. 1993. Aboriginal Australian identity. *History Workshop Journal* 36: 133–161.

Browne, D. R. 1990. Aboriginal radio in Australia: From dreamtime to prime time? *Journal of Communication* 40:111–120.

Brumbaugh, R. 1987. The rainbow serpent on the Upper Sepik. *Anthropos* 82: 25–33.

Brunton, R. 1980a. Correspondence. *Man* 15 (4): 734–735.

———. 1980b. Misconstrued order in Melanesian religion. *Man* 15 (1): 112–128.

———. 1996. The Hindmarsh Island Bridge and the credibility of Australian anthropology. *Anthropology Today* 12 (4): 2–7.

Burridge, K. 1960. *Mambu*. London: Methuen.

Buttimer, A. 1976. Grasping the dynamism of the lifeworld. *Annals of the Association of American Geographers* 66 (2).

Capell, A. 1956. *A new approach to Australian languages*. Oceania Linguistic Monographs, no. 1. Sydney: Oceania Publications.

———. 1972. *Cave painting myths: Northern Kimberley.* Oceania Linguistic Monographs, no. 18. Sydney: Oceania Publications.

Castoriadis, C. 1987. *The imaginary institution of society.* Cambridge, Mass.: MIT Press.

Chaloupka, G. 1993. *Journey in time: The 50,000-year story of the Australian Aboriginal rock art of Arnhem Land*. Kew, Victoria: Reed.

Chatwin, B. 1987. *The songlines*. London: Cape.

Chidester, D., and E. Linenthal, eds. 1995. *American sacred space*. Bloomington: Indiana University Press.

Clark, J. 1993. Gold, sex, and pollution: Male illness and myth at Mt. Kare. *American Ethnologist* 20:742–757.

Clarke, P. 1994. Contact, conflict, and regeneration: Aboriginal cultural geography of the Lower Murray, South Australia. Ph.D. diss., Departments of Geography and Anthropology, University of Adelaide.

Clastres, P. 1977. *Society against the state*. Oxford: Blackwell.

Clifford, J. 1995. Paradise. *Visual Anthropology Review* 11:92–117.

———. 1997. *Routes: Travel and translation in the late twentieth century*. Cambridge: Harvard University Press.

Coate, H. H. C., and E. P. Elkin. 1974. *Ngarinjin-English dictionary*. 2 vols. Oceania Linguistic Monographs, no. 16. Sydney: Oceania Publications.

Cochrane Simons, S., and H. Stevenson, eds. 1990. *Luk luk gen! (Look again!): Contemporary art from PNG*. Townsville: Perc Tucker Regional Gallery.

Craig, B. 1984. Non-violent land rights claims from the centre. *Artlink* 4:19–20.

Craig, B., and D. Hyndman, eds. 1990. *Children of Afek: Tradition and change among the mountain Ok of central New Guinea*. Sydney: Oceania Publications.

Crawford, I. 1968. *The art of the Wandjina: Aboriginal cave paintings in Kimberley, Western Australia*. Melbourne: Oxford University Press.

Croft, B. 1992. A very brief bit of an overview of the Aboriginal arts/cultural industry by a sort of renegade or the cultural correctness of certain issues. *Art Monthly Australia,* no. 56, 20–22.

Crook, T. n.d. On exegesis. Manuscript in author's possession.

———. n.d. On the aesthetics of knowing in Bolivip, Papua New Guinea. Manuscript in author's possession.

Damon, F., and R. Wagner, eds. 1989. *Death rituals and life in the societies of the Kula ring*. DeKalb: Northern Illinois University Press.

Deleuze, G., and F. Guattari. [1972] 1977. *Anti-Oedipus: Capitalism and schizophrenia*. New York: Viking.

———. [1980] 1987. *A thousand plateaus: Capitalism and schizophrenia*. Minneapolis: University of Minnesota Press.

Dissanayake, E. 1988. Coming of age in Papua New Guinea. *Art in America* 76: 45–47.

Dixon, Robert. 1980. *The languages of Australia*. Cambridge: Cambridge University Press.

———. n.d. *Australian Aboriginal languages: Their structure and development*. Forthcoming.

Dubinskas, F., and S. Traweek. 1984. Closer to the ground: A reinterpretation of Walbiri iconography. *Man* (n.s.) 19: 15–30.

Dunbar-Hall, P. 1997. Music and meaning: The Aboriginal rock album. *Australian Aboriginal Studies* 1 (1): 38–47.

Dussart, F. 1997. A body painting in translation. In *Rethinking visual anthropology,* edited by M. Banks and H. Morphy, 186–202. New Haven: Yale University Press.

Dwyer, P. 1996. The invention of nature. In *Redefining nature: Ecology, culture, and domestication,* edited by R. Ellen and K. Fukui, 157–186. Oxford: Berg.

Edwards, R., and J. Stewart, eds. 1980. *Preserving indigenous cultures: A new role for museums*. Canberra: Australian National Commission for UNESCO.

Ehrenzweig, A. 1967. *The hidden order of art.* London: Weidenfield and Nicholson.

Elkin, A. P. 1932. Social organization in the Kimberley division, north-western Australia. *Oceania* 2:296–333.

———. 1933. Totemism in north west Australia. *Oceania* 3:257–296.

———. [1938] 1954. *The Australian Aborigines: How to understand them.* Sydney: Angus and Robertson.

Ellinson, D. 1994. Unauthorised reproduction of traditional Aboriginal art. *University of New South Wales Law Journal* 17:327–344.

Eoe, S. M. 1991. The role of museums in the Pacific: Change or die. In *Museums and cultural centres in the Pacific,* edited by S. M. Eoe and P. Swadling, 1–4. Port Moresby: Papua New Guinea National Museum.

Eoe, S. M., and P. Swadling, eds. 1991. *Museums and cultural centres in the Pacific.* Port Moresby: Papua New Guinea National Museum.

Errington, F. K., and D. B. Gewertz. 1985. The chief of the Chambri: Social change and cultural permeability among a New Guinea people. *American Ethnologist* 12:442–454.

———. 1986. The confluence of powers: Entropy and importation among the Chambri. *Oceania* 57:99–113.

———. 1996. The individuation of tradition in a Papua New Guinea modernity. *American Anthropologist* 98:224–236.

Fairbairn, W. R. D. 1944. Endopsychic structure considered in terms of object-relations. *International Journal of Psycho-Analysis* 25:70–93.

Fajans, J. 1998. Transforming nature, making culture: Why the Baining are not environmentalists. *Social Analysis* 42:12–27.

Fardon, R. 1987. African ethnogenesis. In *Comparative anthropology,* edited by L. Holy, 168–188. Oxford: Blackwell.

———, ed. 1990. *Localizing strategies: Regional traditions of ethnographic writing.* Washington, D.C.: Smithsonian Institution Press, 1990.

Faulstich, P. 1993. "You read 'im this country": Landscape, self, and art in an Aboriginal community. In *Artistic heritage in a changing Pacific,* edited by P. J. C. Dark and R. G. Rose, 149–161. Honolulu: University of Hawai'i Press.

Feld, S. 1990. *Sound and sentiment.* 2d ed. Philadelphia: University of Pennsylvania Press.

———. 1991. Voices of the rainforest. *Public Culture* 4:131–140.

———. 1996. Waterfalls of sound: Acoustemologies of place resounding. In *Senses of place,* edited by S. Feld and K. Basso, 91–136. Santa Fe: School of American Research Press.

Fergie, D. 1994. To all the mothers that were, to all the mothers who are, to all the mothers who will be. Report submitted to the South Australian Aboriginal Legal Rights Movement.

Fernandez, J. 1998. Trees of knowledge of self and other in culture: On models for the moral imagination. In *The social life of trees: Anthropological perspectives on tree symbolism,* edited by L. Rival, 81–110. Oxford: Berg.

Flood, J. 1983. *Archaeology of the dreamtime*. Sydney: Collins.

Foana'ota, L. A. 1994. Solomon Islands national museum and cultural centre policy. In *Culture, kastom, tradition: Developing cultural policy in Melanesia,* edited by L. Lindstrom and G. M. White, 99–102. Suva, Fiji: Institute of Pacific Studies, University of the South Pacific.

Foley, F. 1990. On Aboriginality, art, life, and landscape. *Art Monthly Australia* 30:10–12.

Foley, W. 1986. *The Papuan languages of New Guinea.* Cambridge: Cambridge University Press.

Fortes, M., and E. E. Evans-Pritchard, eds. 1948. *African political systems.* London: Oxford University Press.

Foster, R. 1996/1997. Commercial mass media in Papua New Guinea: Notes on agency, bodies, and commodity consumption. *Visual Anthropology Review* 12:1–17.

———. 1999. Melanesianist anthropology in the era of globalization. *Contemporary Pacific* 11:140–159.

———, ed. 1995. *Nation making: Emergent identities in postcolonial Melanesia.* Ann Arbor: University of Michigan Press.

Fourmile, H. 1994. Aboriginal arts in relation to multiculturalism. In *Culture, difference, and the arts,* edited by S. Gunew and F. Rizvi, 69–85. St. Leonards, Australia: Allen and Unwin.

Fox, J. 1997a. Genealogy and topogeny: Towards an ethnography of Rotinese ritual place names. In *The poetic power of place,* edited by J. Fox, 92–103. Canberra: Australian National University.

———. 1997b. Place and landscape in comparative Austronesian perspective. In *The poetic power of place,* edited by J. Fox, 1–21. Canberra: Australian National University.

———, ed. 1997c. *The poetic power of place: Comparative perspectives on Austronesian ideas of locality.* Canberra: Department of Anthropology, Research School of Pacific and Asian Studies, Australian National University.

Frankel, S. 1986. *The Huli response to illness.* Cambridge: Cambridge University Press.

Fry, T., and A-M. Willis. 1989. Aboriginal art: Symptom or success. *Art in America* 77, no. 7 (July): 108–117, 159–160, 169.

Gell, A. 1980. Correspondence. *Man* 15 (4): 735–737.

Gewertz, D. 1983. *Sepik River societies: A historical ethnography of the Chambri and their neighbours.* New Haven and London: Yale University Press.

Gewertz, D. B., and F. K. Errington. 1991. *Twisted histories, altered contexts: Representing the Chambri in a world system.* Cambridge: Cambridge University Press.

———. 1996. On piety and PepsiCo in a Papua New Guinea "Modernity." *American Ethnologist* 23:476–493.

Giambelli, R. A. 1998. The coconut, the body, and the human being: Metaphors of life and growth in Nusa Penida and Bali. In *The social life of trees:*

Anthropological perspectives on tree symbolism, edited by L. Rival, 133–157. Oxford: Berg.

Ginsburg, F. 1993. Aboriginal media and the Australian imaginary. *Public Culture* 5:557–578.

Goldman, L. 1983. *Talk never dies: The language of Huli disputes*. London: Tavistock Publications.

Goldman, L., and C. Ballard. 1998. *Fluid ontologies: Myth, ritual, and philosophy in the highlands of Papua New Guinea*. Westport: Bergin and Garvey.

Golvan, C. 1992a. Aboriginal art and the protection of indigenous cultural rights. *Aboriginal Law Bulletin* 2:5–8.

———. 1992b. Aboriginal art and the protection of indigenous cultural rights. *European Intellectual Property Review* 14:227–232.

———. 1992c. Tribal ownership of Aboriginal art. *Arts and Entertainment Law Review* (December) 3: 15–17.

Goodale, J. C. 1995. *To sing with pigs is human: The concept of person in Papua New Guinea*. Seattle and London: University of Washington Press.

Gosden, C. 1992. Production systems and the colonisation of the Western Pacific. *World Archaeology* 24:55–69.

———. 1995. Arboriculture and agriculture in coastal Papua New Guinea. In *Transitions: Pleistocene to Holocene in Australia and Papua New Guinea*, edited by J. Allen and J. F. O'Connell. Special issue of Antiquity 69 (265): 807–817.

Gray, S. 1993. Wheeling, dealing, and deconstruction: Aboriginal art and the land post-Mabo. *Aboriginal Law Bulletin* 3:10–12.

———. 1995. Enlightenment or dreaming? Attempting to reconcile Aboriginal art and European law. *Arts and Entertainment Law Review* 2 (April): 18–26.

Gregor, T., and D. Tuzin, eds. In preparation. Gender in Amazonia and Melanesia: An exploration of the comparative method.

Griffin, D. 1996. Introduction. *Museums Australia. Previous possessions, new obligations. A plain English summary of policies for museums in Australia and Aboriginal and Torres Strait Islander Peoples*. Melbourne: Museums Australia.

Guddemi, P. 1992. We came from this: Knowledge, memory, painting, and "play" in the initiation rituals of the Sawiyan of Papua New Guinea. Ph.D. diss., University of Michigan.

Guiart, J. 1951. Forerunners of Melanesian nationalism. *Oceania* 22 (2): 81–90.

Haley, N. 1995. Where ritual roads converge: Exploring some of the myths associated with ritual performance at Gelote. Paper presented at conference, Importing Cultures: Regional Transformations in Myth and Ritual in the Western Highlands of Papua New Guinea, Brisbane.

———. 1996. Revisioning the past, remembering the future: Duna accounts of the world's end. *Oceania* 66:278–285.

Hallam, S. 1975. *Fire and hearth: A study of Aboriginal usage and European usurpation in south-western Australia*. Canberra: Australian Institute of Aboriginal Studies.

Hanks, W. 1996. *Language and communicative practices*. New York: Westview.

Harrison, S. 1990. *Stealing people's names: History and politics in a Sepik River cosmology*. Cambridge: Cambridge University Press.

Hayward, P. 1993. After the record: The *Tabaran* documentary, Papua New Guinea, and inter-cultural relations. *Perfect Beat* 1 (3): 75–85.

———. 1995. A new tradition: Titus Tilly and the development of music video in Papua New Guinea. *Perfect Beat* 2 (2): 1–19.

Head, L. 1994. Landscapes socialised by fire: Post-contact changes in Aboriginal fire use in northern Australia, and implications for prehistory. *Archaeology in Oceania* 29:172–181.

Heelas, P., Lash, S., and P. Morris, eds. 1996. *Detraditionalization: Critical reflections on authority and identity*. Oxford: Blackwell.

Hemming, S. 1994. In the tracks of Ngurunderi: The South Australian Museum's Ngurunderi exhibition and cultural tourism. *Australian Aboriginal Studies*, no. 2:38–46.

Herdt, G. 1990. Secret societies and secret collectives. *Oceania* 60 (4): 361–381.

Hermann, E. 1992. The Yali movement in retrospect: Rewriting history, redefining "cargo cult." *Oceania* 63:55–71.

Hiatt, L. R. 1971. Secret pseudo-procreation rites among the Australian Aborigines. In *Anthropology in Oceania: Essays presented to Ian Hogbin*, edited by L. R. Hiatt and C. Jayawardena, 77–88. Sydney: Angus and Robertson.

———. 1975. Swallowing and regurgitation in Australian myth and rite. In *Australian Aboriginal mythology*, ed. L. R. Hiatt, 143–162. Canberra: Australian Institute of Aboriginal Studies.

Hill, J. D. 1993. *Keepers of the sacred chants: The poetics of ritual in an Amazonian society*. Tucson: University of Arizona Press.

Hollinsworth, D. 1992. Discourse on Aboriginality and the politics of identity in urban Australia. *Oceania* 63:137–155.

Horton, D. 1982. The burning question: Aborigines, fire, and Australian ecosystems. *Mankind* 13:237–251.

Horwitz, P., and B. Knott. 1995. The distribution and spread of the yabby Cherax destructor complex in Australia: Speculations, hypotheses and the need for research. *Freshwater Crayfish* 10:81–91.

Huber, P. 1980. The Anggor bowman: Ritual and society in Melanesia. *American Ethnologist* 7:43–57.

Hynes, R., and A. Chase. 1982. Plants, sites, and domiculture: Aboriginal influence upon plant communities in Cape York Peninsula. *Archaeology in Oceania* 17:38–50.

Ingold, T. 1986. Territoriality and tenure: The appropriation of space in hunting and gathering societies. In T. Ingold, *The appropriation of nature: Essays on human ecology and social relations*, pp. 130–164. Manchester: Manchester University Press.

———. 1994. From trust to domination: An alternative history of human-animal relations. In *Animals and human society: Changing perspectives*, edited by A. Manning and J. Serpell, 1–22. London: Routledge.

———. 1996. Hunting and gathering as ways of perceiving the environment. In

Redefining nature: Ecology, culture, and domestication, edited by R. R. Ellen and K. Fukui, 117–155. Oxford: Berg.

Jacobson, A. 1992. The idolatry of rules: Writing law according to Moses, with reference to other jurisprudences. In *Deconstruction and the possibility of justice,* edited by D. Cornell, M. Rosenfeld, and D. Carlson, 95–151. London: Routledge.

James, R. 1993. The politics of Aboriginality. *Oceania* 63:207–221.

Johnson, V. 1990. Into the urbane: Urban Aboriginal art in the Australian context. *Art Monthly Australia* 30:20–23.

———. 1996. *Copyrites: Aboriginal art in the age of reproductive technologies.* Touring Exhibition 1996 Catalogue. National Indigenous Arts Advocacy Association and Macquarie University.

Jones, P. 1988. Perceptions of Aboriginal art: A history. In *Dreamings,* edited by P. Sutton, 143–179. Ringwood: Viking.

———. 1992. The boomerang in erratic flight: The mutability of ethnographic objects. In *Power, knowledge, and Aborigines,* edited by B. Attwood and J. Arnold, 59–71. Bundoora: La Trobe University Press and the National Centre for Australian Studies, Monash University.

Jones, R. 1969. Fire-stick farming. *Australian Natural History* 16:224–228.

———. 1985. Ordering the landscape. In *Seeing the first Australians,* edited by I. Donaldson and T. Donaldson, 181–209. Sydney: George Allen and Unwin.

———. 1995. The legacy of the firestick. In *Country in flames: Proceedings of the 1994 symposium on biodiversity and fire in north Australia,* edited by D. Rose, 25–31. Canberra and Darwin: Biodiversity Unit, Department of the Environment, Sport, and Territories, and the North Australia Research Unit.

Jones, R., and J. Bowler. 1980. Struggle for the savanna: Northern Australia in ecological and historic perspective. In *Northern Australia: Options and implications,* edited by R. Jones, 3–31. Canberra: Research School of Pacific and Asian Studies.

Jorgensen, D. 1980. What's in a name: The meaning of meaninglessness in Telefolmin. *Ethos* 8:349–366.

———. 1990a. Placing the past and moving the present: Myth and contemporary history in Telefolmin. *Culture* 10:47–56.

———. 1990b. Secrecy's turn. *Canberra Anthropology* 13:40–47.

———. 1998. Whose nature? Invading bush spirits, travelling ancestors, and mining in Telefolmin. *Social Analysis* 42:100–116.

Juillerat, B. 1980. Correspondence. *Man* 15 (4): 732–734.

Kahn, M. 1996. Your place and mine: Sharing emotional landscapes in Wamira, Papua New Guinea. In *Senses of Place,* edited by S. Feld and K. Basso, 167–198. Santa Fe: School of American Research Press.

Kaplan, F. 1994. Introduction. *Museums and the making of "ourselves": The role of objects in national identity,* edited by F. Kaplan, 1–15. London and New York: Leicester University Press.

Kaplan, M. 1995. *Neither cargo nor cult.* Durham, N.C.: Duke University Press.

Kasaherou, E. 1995. The role of the museum in culturally diverse New Caledonia. In *Museums and cross cultural understanding: Papers from the Fifth Regional Assembly of the Asia Pacific Organisation of the International Council of Museums, 24–27 September 1993,* edited by A. Galla, B. Murphy, and D. McMichael, 28–32. Australia: Australian National Committee of International Council of Museums.

Keefe, K. 1988. Aboriginality: Resistence and persistence. *Australian Aboriginal Studies,* no. 1:67–81.

———. 1992. *From the centre to the city.* Canberra: Aboriginal Studies Press.

Keen, I. 1993. Review of "A Place for Strangers." *Australian Journal of Anthropology* 4 (2): 96–110. Sydney: Anthropology Society of New South Wales.

———. 1994. *Knowledge and secrecy in an Aboriginal religion.* Oxford: Clarendon Press.

Kimber, R. 1976. Beginnings of farming? Some man-plant-animal relationships in central Australia. *Mankind* 10 (3): 142–151.

———. 1983. Black lightning: Aborigines and fire in Central Australia and the western desert. *Archaeology in Oceania* 18:38–45.

———. 1995. Politics of the secret in contemporary western desert art. In *Politics of the secret,* edited by C. Anderson, 123–142. Sydney: University of Sydney.

Kimber, R., and M. Smith. 1987. An Aranda ceremony. In *Australians to 1788,* edited by E. Mulvaney and J. White, 220–237. Sydney: Fairfax, Syme, and Weldon Associates.

Knauft, B. 1993. *South coast New Guinea cultures: History, comparison, dialectic.* Cambridge: Cambridge University Press.

——— 1996. *Genealogies for the present in cultural anthropology.* New York: Routledge.

Kolig, E. 1981. *The silent revolution: The effects of modernisation on Australian Aboriginal religions.* Philadelphia: Institute for the Study of Human Issues.

Kulick, D., and C. Stroud. 1990. Christianity, cargo, and ideas of self: Patterns of literacy in a Papua New Guinean village. *Man,* n.s., 25: 286–304.

La Flesche, F. 1925. *The Osage tribe: The rite of vigil.* 39th Annual Report. Washington: Bureau of American Ethnology.

Lambek, M., and A. Strathern, eds. 1998. *Bodies and persons: Comparative perspectives from Africa and Melanesia.* Cambridge: Cambridge University Press.

Lancy. D. F., and A. Strathern. 1981. "Making twos": Pairing as an alternative to the taxonomic mode of representation. *American Anthropologist* 83: 773–795.

Langton, M. 1994. Aboriginal art and film: The politics of representation. *Race and Class* 35:89–106.

Lattas, A. 1989. Trickery and sacrifice: Tambarans and the appropriation of female reproductive power in male initiation ceremonies in West New Britain. *Man* 24 (3): 451–469.

———. 1992a. Primitivism, nationalism, and individualism in Australian popular culture. In *Power, knowledge and Aborigines,* edited by B. Attwood and J. Arnold, 45–58. Bundoora: La Trobe University Press and the National Centre for Australian Studies, Monash University.

———. 1992b. Wiping the blood off Aboriginality: The politics of Aboriginal embodiment in contemporary intellectual debate. *Oceania* 63:160–164.

———. 1992c. The punishment of masks. *Canberra Anthropology* 15(2):69–88.

———. 1993. Essentialism, memory, and resistance: Aboriginality and the politics of authenticity. *Oceania* 63:240–267.

———. 1996. Colonialism, Aborigines, and the politics of time and space: The placing of strangers and the placing of oneself. *Social Analysis* 40:20–42.

———. 1998. *Cultures of secrecy: Reinventing race in bush Kaliai.* Madison: University of Wisconsin Press.

Latz, P. 1995. Fire in the desert: Increasing biodiversity in the short term, decreasing it in the long term. In *Country in flames: Proceedings of the 1994 symposium on biodiversity and fire in north Australia,* edited by D. Rose, 77–86. Canberra and Darwin: Biodiversity Unit, Department of the Environment, Sport, and Territories, and the North Australia Research Unit.

Lawrence, P. 1964. *Road belong cargo.* Melbourne: Melbourne University Press.

Laycock, D. 1979. Linguistic boundaries and unsolved problems in Papua New Guinea. In *New Guinea and neighbouring areas: A sociolinguistic laboratory,* edited by S. Wurm, 81–99. The Hague: Mouton.

Layton, R. 1995. Relating to the country in the western desert. In *The anthropology of landscape: Perspectives on place and space,* edited by E. Hirsch and M. O'Hanlon, 210–231. Oxford: Clarendon Press.

Leach, Jerry, and Edmund Leach, eds. 1983. *The Kula: New perspectives on Massim exchange.* Cambridge: Cambridge University Press.

Lederman, R. 1998. Globalization and the future of culture areas: Melanesianist anthropology in transition. *Annual Review of Anthropology* 27:427–449.

Leopold, A. [1949] 1976. *A sand county almanac, and sketches here and there.* London: Oxford University Press.

Lester, Y. 1994. Understanding country: Dialogue can resolve differences. *Weekend Australian,* July 30–31, 1994, 16.

Lévi-Strauss, C. 1963. *Structural anthropology.* New York: Basic Books.

———. 1965. The future of kinship studies. In *Proceedings of the Royal Anthropological Institute of Great Britain and Ireland for 1965,* 12–22.

———. 1966. *The savage mind.* Chicago: University of Chicago Press.

———. [1949] 1969. *The elementary structures of kinship.* Boston: Beacon.

Lewis, P. 1990. Tourist art, traditional art, and the museum in Papua New Guinea. In *Art and identity in Oceania,* edited by A. Hanson and L. Hanson, 149–163. Honolulu: University of Hawai'i Press.

Lindstrom, L. 1990. *Knowledge and power in a South Pacific society.* Washington, D.C.: Smithsonian Institution Press.

———. 1993. *Cargo cult: Strange stories of desire from Melanesia and beyond.* Honolulu: University of Hawai'i Press.

Linton, R. 1959. *The tree of culture*. New York: Knopf.

Lommel, A. [1952] 1969. Die Unambal, ein Stamm in Nordwest-Australien. Homburg: Monographien zur Volkerkunde. Unpublished English translation by F. Zandvoort, 1997.

Lutkehaus, N., C. Kaufmann, W. Mitchell, D. Newton, L. Osmundsen, and M. Schuster, eds. 1990. *Sepik heritage: Tradition and change in Papua New Guinea*. Durham, N.C.: Carolina Academic Press.

Macknight, C. C. 1976. *The voyage to Marege': Macassan trepangers in northern Australia*. Melbourne: Melbourne University Press.

———. 1986. Macassans and the Aboriginal past. In C. C. Macknight and J. P. White, eds., *Papers presented to John Mulvaney. Archaeology in Oceania* 21 (1): 69–75.

Maddock, K. 1972. *The Australian Aborigines: A portrait of their society*. London: Allen Lane.

———. 1980. *Anthropology, law, and the definition of Australian Aboriginal rights to land*. Nijmegan: Catholic University.

———. 1988. Copyright and traditional designs: An Aborignal dilemma. *Aboriginal Law Bulletin* 2:8–9.

Magowan, F. 1994. Melodies of mourning. Ph.D. diss., Oxford University.

Marrie, A. 1985. Killing me softly: Aboriginal art and Western critics. *Art Network* 14:17–21.

Maschio, T. 1994. *To remember the faces of the dead*. Madison: University of Wisconsin Press.

Mathews, J. 1996. Commonwealth Hindmarsh Island report. Canberra: Commonwealth Government of Australia.

McConvell, P., and N. Evans, eds. 1997. *Archaeology and linguistics: Aboriginal Australia in global perspective*. Melbourne: Oxford University Press.

McDowell, N. 1985. Past and future: The nature of episodic time in Bun. In *History and ethnohistory in Papua New Guinea,* edited by D. Gewertz and E. Schieffelin, 26–39. Oceania Monograph, no. 28. Sydney: Oceania Publications.

Mead, M. 1933–1934. The Marsalai cult among the Arapesh, with special reference to the rainbow serpent beliefs of the Australian Aborigines. *Oceania* 4:37–53.

———. [1938] 1970. *The mountain Arapesh*. Vol. 2, Arts and supernaturalism. Garden City, N.Y.: Natural History Press.

Megaw, J. V. S. 1982. Western desert acrylic painting: Artifact or art? *Art History* 5:205–218.

———. 1990. Art as identity: Aspects of contemporary Aboriginal art. In *Art and identity in Oceania,* edited by A. Hanson and L. Hanson, 282–292. Honolulu: University of Hawai'i Press.

Megaw, M. R., and J. V. S. Megaw. 1993. Black art and white society: Some bicentennial observations on contemporary Australian Aboriginal art. In *Artistic heritage in a changing Pacific,* edited by P. J. C. Dark and R. G. Rose. Honolulu: University of Hawai'i Press.

Meggitt, M. J. 1962. *Desert people: A study of the Walbiri Aborigines of Central Australia*. Sydney: Angus and Robertson.

Merlan, F. 1997. Fighting over country. Four commonplaces. In *Fighting over country: Anthropological perspectives,* edited by D. E. Smith and J. Finlayson, CAEPR Research Monograph no. 12:1–15. Canberra: Centre for Aboriginal Economic Policy Research.

———. 1998. *Caging the rainbow: Places, politics, and Aborigines in a north Australian town.* Honolulu: University of Hawai'i Press.

Merlan, F., and A. Rumsey 1991. *Ku Waru: Language and segmentary politics in the western Nebilyer Valley, Papua New Guinea.* Cambridge: Cambridge University Press.

Michaels, E. 1988. Bad Aboriginal art. *Art and Text* 28:59–73. Reprinted in Michaels 1994:142–162.

———. 1994. *Bad Aboriginal art: Tradition, media, and technological horizons.* Minneapolis: University of Minnesota Press.

Mimica, J. 1988. *Intimations of infinity.* Oxford: Berg.

Mitchell, J., ed. 1991. *The Selected Melanie Klein.* Harmondsworth, U.K.: Penguin.

Mitchell, T. 1992. World music, indigenous music, and music television in Australia. *Perfect Beat* 1 (1): 1–16.

———. 1996. *Popular music and local identity: Rock, pop, and rap in Europe and Oceania.* London: Leicester University Press.

Montagu, A. 1974. *Coming into being among the Australian Aborigines: The procreative beliefs of the Australian Aborigines.* 2d ed. London: Routledge and Kegan Paul.

Morgan, S. 1988. *My place.* Freemantle: Freemantle Arts Centre Press.

Morphy, H. 1983. "Now you understand": An analysis of the way Yolngu have used sacred knowledge to retain their autonomy. In *Aborigines, land, and land rights,* edited by N. Peterson and M. Langton, 110–133. Canberra: Australian Institute of Aboriginal Studies.

———. 1991. *Ancestral connections: Art and an Aboriginal system of knowledge.* Chicago: University of Chicago Press.

———. 1994. The interpretation of ritual: Reflections from film on anthropological practice. *Man* 29:117–146.

———. 1995. Landscape and the reproduction of the ancestral past. In *The Anthropology of Landscape,* edited by E. Hirsch and M. O'Hanlon, 184–209. Oxford: Oxford University Press.

———. 1996. Empiricism to metaphysics: In defence of the concept of the dreamtime. In *Prehistory to politics: John Mulvaney, the humanities, and the public intellectual,* edited by T. Bonyhady and Tom Griffiths, 163–189. Melbourne: Melbourne University Press.

Morson, G., and C. Emerson. 1990. *Mikhail Bakhtin: Creation of a prosaics.* Stanford: Stanford University Press.

Morton, J. 1987. Singing subjects and sacred objects: More of Munn's "transformation of subjects into objects" in Central Australian myth. *Oceania* 58:100–118.

———. 1989. Singing subjects and sacred objects: A psychological interpretation of the "transformation of subjects into objects" in Central Australian myth. *Oceania* 59:280–297.

———. 1997. Totemism now and then: A natural science of society? In *Scholar and sceptic: Australian Aboriginal studies in honour of Les Hiatt*, edited by F. Merlan, J. Morton, and A. Rumsey, 151–170. Canberra: Aboriginal Studies Press.

Mowaljarlai, D., and J. Malnic. 1993. *Yorro Yorro: The spirit of the Kimberleys.* Broome: Magabala Books.

Mowaljarlai, D., and P. Vinnicombe. 1995. That rock that is a cloud: Concepts associated with rock images in the Kimberley region of Western Australia. In *Perceiving rock art: Social and Political Perspectives*, edited by K. Helskog and B. Olsen. Oslo: Novus Forlag, Instituttet for Sammenlignende Kulturforskning.

Moyle, R. 1983. Songs, ceremonies, and sites: The Agharringa case. In *Aborigines, land, and land rights*, edited by N. Peterson and M. Langton, 66–93. Canberra: Australian Institute of Aboriginal Studies.

Muecke, S. 1992. *Textual spaces: Aboriginality and cultural studies.* Sydney: New South Wales University Press.

———. 1997. *No road: Bitumen all the way.* Freemantle: Freemantle Arts Centre Press.

Muecke, S., K. Benterrak, and P. Roe. 1984. *Reading the country: Introduction to nomadology.* Freemantle: Freemantle Arts Centre Press.

Mulvaney, D. J., H. Morphy, and A. Petch, eds. 1997. *"My Dear Spencer": The letters of F. J. Gillen to Baldwin Spencer.* South Melbourne: Hyland House.

Munn, N. 1964. Totemic designs and group continuity in Walbiri and Pitjantjatjara myth. In *Australian Aboriginal anthropology*, edited by R. M. Berndt, 83–100. Nedlands, Western Australia: University of Western Australia Press.

———. 1969. The effectiveness of symbols in Murngin rite and myth. In *Forms of symbolic action*, edited by R. F. Spencer, 178–207. Seattle: American Ethnological Society.

———. 1970. The transformation of subjects into objects in Walbiri and Pitjantjatjara myth. In *Australian Aboriginal anthropology: Modern studies in the social anthropology of the Australian Aborigines*, edited by R. M. Berndt, 141–163. Nedlands, Western Australia: University of Western Australia Press.

———. 1973a. The spatial presentation of cosmic order in Walbiri iconography. In *Primitive art and society*, edited by A. Forge, 193–220. London: Tavistock.

———. 1973b. *Walbiri iconography: Graphic representation and cultural symbolism in a central Australian society.* Ithaca: Cornell University Press.

———. 1996. Excluded spaces: The figure in the Australian Aboriginal landscape. *Critical Inquiry* 22:446–465.

Museums Australia. 1996. *Previous possessions, new obligations: A plain English summary of policies for museums in Australia and Aboriginal and Torres Strait Islander peoples.* Melbourne: Museums Australia.

Myers, F. 1986. *Pintupi country, Pintupi self: Sentiment, place, and politics among western desert Aborigines*. Washington, D.C.: Smithsonian Institution Press.

———. 1989. Truth, beauty, and Pintupi painting. *Visual Anthropology* 2:163–195.

———. 1991. Representing culture: The production of discourse(s) for Aboriginal acrylic painting. *Cultural Anthropology* 6:26–62.

———. 1994. Beyond the intentional fallacy: Art criticism and the ethnography of Aboriginal acrylic painting. *Visual Anthropology Review* 10:10–43.

Nakinch, T. 1977. The origin and formation of the Ulga and Upuka people in the Nebilyer area of Mt. Hagen. Institute of Applied Social and Economic Research occasional paper. Port Moresby: Institute of Applied Social and Economic Research.

Newsome, A. 1980. The eco-mythology of the red kangaroo in central Australia. *Mankind* 12 (4): 327–334.

Niles, D. 1996. Questions of music in Papua New Guinea. *Perfect Beat* 2 (4): 58–62.

Nuenfeldt, K. 1993. The essentialistic, the exotic, the equivocal, and the absurd: The cultural production and use of the didjeridu in world music. *Perfect Beat* 2 (1): 88–104.

———, ed. 1997. *The didjeridu: From Arnhem Land to Internet*. Sydney: John Libbey.

O'Connell, J. F., and J. Allen. 1998. When did humans first arrive in Australia and why is it important to know? *Evolutionary Anthropology* 6:132–146.

O'Hanlon, M. 1993. *Paradise: Portraying the New Guinea highlands*. London: British Museum Press.

———. 1995. Modernity and the "graphicalization" of meaning: New Guinea highland shield design in historical perspective. *Journal of the Royal Anthropological Institute* 1:469–493.

Onus, L. 1990a. Copyright and issues of appropriation. *Artlink* 10 (1–2): 38–39.

———. 1990b. Language and lasers. *Art Monthly Australia* 30:14–19.

Otto, T., and N. Thomas, eds. 1997. *Narratives of nation in the South Pacific*. Amsterdam: Harwood.

Palmer, K. 1995. Religious knowledge and the politics of continuity and change. In *Politics of the secret*, edited by C. Anderson, 15–26. Oceania Monographs, no. 45. Sydney: Oceania Publications.

Pannell, S. 1994. Mabo and museums: "The indigenous (re)appropriation of indigenous things." *Oceania* 65:18–39.

Panoff, M. 1968. The notion of double self among the Maenge people of New Britain. *Journal Polynesian Society* 77:275–296.

Parkin, D. 1987. Comparison as the search for continuity. In *Comparative anthropology*, edited by L. Holy. Oxford: Blackwell.

Paulius, N. E. 1991. The cultural heritage of the Pacific: Preservation, development, and promotion. In *Museums and cultural centres in the Pacific*, edited by S. M. Eoe and P. Swadling, 5–14. Port Moresby: Papua New Guinea National Museum.

Pentony, P. 1961. Dreams and dream beliefs in North Western Australia. *Oceania* 32:144–149.

Peterson, N. 1976. The natural and cultural areas of Aboriginal Australia: A preliminary analysis of population groupings with adaptive significance. In *Tribes and boundaries in Australia,* edited by N. Peterson, 50–71. Canberra: Australian Institute of Aboriginal Studies.

———. 1995. "Peoples," "islands," and "succession." In *Anthropology in the Native Title era,* edited by J. Fingleton and J. Finlayson, 11–18. Canberra: Native Title Research Unit, Australian Institute of Aboriginal and Torres Strait Islander Studies.

Pockley, S. 1998. The flight of the ducks. Ph.D. diss., Centre for Animation and Interactive Multimedia. http://www.cinemedia.net/FOD.

Povinelli, E. 1993. *Labor's lot: The power, history, and culture of Aboriginal action.* Chicago: University of Chicago Press.

———. 1995. Do rocks listen? The cultural politics of apprehending Australian Aboriginal labor. *American Anthropologist* 97:505–518.

Price-Williams, D., and R. Gaines. 1994. The dreamtime and dreams of northern Australian Aboriginal artists. *Ethos* 22:373–388.

Puri, K. 1992. Protection for Aboriginal folklore. *Australian Folklore* 7:1–17.

———. 1993. Copyright protection for Australian Aborigines in the light of Mabo. In *Mabo: A judicial revolution,* edited by M. A. Stephenson and S. Ratnapala, 132–164. St. Lucia: University of Queensland Press.

Raabe, E. C. 1995. Modernism or folk art? The reception of Pacific art in Europe. *Art and Asia Pacific* 2:96–103.

Radcliffe-Brown, A. R. 1913. Three tribes of Western Australia. *Journal of the Royal Anthropological Institute* 43:143–194.

———. 1930–1931. The social organization of the Australian tribes. *Oceania* 1:34–63, 206–246, 232–341, 426–456.

Regenvanu, R. 1997. Preface to *Vanuatu Kunst aus der Südsee: Eine Einführung,* by C. Kaufmann. Basel: Museum der Kulturen and Christoph Merian Verlag.

Rodman, M. C. 1998. Creating historic sites in Vanuatu. *Social Analysis* 42 (3): 117–134.

Rolls, E. 1981. *A million wild acres.* Ringwood, Victoria: Penguin.

Rose, D. 1988. Exploring an Aboriginal land ethic. *Meanjin* 47 (3): 378–387.

———. 1992. *Dingo makes us human: Life and land in an Aboriginal Australian culture.* Cambridge: Cambridge University Press.

———. 1994. Whose confidentiality? Whose intellectual property? In *Claims to knowledge, claims to country, Native Title, Native Title claims, and the role of the anthropologists,* edited by M. Edmunds, 1–12. Canberra: Native Title Research Unit, Australian Institute of Aboriginal and Torres Strait Islander Studies.

———. 1996. *Nourishing terrains: Australian Aboriginal views of landscape and wilderness.* Canberra: Australian Heritage Commission.

———. 1999. Indigenous ecologies and the ethic of connection. In *Global ethics for the twenty-first century,* edited by N. Low, 175–186. London: Routledge.

Rowse, T. 1993. *After Mabo: Interpreting indigenous traditions.* Melbourne: Melbourne University Press.

Rubinstein, M. R. 1989. Outstations of the postmodern: Aboriginal acrylic painting of the western Australian desert. *Arts Magazine* 63:40–47.

Rumsey, A. 1989. Language groups in Aboriginal land claims. *Anthropological Forum* 6:69–79.

———. 1993. Language and territoriality in Aboriginal Australia. In *Language and culture in Aboriginal Australia,* edited by M. Walsh and C. Yallop, 191–206. Canberra: Aboriginal Studies Press.

———. 1994. The dreaming, human agency, and inscriptive practice. *Oceania* 65:116–130.

———. 1995. Pairing and parallelism in the New Guinea highlands. In *SALSA II: Proceedings of the second annual symposium about language and society,* Austin (Texas Linguistic Forum 34), edited by P. Silberman and J. Loftlin, 108–118. Austin: University of Texas.

———. 1996. Aspects of Native Title and social identity in the Kimberleys and beyond. *Australian Aboriginal Studies,* no. 1:2–10.

———. 1999a. The White man as cannibal in the New Guinea Highlands. In *The anthropology of cannibalism*, edited by L. Goldman, 105–121. Westport: Bergin and Garvey.

———. 1999b. Comment on D. J. Mulvaney, H. Morphy, and A. Petch, *"My dear Spencer,"* and review of it by Diane Austin-Broos. *Oceania* 70: 177–178.

Russell-Smith, J., and D. Bowman. 1992. Conservation of monsoon rainforest isolates in the Northern Territory, Australia. *Biological Conservation* 59: 51–63.

Sackett, L. 1991. Promoting primitivism: Conservationist depictions of Aboriginal Australians. *Australian Journal of Anthropology* 2:233–246.

Sagir, B. In press. The politics of petroleum extraction and royalty distribution in Kutubu. In *Mining and indigenous lifeworlds in Australia and Papua New Guinea*, edited by A. Rumsey and J. Weiner. Adelaide: Crawford House Publishing.

Sahlins, M. 1968. *Tribesmen.* Englewood Cliffs, N.J.: Prentice-Hall.

———. 1985. *Islands of history.* Chicago: University of Chicago Press.

Sam, J. 1996. Audiovisual documentation of living cultures as a major task for the Vanuatu Cultural Centre. In *Arts of Vanuatu,* edited by J. Bonnemaison, C. Kaufmann, K. Huffman, and D. Tryon, 288–289. Bathurst: Crawford House Publishing.

Schneider, D. 1965. Some muddles in the models, or, how the system really works. In *The relevance of models for social anthropology,* edited by M. Banton, 25–85. London: Tavistock.

Schwimmer, E., ed. 1977. *F. E. Williams: "The Vailala madness" and other essays.* Honolulu: University of Hawai'i Press.

Scoditti, G. 1996. *Kitawa oral poetry: An example from Melanesia.* Pacific Linguistics Series D-87. Canberra: Department of Linguistics, Research School of Pacific and Asian Studies, Australian National University.

Scott, C. 1996. Science for the West, myth for the rest? The case of James Bay Cree knowledge construction. In *Naked science: Anthropological inquiry into boundaries, power, and knowledge,* edited by L. Nader, 69–86. New York: Routledge.

Scott-Mundine, D. 1990. Black on black: An Aboriginal perspective on Koori art. *Art Monthly Australia* 30:7–9.

Sculthorpe, G. 1993. Interpreting Aboriginal history in a museum context. *Museums Australia Journal* 2–3:49–55.

Service, E. 1966. *The hunters.* Englewood Cliffs, N.J.: Prentice-Hall.

Shapiro, W. 1989. The theoretical importance of pseudo-procreative symbolism. *The Psychoanalytic Study of Society* 14:71–88.

Sharp, R. L. 1952. Steel axes for stone-age Australians. *Human Organization* 12:17–22.

Sherman, B. 1994. From the non-original to the Ab-original: A history. In *Of authors and origins: Essays on law,* edited by B. Sherman and A. Strowe, 111–130. Oxford: Clarendon Press.

Sillitoe, P. 1993. Forest and demons in the Papua New Guinea highlands. *Australian Journal of Anthropology* 4:220–232.

Silverman, E. 1996. The gender of the cosmos: Totemism, society, and embodiment in the Sepik River. *Oceania* 67:30–49.

———. 1997a. Art, authenticity, and other transnational dilemmas: Lessons from Sepik River tourism, Shona sculpture, and the New Guinea Sculpture Garden at Stanford University. Paper delivered at the annual meeting of the American Anthropological Association, Washington, D.C.

——— 1997b. Politics, gender, and time in Melanesia and Aboriginal Australia. *Ethnology* 36:101–121.

——— 1999. Art, tourism, and the crafting of identity in the Sepik River (Papua New Guinea). In *Unpacking culture: Art and commodity in colonial and postcolonial worlds,* edited by R. Phillips and C. Steiner, 51–66. Berkeley: University of California Press.

Simons, S. C. 1993. Strong ai bilong em: A comparison of Papua New Guinean urban artists and Australian Aboriginal urban artists. In *Artistic heritage in a changing Pacific,* edited by P. J. C. Dark and R. G. Rose, 173–184. Honolulu: University of Hawai'i Press.

Smith, M. A., M. Spriggs, and B. Fankhauser, eds. 1993. *Sahul in review: Pleistocene archaeology in Australia, New Guinea, and Island Melanesia.* Occasional Papers in Prehistory, no. 24. Canberra: Department of Prehistory, Research School of Pacific Studies, Australian National University.

Spearritt, G. 1979. The music of the Iatmul people of the Middle Sepik River (Papua New Guinea) with special reference to instrumental music at Kandangai and Aibom. Manuscript.

Specht, J. R. 1979. Anthropology. In *Rare and curious specimens: An illustrated history of the Australian Museum 1827–1979,* edited by R. Strahan, 141–150. Sydney: Trustees of the Australian Museum.

Specht, J., and C. MacLulich. 1996. Changes and challenges: The Australian Museum and indigenous communities. In *Archaeological displays and the public,* edited by P. McManus, 27–49. London: Institute of Archaeology and University College.

Spencer, B., and F. Gillen. 1899. *The native tribes of central Australia*. London: Macmillan.

Spriggs, M. 1997. *The island Melanesians*. Oxford: Blackwell.

Stanek, M. 1983. *Sozialordnung und Mythik in Palimbei*. Basel: Wepf.

Stanner, W. E. H. 1956. The dreaming. In *Australian signpost: An anthology,* edited for the Canberra Fellowship of Australian Writers by T. Hunderford, 51–65. Melbourne: Chesire.

———. 1963. On Aboriginal religion. VI. Cosmos and society made correlative. *Oceania* 33:239–273.

———. 1966. *On Aboriginal religion*. Sydney: Oceania Publications.

———. 1979. *White man got no dreaming*. Canberra: Australian National University Press.

Steiner, C. B. 1994. *African art in transit*. Cambridge: Cambridge University Press.

Stephen, M. 1979. Dreams of change: The innovative role of altered states of consciousness in traditional Melanesian religion. *Oceania* 50 (1): 3–22.

———. 1982. "Dreaming is another power": The social significance of dreams among the Mekeo of Papua New Guinea. *Oceania* 53:106–122.

Stewart, P. J. 1998. Ritual trackways and sacred paths of fertility. *Proceedings of the 1997 Perspectives on the Bird's Head of Irian Jaya, Indonesia, ISIR conference*. Amsterdam: Rodopi.

Stewart, P. J., and A. Strathern. 1997. Transecting bisects: Female spirit cults as a prism of cultural performance in the Hagen, Pangia, and Duna areas of Papua New Guinea. Okari Research Group Working Paper, no. 1.

Strathern, A. J. 1972. *One father, one blood: Descent and group structure among the Melpa people*. Canberra: Australian National University Press.

———. 1990. Fertility and salvation: The conflict between spirit cult and Christian sect in Mt. Hagen. *Journal of Ritual Studies* 5 (1): 51–64.

———. 1993. Big-man, great-man, leader: The link of ritual power. *Journal de la Sociètè des Ocèanistes* (2): 145–158.

Strathern, A., and P. J. Stewart. 1997. The efficacy-entertainment braid revisited: From ritual to commerce in Papua New Guinea. *Journal of Ritual Studies* 11 (1): 55–63.

———. 1998. Shifting places, contested spaces: Land and identity politics in the Pacific. *The Australian Journal of Anthropology* 9(2): 209–224.

———. 1999a. The spirit is coming! A photographic-textual exposition of the female spirit cult performance in Mt. Hagen. Ritual Studies Monograph Series, no. 1. Pittsburgh: Department of Anthropology, University of Pittsburgh.

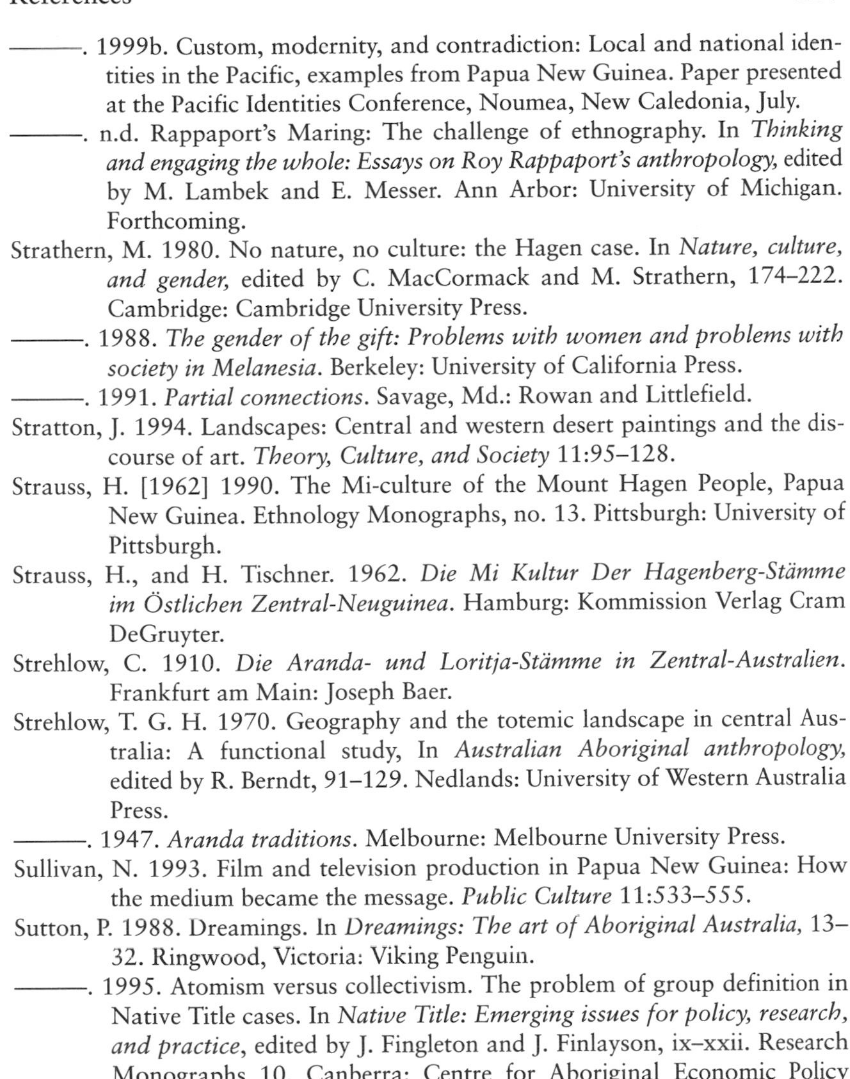

———. 1999b. Custom, modernity, and contradiction: Local and national identities in the Pacific, examples from Papua New Guinea. Paper presented at the Pacific Identities Conference, Noumea, New Caledonia, July.

———. n.d. Rappaport's Maring: The challenge of ethnography. In *Thinking and engaging the whole: Essays on Roy Rappaport's anthropology,* edited by M. Lambek and E. Messer. Ann Arbor: University of Michigan. Forthcoming.

Strathern, M. 1980. No nature, no culture: the Hagen case. In *Nature, culture, and gender,* edited by C. MacCormack and M. Strathern, 174–222. Cambridge: Cambridge University Press.

———. 1988. *The gender of the gift: Problems with women and problems with society in Melanesia.* Berkeley: University of California Press.

———. 1991. *Partial connections.* Savage, Md.: Rowan and Littlefield.

Stratton, J. 1994. Landscapes: Central and western desert paintings and the discourse of art. *Theory, Culture, and Society* 11:95–128.

Strauss, H. [1962] 1990. The Mi-culture of the Mount Hagen People, Papua New Guinea. Ethnology Monographs, no. 13. Pittsburgh: University of Pittsburgh.

Strauss, H., and H. Tischner. 1962. *Die Mi Kultur Der Hagenberg-Stämme im Östlichen Zentral-Neuguinea.* Hamburg: Kommission Verlag Cram DeGruyter.

Strehlow, C. 1910. *Die Aranda- und Loritja-Stämme in Zentral-Australien.* Frankfurt am Main: Joseph Baer.

Strehlow, T. G. H. 1970. Geography and the totemic landscape in central Australia: A functional study, In *Australian Aboriginal anthropology,* edited by R. Berndt, 91–129. Nedlands: University of Western Australia Press.

———. 1947. *Aranda traditions.* Melbourne: Melbourne University Press.

Sullivan, N. 1993. Film and television production in Papua New Guinea: How the medium became the message. *Public Culture* 11:533–555.

Sutton, P. 1988. Dreamings. In *Dreamings: The art of Aboriginal Australia,* 13–32. Ringwood, Victoria: Viking Penguin.

———. 1995. Atomism versus collectivism. The problem of group definition in Native Title cases. In *Native Title: Emerging issues for policy, research, and practice*, edited by J. Fingleton and J. Finlayson, ix–xxii. Research Monographs 10. Canberra: Centre for Aboriginal Economic Policy Research.

———. 1997. Materialism, sacred myth, and pluralism: Competing theories of the origin of Australian languages. In *Scholar and sceptic: Australian Aboriginal studies in honour of L. R. Hiatt,* edited by Francesca Merlan, John Morton, and Alan Rumsey, 211–242. Canberra: Aboriginal Studies Press.

Swadling, P. 1996. *Plumes from paradise: Trade cycles in outer Southeast Asia and their impact on New Guinea and nearby islands until 1920.* Boroko (National Capital District): Papua New Guinea National Museum, in association with Robert Brown and Associates.

Swain, T. 1993. *A place for strangers: Towards a history of Australian Aboriginal being*. Cambridge: Cambridge University Press.

Tamisari, F. 1997. Body, vision, and movement: In the footprints of the ancestors. Manuscript.

Taussig, M. 1980. *The devil and commodity fetishism in South America*. Chapel Hill: University of North Carolina Press.

———. 1987. *Shamanism, colonialism, and the wild man*. Chicago: University of Chicago Press.

Taylor, L. 1988. The aesthetics of Toas. *Canberra Anthropology* 11:86–99.

———. 1989. Aboriginal artists and the market: Two case studies in cultural adaptation. In *Emergent inequalities in Aboriginal Australia,* edited by L. Taylor, 119–140. Sydney: University of Sydney.

———. 1990. The rainbow serpent as visual metaphor in western Arnhem Land. *Oceania* 60:329–344.

———. 1996. *Seeing the inside: Bark painting in western Arnhem Land*. Oxford: Clarendon Press.

Tehan, M. 1997. Co-existence of interests in land: A dominant feature of the common law. *Land, rights, laws: Issues of Native Title,* no. 12. Native Titles Research Unit. Australian Institute of Aboriginal and Torres Strait Islander Studies. http://aiatsis.gov.au/ntpapers/ntip12.htm.

Tonkinson, M. E. 1990. Is it in the blood? Australian Aboriginal identity. In *Cultural identity and ethnicity in the Pacific,* edited by J. Linnekin and L. Poyer, 191–218. Honolulu: University of Hawai'i Press.

Tonkinson, R. 1974. *Aboriginal victors of the Desert Crusade*. Menlo Park: Cummings.

———. 1978. Semen versus spirit-child in a western desert culture. In *Australian Aboriginal concepts,* edited by L. R. Hiatt, 81–91. Canberra: Australian Institute for Aboriginal Studies Press.

———. 1996. Anthropology and Aboriginal traditions: The Hindmarsh Island Bridge affair and the politics of interpretation. Paper presented at the annual meeting of the Association for Social Anthropology in Oceania, Kona, Hawaii, February.

———. 1997. Anthropology and Aboriginal tradition: The Hindmarsh Island Bridge affair. *Oceania* 68:1–26.

Tully, J. 1994. Aboriginal property and western theory: Recovering a middle ground. *Social Philosophy and Policy* 11:153–180.

Tuzin, D. 1992. Revelation and concealment in the cultural organization of meaning: A methodological note. In *Shooting the sun: Ritual and meaning in West Sepik,* edited by B. Juillerat, 251–259. Washington, D.C.: Smithsonian Institution Press.

van der Leeden, A. C. 1960. Social structure in New Guinea. *Bijdragen tot de Taal-, Land- en Volkenkunde* 116: 119–149.

———. 1970. Australia and Melanesia: Propositions regarding comparative research. In *Anniversary contributions to anthropology: Twelve essays published on the occasion of the 40th anniversary of the Leiden Anthropological Society,* 78–91. Leiden: Brill.

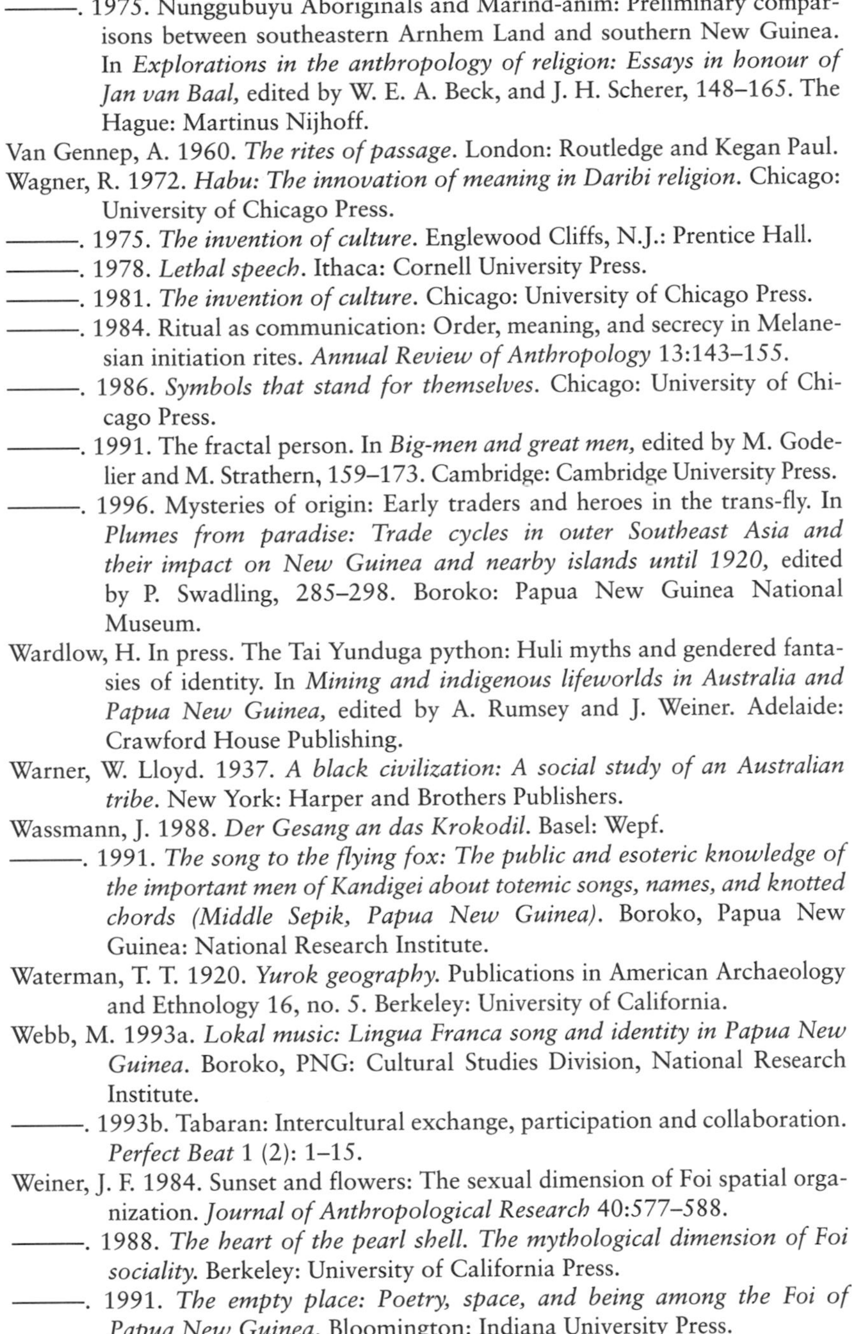

———. 1975. Nunggubuyu Aboriginals and Marind-anim: Preliminary comparisons between southeastern Arnhem Land and southern New Guinea. In *Explorations in the anthropology of religion: Essays in honour of Jan van Baal,* edited by W. E. A. Beck, and J. H. Scherer, 148–165. The Hague: Martinus Nijhoff.

Van Gennep, A. 1960. *The rites of passage.* London: Routledge and Kegan Paul.

Wagner, R. 1972. *Habu: The innovation of meaning in Daribi religion.* Chicago: University of Chicago Press.

———. 1975. *The invention of culture.* Englewood Cliffs, N.J.: Prentice Hall.

———. 1978. *Lethal speech.* Ithaca: Cornell University Press.

———. 1981. *The invention of culture.* Chicago: University of Chicago Press.

———. 1984. Ritual as communication: Order, meaning, and secrecy in Melanesian initiation rites. *Annual Review of Anthropology* 13:143–155.

———. 1986. *Symbols that stand for themselves.* Chicago: University of Chicago Press.

———. 1991. The fractal person. In *Big-men and great men,* edited by M. Godelier and M. Strathern, 159–173. Cambridge: Cambridge University Press.

———. 1996. Mysteries of origin: Early traders and heroes in the trans-fly. In *Plumes from paradise: Trade cycles in outer Southeast Asia and their impact on New Guinea and nearby islands until 1920,* edited by P. Swadling, 285–298. Boroko: Papua New Guinea National Museum.

Wardlow, H. In press. The Tai Yunduga python: Huli myths and gendered fantasies of identity. In *Mining and indigenous lifeworlds in Australia and Papua New Guinea,* edited by A. Rumsey and J. Weiner. Adelaide: Crawford House Publishing.

Warner, W. Lloyd. 1937. *A black civilization: A social study of an Australian tribe.* New York: Harper and Brothers Publishers.

Wassmann, J. 1988. *Der Gesang an das Krokodil.* Basel: Wepf.

———. 1991. *The song to the flying fox: The public and esoteric knowledge of the important men of Kandigei about totemic songs, names, and knotted chords (Middle Sepik, Papua New Guinea).* Boroko, Papua New Guinea: National Research Institute.

Waterman, T. T. 1920. *Yurok geography.* Publications in American Archaeology and Ethnology 16, no. 5. Berkeley: University of California.

Webb, M. 1993a. *Lokal music: Lingua Franca song and identity in Papua New Guinea.* Boroko, PNG: Cultural Studies Division, National Research Institute.

———. 1993b. Tabaran: Intercultural exchange, participation and collaboration. *Perfect Beat* 1 (2): 1–15.

Weiner, J. F. 1984. Sunset and flowers: The sexual dimension of Foi spatial organization. *Journal of Anthropological Research* 40:577–588.

———. 1988. *The heart of the pearl shell. The mythological dimension of Foi sociality.* Berkeley: University of California Press.

———. 1991. *The empty place: Poetry, space, and being among the Foi of Papua New Guinea.* Bloomington: Indiana University Press.

———. 1995a. Anthropologists, historians and the secret of social knowledge. *Anthropology Today* 11:3–7.
———. 1995b. Technology and *techne* in Trobriand and Yolngu art. In *Too many meanings: A critique of the anthropology of aesthetics,* edited by J. Weiner. Special issue of *Social Analysis* 38:32–46.
———. 1995c. *The lost drum: The myth of sexuality in Papua New Guinea and beyond.* Madison: University of Wisconsin Press.
——— 1995d. The secret of the Ngarrindjeri: The fabrication of social knowledge. *Arena Journal* 5:17–32.
——— 1997. "Bad Aboriginal" anthropology: A reply to Ron Brunton. *Anthropology Today* 13 (4): 5–8.
——— 1999. Culture in a Sealed Envelope: The Concealment of Aboriginal Heritage and Tradition in the Hindmarsh Island bridge Affair. *Journal of the Royal Anthropological Institute* 5 (2): 193–210.
Wendt, A. 1976. Towards a New Oceania. *Mana Review: A South Pacific Journal of Language and Literature* 1 (1): 49–60.
White, J. P. 1996. Paleolithic colonization in Sahul land. In *Prehistoric Mongoloid dispersals,* edited by T. Akazawa and E. J. E. Szathmáry, 303–308. Oxford: Oxford University Press.
Whittaker, E. 1994. Public discourse on sacredness: The transfer of Ayers Rock to Aboriginal ownership. *American Ethnologist* 21:310–334.
Williams, F. E. 1936. *Papuans of the trans-fly.* Oxford: Clarendon Press.
Williams, N. M. 1976. Australian Aboriginal art at Yirrkala: The introduction and development of marketing. In *Ethnic and tourist arts,* edited by N. H. H. Graburn, 266–284. Berkeley: University of California Press.
———. 1986. *The Yolngu and their land: A system of land tenure and the fight for its recognition.* Stanford: Stanford University Press.
Williams, N., and G. Baines. 1993. *Traditional ecological knowledge.* Canberra: Centre for Resource and Environmental Studies, Australian National University.
Williams, N., and E. Hunn. 1982. *Resource managers: North American and Australian hunter-gatherers.* Washington, D.C.: American Association for the Advancement of Science.
Worsley, P. 1955. Totemism in a changing society. *American Anthropologist* 57: 851–861.
———. [1957] 1970. *The trumpet shall sound.* London: Paladin.
———. 1967. Groote Eylandt Totemism and Le Totemisme Aujourd'hui. In *The structural study of myth and totemism,* edited by E. Leach, 141–159. London: Tavistock.
Young, M. 1983. *Magicians of Manumanua.* Berkeley: University of California Press.

CONTRIBUTORS

Lissant Bolton is the curator of the Pacific and Australian Collections in the Department of Ethnography at the British Museum. She has done long-term fieldwork in Vanuatu, in collaboration with the Vanuatu Cultural Centre. She is the editor of the volume *Fieldwork and Fieldworkers: Developments in Vanuatu Research* (special issue of *Oceania,* September 1999) and is currently working on a book titled *Unfolding the Moon: Women, Textiles, and Kastom in Vanuatu.* Her e-mail address is lbolton@british-museum.ac.uk.

Andrew Lattas is a former Australian Research Council fellow and a current lecturer in anthropology at the University of Newcastle. He has written extensively on race relations in Australian society. He has also conducted fieldwork for many years in New Britain, Papua New Guinea, and is the author of *Cultures of Secrecy* (1998), a study of cargo cult practices in the area. His e-mail address is alattas@socanth.newcastle.edu.au.

Anthony Redmond is a doctoral candidate in the Department of Anthropology at the University of Sydney, where he is writing his dissertation on the mythology, art, and cosmology of the Ngarinyin people of northwestern Australia. He has done several years of fieldwork in Aboriginal settlements in the region and has worked for the Kamali and Kimberley land councils, in collaboration with Alan Rumsey, on the preparation of a land claim by the Ngarinyin to be heard by the Federal Court of Australia. His e-mail address is redmond@idl.hct.au.

DEBORAH BIRD ROSE is a senior research fellow in the Centre for Resource and Environmental Studies at Australian National University. She writes in the fields of anthropology, history, environmental knowledge, and religious studies, focusing on social and ecological justice in frontier zones where issues of European-Aboriginal reconciliation are both urgent and deeply problematic. Her books include *Hidden Histories* (1991), *Dingo Makes Us Human* (1992), and *Nourishing Terrains: Australian Aboriginal Views of Landscape and Wilderness* (1996). Her e-mail address is deborah.rose@anu.edu.au.

ALAN RUMSEY is a fellow in the Department of Anthropology, Research School of Pacific and Asian Studies, Australian National University. He has done fieldwork in Highland New Guinea and Northern Australia. He is the author of many publications on Ngarinyin, Bunuba, and Ku Waru language and social life and is the coauthor, with Francesca Merlan, of the book *Ku Waru: Language and Segmentary Politics in the Western Nebilyer Valley, Papua New Guinea* (1991). His e-mail address is alan.rumsey@anu.edu.au.

ERIC KLINE SILVERMAN is an assistant professor of anthropology at DePauw University. He has done fieldwork in the Middle Sepik region of Papua New Guinea, and has published material about that area and compared it with Aboriginal Australia. With the aid of a fellowship from the National Endowment for the Humanities, he is currently writing a book on Jewish circumcision that will draw on many ritual, bodily, and mythic themes that are relevant to Melanesia and Australia. His e-mail address is erics@depauw.edu.

PAMELA J. STEWART is a research associate in the Departments of Anthropology and Religious Studies at the University of Pittsburgh and is an adjunct lecturer in anthropology at James Cook University (Townsville, Australia). She works with her husband and collaborator, Andrew Strathern, in the Duna, Hagen, and Pangia areas of Papua New Guinea. Her most recent coauthored books are *Curing and Heal-*

ing: Medical Anthropology in Global Perspective (1999) and *The Python's Back: Pathways of Comparison between Indonesia and Melanesia* (forthcoming). Her e-mail address is pamjan@pitt.edu.

ANDREW STRATHERN is Andrew Mellon Professor of Anthropology at the University of Pittsburgh. He has been doing fieldwork in the Western and Southern Highlands of Papua New Guinea since 1964 and is the author of many books and articles based on that work. His most recent books, coauthored with his wife and collaborator, Pamela J. Stewart, are *Kuk Heritage: Issues and Debates in Papua New Guinea* (1998) and *Collaborations and Conflict: A Leader Through Time* (1999). His e-mail address is strather+@pitt.edu.

ROY WAGNER is a professor in the Department of Anthropology at the University of Virginia. He has carried out fieldwork among the Daribi and Usen Barok of Papua New Guinea and is the author of such renowned works as *The Curse of Souw* (1967), *Habu* (1974), *The Invention of Culture* (1975), *Lethal Speech* (1978), *Asiwinarong* (1986), and *Symbols that Stand for Themselves* (1986). His latest book, *An Anthropology of the Subject,* is currently in press.

JÜRG WASSMANN is professor of anthropology and director of the Institute of Ethnology at the University of Heidelberg. He has a strong interest in cognitive anthropology and has conducted field research in Papua New Guinea (Iatmul, Yupno) and Bali. He has published major articles on his cognitive anthropological research, as well as the books *Der Gesang an das Krokodil* (1988), *The Song to the Flying Fox* (1991), and *Das Ideal des Leicht Gebeugten Menschen* (1993). His e-mail address is Juerg.Wassmann@urz.uni-heidelberg.de.

JAMES F. WEINER is a visiting fellow in the Department of Anthropology, Research School of Pacific and Asian Studies, Australian National University. He has worked with the Foi since 1979 and is the author of *The Heart of the Pearl Shell* (1988), *The Empty Place* (1991), *The Lost Drum* (1995), and numerous articles on the Foi. He has also conducted Native Title research in southeastern Queensland. His latest monograph, *Tree Leaf Talk: Heidegger, Anthropology, and the Work of Concealment in Human Culture,* is currently under review. His e-mail address is james.weiner@anu.edu.au.

INDEX